Across the Pond

Chapters from the Atlantic

Malcolm Archibald

Whittles Publishing

Typeset by
Whittles Publishing Services

Published by
Whittles Publishing
Roseleigh House,
Latheronwheel,
Caithness, KW5 6DW,
Scotland, UK

ISBN 1-870325-33-8

Printed by Interprint Ltd., Malta

Contents

The Statue of Liberty, circa 1886. In the forefront is a Hudson River sloop, a type of vessel which regularly crosssed the Atlantic and even travelled as far as China. Courtesy New York Public Library.

Introduction

'Think of the broad Atlantic, that terrible waste of desolate water, tossing in tumult in repeated, almost ceaseless storms, and shrouded with an unbroken canopy of mist.'
Winston Churchill

To stand on the western rim of Europe and witness an Atlantic sunset is to become immersed in one of the most beautiful sights in creation. On a calm day the sense of peace, enhanced rather than disturbed by the hush of the sea, sinks deep into the soul, while a wild winter of driving waves with the glowing sun barely glimpsed between brooding clouds invokes a sense of awe. Either way, the experience is so satisfying that it is nearly spiritual. To the ancient peoples staring out into this vast beyond, the sense of mystery and everlasting power must have been immeasurable. Yet although they would have felt dwarfed by the sheer immensity of the ocean, they would be unaware of just how big their neighbouring sea was, and how important it was to become.

If the geologists are correct, at one time there were only two vast continents in the world, intriguingly labelled Laurasia and Gondwanaland and separated by some form of sea. Around 150 million years ago the northern supercontinent split and the Americas drifted apart from Eurasia. A ridge 6000 feet in height marks this geographical divide which continues to widen at the rate of approximately two inches every year, however much electronic communications press a bland global monoculture on a once fascinatingly varied world. The Atlantic Ocean quickly filled the space in between the drifting continents.

The second largest ocean in the world, the Atlantic stretches between Africa and the Americas and from the Arctic to the Antarctic. The equator is used as an arbitrary line to divide this massive area of water into the South and North Atlantic. At its maximum the North Atlantic covers 16,500,000 square miles and even excluding ancillary seas such as the Caribbean and Baltic it covers 10,588,000 square miles. Even where the ocean is narrowest, between Brazil and Africa, there are 1,700 miles to cross, while at the widest 4000 miles of unbroken water divide the New World from the Old. Soundings by USS *Milwaukee* obtained a depth of 5049 fathoms, around 30,246 feet, in the Puerto Rico trough off Guyana. The average depth, however, is about 13,000 feet.

Submarine ridges and lifts divide the ocean floors on either side of the Mid Atlantic ridge into a number of basins, while there are shelves on the continental coasts. Further out, large islands erupt above the surface of the ocean: Newfoundland, Iceland, the British Isles and the massively-iced bulk of Greenland. Other, smaller, island groups include the Orkney and Shetland islands north of Scotland, the Faroe Islands between Shetland and Iceland and Bermuda off the coast of the United States. Sable Island, sitting 100 miles east of Nova Scotia, has a unique position and a history all of its own.

There are no immediately obvious boundaries between the Atlantic and the Arctic Ocean, but scientists have discovered a number of submarine ridges between Scotland, Greenland and Baffin Island. On the west the Caribbean basks in tropical sun, hiding its history of buccaneer, galleon and slavery behind an Antillean screen composed of some of the world's most lushly beautiful islands. To the east, the Rock of Gibraltar stands as a dramatic full stop to the Atlantic and a marker for the central sea of the Mediterranean, where so much of western civilisation was born. Fittingly, it was people from this Mediterranean melting pot who named the Atlantic, for legend claims that the mighty western ocean was named after Atlas, the god who became a mountain to uphold the heavens. His name is enduringly connected to the Atlas Mountains that burst upward from the north-western fringe of Africa. The Greeks referred to the western exit of the Mediterranean as *atlantikos* and by a process of association that adjective became attached to the surging ocean outside. Its seemingly limitless extent led to myths of mysterious lands, from Avalon to Atlantis, the Isles of the Blessed to Hy Brasil. Atlantis was a transposed myth, the Celtic Lands of the Blessed a story, but all were to be surpassed by the reality of the Americas, that huge golden land that was possibly hinted at by ancient dreams.

As invisible but more real than any mythical island, is the tropic high-pressure belt that forms above the expanse of ocean around the equator. Together with the Arctic chill and the influence of the landmasses on temperature, this belt creates an anti-cyclonic area with air movement that can veer between enthusiastic and frantic. In the North Atlantic, air that is constantly surging in to occupy the low pressure areas created by the temperature rises of the landmasses creates cyclonic conditions that generate vicious gales, making these seas amongst the most dangerous in the world.

Helped by the rotation of the earth, the anti-cyclonic areas on either side of the equator generate trade winds that produce a clockwise current system. On the southern side of the equator a mid-Atlantic current crosses to South America, dividing as it reaches the vicinity of Cape Sao Roque. The Brazil current slides south towards the mouth of the River Plate, while the South Equatorial Current drifts north toward the Caribbean. Here it merges with the North Equatorial Current and the consequential rise of the Caribbean Sea level gives rise to a counter current. This North Atlantic

Drift from Caribbean to north-western Europe raises the temperature of the British Isles and keeps the seaports ice-free in winter, but a split in the current produces the cold Canaries Current that pushes south off north-west Africa. Another cold current, the Labrador, punches down from the Arctic to separate the Gulf Stream from the eastern seaboard of North America.

Eerily calm waters and stretches of brown or yellow gulfweed epitomises that section of the Atlantic bounded by the West Indian islands, the Azores, and the Gulf Stream. This area has become known as the Sargasso Sea from *Sargassum*, the scholarly name of the gulfweed. The early mariners told tales of ships rotting in the placid seas with their progress halted by clinging weed, but even though the *Sargassum* covered a far more extensive area then, there seems never to have been any danger of ships being trapped. Today the presence of oil rigs is a constant reminder of the more definite threat of pollution.

The North Atlantic contains some of the best fisheries in the world and some of the most over-fished. For centuries European fishermen, using ever more sophisticated equipment, exploited the waters off Europe and the seas off Iceland. The discovery of the riches of the Grand Banks of Newfoundland sent a deluge of European fishermen west to the Banks, a submarine plateau covering thousands of square miles, where the warm waters of the North Atlantic Drift meet the cool Labrador Current. This combination of temperatures, augmented by shallow seas warmed by the sun, encourages the breeding of plankton on which fish feed. However, the fishermen who exploit these waters have to contend with the notorious fogs, while there is constant danger from icebergs drifting from the north. Yet at one time up to 100,000 fishermen, from the Nova Scotia schooner captains to the Basques from the Bay of Biscay, hauled cod from the Banks.

Fogs, icebergs and storms highlight the dangers of the North Atlantic, and there are many areas notorious for shipwrecks. Both Sable Island and Newfoundland share the epithet 'Graveyard of the Atlantic' with good reason. In a single violent day in 1804 as many as 80 ships foundered on the Newfoundland coasts and the Atlantic has seen a constant trickle of casualties, in peace or war. Any coast could be lethal; one particularly grim day saw a gale strike west Wales, wreck over 100 vessels, and wash away the church of St Brent near Brynhellan.

If commerce has carried some of the world's richest cargoes across the Atlantic, then humanity has also shamed the seas with the press-gang and the slave trade with callous unconcern for the seamen that worked the ships and the unimaginable horror of warfare. Men have fought and died for control of this ocean, for freedom of the seas or freedom to control the seas and blood from torn seamen has added to the salt content of this most saline of all oceans.

This was the Ocean Sea, the forbidding water that encircled the world of the ancients and prevented them from expanding from their central, Mediterranean lands. It was to become the greatest challenge in the world, and the greatest highway. It is the Atlantic.

Acknowledgements

I would like to thank sincerely the following people: Chris Young of SS *Great Britain* Project, Bristol for the magnificent illustrations of *Great Britain* and *Matthew*; Peter J. Stuckey, Editor of the *Bristol Shiplover* for putting me in touch with the above. P.J.H. Tebay of the Liverpool Nautical Research Society; Chaplain William Donnelly of New York City (ex-USN) for his constant encouragement – 'hang in there'– help and advice. Billie Love of the Billie Love Historical Collection for her superb range of photographs and, above all and always, my wife Cathy and children Alexander and Hannah for putting up with the many hours I spent huddled over either a book or a computer. Illustrations on pages 91, 110, 116, 153, and 181 courtesy of IMSI Masterclips and MasterPhotos Premium Image Collection, 75 Rowland Way, Novato Ca. 94945, USA.

for Cathy

Chapter 1

Out of the Central Sea

'Not easy is it to travel the inaccessible sea
Beyond the columns of Heracles ...'

Pindar

Western civilisation as we understand it was born in the lands around the Mediterranean Sea and transported in myriad voyages by mainly forgotten mariners. This relatively small area of water connects three continents and many cultures, but for many millennia it was the larger eastern section that was the most important. Here the long finger of the Adriatic points to fertile northern Italy while the island-specked Aegean protects the dangerous access to the Sea of Marmora and the Black Sea. The Aegean seems to have been originally populated by farmers from Asia Minor, possibly in a slow spreading from island to visible island when family growth reduced the availability of arable land. Gradually, experience of their environment helped consummate the marriage between humanity and the sea until an infant maritime culture was spawned on the long island of Crete at the very southern entrance to the Aegean.

From his palace at Knossos, King Minos dominated the eastern Mediterranean so the Minoans could thumb nautical noses at their land-based neighbours and the ancient city-states of the fertile crescent. Far up the Nile at royal Thebes, the tomb of Rekh-mi-Re, vizier to Thothmes III, boasts a carving showing various peoples paying tribute. Among these people is the mysterious 'Kftiu of the lands in the heart of the Great Green Sea', according to the hieroglyphics, and these may well be the Minoans. It is interesting to recreate mentally the voyage of the Minoans as they left Crete, coasted down the Levant and rowed up the fertile Nile, so different from their northern island. Perhaps they marvelled at the wonders of Egyptian civilisation, or maybe they felt discomfort at being so far from the sea. Either way it is possible that the Minoans sailed north of Crete as well as south, threading through the Aegean islands into the

Dardanelles, or westward to the Adriatic from where southern Italy is visible. Adding legendary credence to absolute speculation, the Greeks had a legend that Daedalus of Crete fled westward to Sicily with King Minos in pursuit. Although this may indicate a Minoan presence as far west as Sicily, it seems unlikely that they ventured any further.

After the Minoans, the Phoenicians and the Mycenean Greeks kept the seafaring tradition alive. It was during the Mycenean period that the famous siege of Troy occurred and the wanderings of Odysseus are a reminder of just how esoteric the western Mediterranean was. Odysseus was between Crete and the Greek mainland when an easterly wind blew him to a land of lotus-eaters who may have been the date-eating inhabitants of Tunisia, the furthest west of the familiar Greek world. If this is accepted, then his following adventures occurred in the western Mediterranean, or perhaps beyond. The mythical Charybdis, which three times a day sucked away the salt water to expose the sea bottom, may have been an attempt to explain the phenomenon of Atlantic tides to the people of the near tideless Mediterranean.

In ancient Greece sea travel was not only faster, it was frequently much safer than land travel, as the peoples who infested the tangled hills north and west of Greece were not renowned for their friendliness. So it was not a desire to broaden their minds that encouraged the Greeks to venture overseas but a desire for trade and a need for space. Almost certainly overpopulation explains the rolling programme of colonisation that distributed Greeks from the Asiatic shores of the Black Sea to southern France. When the need for colonisation was created the city would elect a leader, supply him with ships and colonists and send him into the Mediterranean. Rather than travel blind, the prospective colonists would have sought the advice of the gods and, more practically, would have consulted mariners who knew the area in which they proposed to settle. Around 750 BC the Greeks founded their first colonies outside the Aegean; Cumae just north of Naples on the western coast of Italy, and Sinope in the Black Sea. Cumae would be a staging post on the route to the mines of Tuscany, a function that Sinope would fulfil toward the mines of Transcaucasia. Perhaps Jason, seeker of the Golden Fleece, was a representation of the early explorers of the Black Sea. These were tentative ventures, followed by more intensive spreading as the Greek world expanded east and west. By 550 BC there were Greek colonies all along eastern Sicily and southern Italy, at Cyrenaica in Libya, on the northern shore of the Black Sea and, significantly, at Massilia in southern France.

Born in the Greek colony of Halicarnassus on the Anatolian coast around 485 BC, Herodotus was a well-travelled man whose historical writings earned him the title 'the father of history'. It was Herodotus who claimed that the Phocaeans, a Greek people from the area in the Gulf of Smyrnia, now Izmir in Turkey, 'were the first of the Greeks to undertake long sea voyages.' According to Herodotus, these Phocaeans were the first to venture into 'Adria...and Tyrrhenia, and Iberia and Tartessos.' If Adria is taken to mean the Italian coast of the Adriatic, Tyrrhenia as the western Italian coast and Iberia as Spain, then the Phocaean Greeks virtually opened up the western Mediterranean, thus making the discovery of the Strait of Gibraltar and the Atlantic

Ocean a virtual certainty. Herodotus named the Phocaean ships as pentecosters, a name that referred to their 50 oars. They were long ships, narrow, with a distinct keel and although they possessed a cloth sail the northerly wind prevalent in the Aegean summer did not encourage the development of this method of propulsion.

Herodotus claimed that a Mediterranean storm carried a man named Kolaios right out of the Mediterranean until he 'passed out between the Pillars of Heracles and came to Tartessos.' This may not be correct, for it is unlikely that a storm drove the unfortunate Kolaios around 1500 miles through the island-studded Mediterranean. To travel to Iberia the Phocaeans may have coasted up Italy to Elba, then possibly crossed the open sea to the northern spur of Corsica, following the rocky shoreline south to the larger island of Sardinia. With the Mediterranean so familiar today, it is hard to imagine it as being unknown. It would be a fascinating voyage for these Greeks, with every sweaty pull of the oars revealing some new wonder and the captain standing in the curved bow, intently studying the water in fear of shallows or rocks. If there were any signs of danger he would negotiate the ranks of gasping, naked oarsmen to reach the stern and steer his ship clear.

Around 650 years before the birth of Christ, the Phocaeans founded the nearly-forgotten colony of Hemeroskeion in Majorca, a couple of hundred miles from Sardinia, and possibly from here they probed the Spanish coast. South and west, pulling at the oars until, if Herodotus was correct, they discovered Tartessos. Whoever it was that penetrated through the Strait of Gibraltar, the sight of an unaccustomed horizon and the huge swells of the Ocean Sea must have been as frightening as it was perplexing. Would that mariner have realised that until his voyage the glory of Greece had glittered in a sea that was little more than a pond in comparison to the vastness that lay beyond the Rock? The Greeks knew about the East, they had sailed to India and possibly beyond, but this Ocean was an unknown entity.

However they came, the Greeks who reached Tartessos developed a friendship with a king named Arganthonius. The location of Tartessos is as uncertain as its description, but many scholars believe it to have been situated on the river Guadalquivir, with a native name of Tertis. Legend and myth have hazed this place with dazzling glamour for while some thought it a silver city, cruel reality reveals only minor settlements and commercial enterprise. Even silver mines did not necessarily mean prosperity for the men who wielded the pickaxes and whatever profits were made were not reflected in amazing architecture. Iberia was at least part Celtic, and the Celts were never renowned for their urban civilisation. A settlement, a large hill fort or a loose confederation of tribes perhaps, but certainly never a city in the Greek sense.

If the Phocaeans rowed their ships up the Guadalquivir river they might have rested at Cadiz, where in 1938 a late 7th century BC bronze Greek helmet was recovered. It is possible that the Greek stories of the splendour of Tartessos are responsible for some of the legends of Atlantis, but around a hundred years after the Greek discovery, Phoenician ships and their Carthaginian offspring claimed this western Mediterranean as their own. The Phoenicians came from the Levant, south and east of the homeland of the Phocaean Greeks. After the close relation of trading partners, Tartessos was relegated to a place of legend as the Greeks turned east and Carthage replaced them as the major power in the west.

The latest Greek find on the Atlantic coast of Spain was another helmet of the late 6th century BC, which possibly reveals the latest extent of Greek influence in the area. In the 5th century BC the Greek states were heavily involved in the war with Persia and her ally, Phoenicia, whose Carthaginian colony closed the strait between the Mediterranean and Atlantic by garrisoning the larger island in a bay not far from the mouth of the Guadalquivir. With their genius for austere names, the Carthaginians called this base Gadir, which meant stronghold, and in time the Roman version, Gades, became Cadiz. From Gadir the Carthaginians could prevent any Greek merchant vessels from penetrating the strait. Algeciras, opposite Gibraltar, might have been an additional base for Carthaginian warships. Despite being defeated by the Phocaeans off Corsica in 535 BC, Carthage continued to control the strait, and therefore dominated the Atlantic trade routes. Nonetheless the Phocaeans retained their major colony of Massalia in southern France, and traded along the Iberian coast.

If the Greeks have the gloss of romance around their exploits, the Phoenicians were the seafaring professionals. They were never a united single people for they owed allegiance only to their individual city-states that clung to the rocky coast of Lebanon, but the sea was their life. They were traders who carried cargoes of carved ivory and coloured glass, fabrics dyed with Tyrian purple and ingots of smelted metal but they were also noted slavers and pirates. Phoenician exploration was commercially based as they searched for new trading outlets.

There were two types of Phoenician ships, long ships for warfare and round ships for trade. The trading ships were the smaller, with a rounded stem and stern, a broad beam and a deep hold. Purely muscle powered, they had perhaps six oars on each side in one or two banks, and lacked a mast or sail. Warships also had two banks of oars while the long pointed bow thrust arrogantly forward to act as a ram in the close combat that characterised naval warfare of the period. When the explorer-historian Tim Severin constructed a vessel to retrace the route of Jason into the Black Sea, the ram also made a 'marked improvement in the galley's behaviour', helping her slip through the water and flattening the bow wave so the oarsmen could row in smoother water. Although most Mediterranean warships utilised the ram, the black pitch that sealed the ships from the water was purely Phoenician and ensured the distinctiveness of their vessels.

The helmsman stood in the convex stern, using the steering oar that plunged into the sea over one quarter as he watched both the set of the sail on its central mast and the labouring oarsmen. The ship's captain would know the season for the winds, would be aware of the drift of the currents, the way of the stars and the position of headlands and islands. He would also watch the flights of birds. If the men had to fight they would don their linen corselets, slip a bronze helmet over their head and grip a javelin in calloused hands. About 700 BC the trireme, with three banks of oars, made its appearance, adding to the speed of the ships. With the Phoenicians owning fleets of

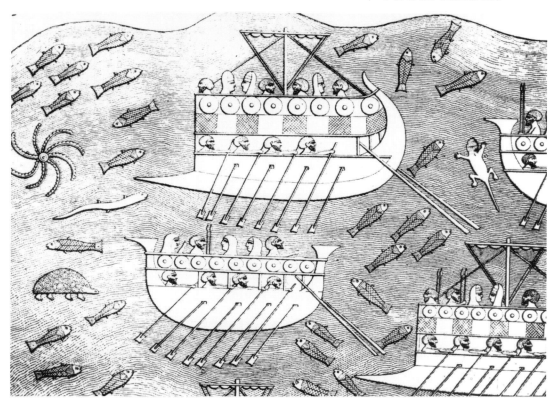

'*...the Phoenicians were the seafaring profesonals.*' Courtesy of the Billie Love Collection, Isle of Wight.

perhaps 150 or 200 of these vessels it was not surprising that Persians and other land-based powers employed them as mercenaries.

For many centuries the Egyptians had been trading down the Red Sea to Arabia and the coast of east Africa, and as knowledge of the discovery of the Atlantic spread, it seemed obvious that the world was completely surrounded by water. There was an Ocean River whose current ran down the east coast of Africa and poured into the Mediterranean through the Strait of Gibraltar. Within this Ocean River sat the disc of the world, with the Mediterranean a central sea. When Herodotus visited the Greek trading post of Naukratis on the Nile, he was told about Pharaoh Necho of Egypt who sometime around the 6th century BC sent Phoenician seamen to follow this Ocean River.

According to the story, the Phoenicians travelled during the summer, planted grain in autumn and spent the winter ashore while their crops ripened. After two years of journeying, they reached the Pillars of Heracles and another year brought them back to Egypt. As a story it surely ranks alongside the Odyssey, but Herodotus inserted one significant sentence. At one stage, he informs us, the mariners 'had the sun on their right hand as they sailed along the African coast'. This may mean that at one point the Phoenicians were in the Southern Hemisphere and sailing west, which would certainly be possible on the eastern coast of South Africa. If they circumnavigated Africa, these Phoenicians would have been the first known people to navigate on the Atlantic, but no known epic commemorates their achievement; only the brief words of Herodotus.

But was this journey possible? As these would be picked and experienced seamen, used to the perils of rowing along sometimes dangerous coasts, there is no reason that the distance could not be achieved, given enough time. From Egypt to the Horn of Africa the Red Sea was as familiar as the Mediterranean while south of Cape Guardafui the northeast monsoon thrusts any sailed craft down the 3000 miles toward Mozambique, where the Agulhas Current would take over. The southern tip of Africa would have posed problems, for the Portuguese had good reason for naming this the Cape of Storms, but after that the Benguela Current would help the Phoenicians past the horrors of the Skeleton Coast. The Southeast Trades would help push the Phoenicians northward to the equator, but the currents and wind systems of the North Atlantic are less sympathetic. Off the western bulge of Africa the winds come from the north and they would be rowing against the current, but by now the stars at least would be friendly. Once through the strait, the eastward passage along the Mediterranean would feel like a pleasure cruise. But who would believe the tales these men had to tell? Amazing though this voyage might have been, it did not lead to a spate of emulators: the Phoenicians were businessmen and travel without commerce was a waste of time.

As Herodotus is silent about Hanno, his circumnavigation attempt probably took place after the historian's death, possibly toward the end of the 5th century BC. With the Levantine city-states under the heel of Persia, Phoenician power was concentrated in its sea-colony of Carthage. Strategically situated at the Strait of Tunisia, Carthage squatted inside the shelter of Cape Bon, possibly based around the sandy beaches of what is today the suburb of Le Kram. The name Carthage may derive from *qart hadasht*, meaning new town; a fitting name for surely one of the more successful of Phoenician colonies. As a reminder of the nature of these black-shipped seamen, archaeologists have unearthed thousands of urns that contained sacrificial ashes, for first-born children were sacrificed to Tanit or Moloch, god of fertility. There were two sections in the harbour of Carthage – a southern commercial section and a northern, military section. From an island in the northern harbour an Admiral controlled the sleek warships that kept the Greek vessels out of the western Mediterranean and sent vessels to conquer Sardinia, fight in Sicily and to trade from Tyre to the tin land of Cornwall.

Simultaneous to Greek defeat of a joint Persian-Phoenician fleet at the battle of Salamis, a Carthaginian army failed in Sicily. Baulked in the east, Carthage faced west, sending Hanno to sail down and around the African coast. Some details of this voyage were carved on the Carthaginian temple of Kronos and a version was copied in the 10th century AD and preserved in the University of Heidelberg. According to the surviving account, Hanno sailed with 60 pentecosters and 30,000 men and women. Presumably he left the majority of these settlers at the six cities he is claimed to have founded on the African coast. There is mention of the large river Lixos that flowed from Libya 'beside which nomads called Lixitae pastured their flocks'. The Phoenicians explored inland, meeting 'inhospitable Ethiopians' and wild animals. Further south they left a settlement on an island they named Cerne, and beyond that was a large river called Chretes.

Twelve days south of Cerne was another river, populated with 'crocodiles and hippopotamuses' and further south yet was a 'fiery coast' where 'great streams of fire and lava poured down into the sea'. They sailed on, past a mountain with the evocative name of Chariot of the Gods to a gulf they termed Horn of the South where there was an island containing a lake. On that lake was another island containing what the Phoenicians thought were savages, mainly 'women with shaggy bodies' that the African guides called gorillas. The Phoenicians caught, killed and flayed three of these gorillas and, as their provisions were short, returned with the skins to Carthage.

Historians have identified the River Lixos as the River Draa in southern Morocco and the Lixitae as Berbers. Cerne appears to be the most southern settlement of either Phoenicians or Carthaginians, and could be anywhere between the western Sahara and the delta of the Senegal River, which river has been identified with the Chretes. The mountain named Chariot of the Gods may be Mount Cameroon, at over 13,000 feet, or Kakulima at nearly 3000 feet in Guinea. To sight either peak reveals that the Carthaginians were notable seamen, but that was not an end to their nautical exploits for Carthaginian coins of the 3rd century BC were discovered on the Azores in 1749.

Pliny wrote of a Carthaginian named Himilco who was sent to explore 'the parts beyond Europe' and pushed past the Pillars of Heracles. He sailed northward around Spain and Portugal to the coast of Brittany, the Oestrymnian promontory, from where men sailed to Ireland in skin covered boats. From Brittany it was a relatively short distance to Britain, and legend credits Himilco with being the first Carthaginian to become involved in the Cornish tin trade.

It could have been around 308 BC, when Carthage was distracted by a Sicilian war, or around 240 BC, when Rome weakened the city, that Pytheas of Massalia slipped past the Gades garrison and into the Atlantic. To an extent the date is irrelevant, for it is the voyage that reveals the maritime ability of the Phocaean. Pytheas probably sailed in a Massalian merchant vessel, the largest of which were about 150 feet long, 500 tons in weight and drew 12 feet of water. After coasting along Mediterranean Spain he steered past the Pillar of Heracles, cheekily put into Gades to stock up for the voyage ahead and headed west along the rocky coastline that had known only Carthaginian ships for so long. Avoiding the tumultuous seas at Cape St Vincent, Pytheas sailed past Portugal and along the northern Iberian coast to the great bite of the Bay of Biscay. He passed the estuaries of the Gironde and the Loire and from the isle of Uxisame, possibly off Britanny, he sailed into the open sea to Cornwall.

To have the confidence to leave the coast, Pytheas must have had some knowledge of his route, or perhaps a local Celtic pilot. From Cornwall, he coasted northward into the volatile waters of the Irish Sea and onward, around the Mull of Galloway, threaded through the Hebrides to the 'very ends of the habitable world' where the great green rollers of the North Atlantic explode against the cliffs of Cape Wrath. Not surprisingly, Pytheas was alarmed by the eddies and swift current of the Pentland Firth between Scotland and Orkney, but he learned of an island six day's voyage further north and heard reports of midsummer days with 20 hours of daylight. Probably he was at Shetland, whose windswept austerity would appear bleak to his Mediterranean eyes and may even have voyaged to the frozen sea that lay somewhere north of the Faroe Islands.

From the north-eastern tip of Scotland Pytheas seems to have headed east across the North Sea, for there are claims he reached the source of the amber trade at the entrance of the Baltic Sea. Perhaps he threaded past the Kattegat, more likely he touched on Jutland before recrossing to Britain. 'This island' he stated 'is densely inhabited, but has a very cold climate...there are many chieftains and rulers; but these for the most part live in peace with one another'. Surely one of the most daring of early maritime explorers, Pytheas completed his circumnavigation of Britain, crossed the Strait of Dover and then faded into obscurity. If there had been a Homer to add drama to the bare bones of a stupendous voyage, Pytheas might have been as well remembered as Odysseus.

Pytheas was more than just a seaman who sailed to landfalls that no other southerner was to see for centuries. He was also one of the first men to use observations of the sun's altitude to fix the latitude of places he visited and the first Greek to understand the moon's influence on the tide. It was unfortunate that his explorations were not followed up and no Mediterranean trading fleet ventured to the coasts of Scotland or Ireland.

After Rome razed Carthage in 146 BC the passage to the Atlantic was free. A comparative flood of sailors poured through the strait. There was Midariyus, that Pliny claimed was 'the first to import lead from the Tin Land'. There was Euthymenes, another Phocaean from Massalia who sailed south along the African coast until he reached a crocodile-infested river that he thought was the Nile. There was Polybius of Megalopolis who took a Roman fleet through the strait and sailed south until he came to the Carthaginian settlement established by Hanno. There was the remarkable Eudoxus of Cyzicus in the Black Sea, who already had made the round trip to India and back twice. However, he disliked handing over his profits to the Ptolemaic rulers of Egypt and decided to sail home by circumnavigating Africa. With a varied crew that included physicians, dancing girls and artisans, Eudoxus was forced aground on his first attempt, travelled further on his second and vanished on his third.

Once the Carthaginians were quashed it was obvious that the Romans would head west. While the legions marched on land, the Roman ships, steadily unspectacular, thrust into the Atlantic, meeting the local mariners and either defeating or absorbing them. After Gaul, remorseless Rome targeted Britain, with Agricola's fleet ploughing along the Scottish east coast. There seems to have been a landing in Orkney, for the local chief submitted, and the Romans continued their exploration until *dispecta est Thule* – even Thule was seen. In this case Thule may have been Shetland, 50 miles to the north. From that northern point the Romans rounded Cape Wrath and slipped south to safer waters. Now all western Europe south of Scandanavia had been explored, and the surf of the eastern Atlantic pounded on familiar shores. Yet it was to be some hundreds of years before Europe crossed the next obstacle and faced the daunting width of the Atlantic.

Chapter 2

By Curragh and Knorr

'I pray the blameless monk-prover
Our Father, my journey to further
Heaven's Lord may he bless and let hover
His hawk-perching hand over my head.
Hafgerdingadrapa (The Lay of the Towering Waves)
Norse, 10th century AD.

At Cossans in Scotland the nine foot tall Standing Stone of Saint Orland carries carvings of a Dark Age boat. High-prowed and wooden-built, this vessel has a steering oar, a crew of five and tells something of the long maritime tradition of Scotland. When the earliest settlers arrived, sometime before 6500 BC, they may have used the heavy dugout canoes that have been unearthed from time to time but presumably the next wave of farmer immigrants sailed in something large enough to carry livestock. They may have used the leather curragh of the Celt, or boats built of hewn planks, and they were augmented by a race of people who traded in the stone axes that were essential for clearing the dense Caledonian forest. Whoever they were, the axe traders were skilled seamen who travelled between mainland Europe and Britain and erected the best of their existing monuments on the islands of the north. Given the difficulties of land transport with dense forest, wild animals and water-logged lowlands the sea was a natural highway.

There was significant settlement on the nautical crossroads of Orkney, that scattering of islands besieged by Atlantic surf, battered by Arctic gales and facing the North Sea that stretched to the coasts of Scandinavia. Of the Neolithic settlements in these northern isles probably the best known is Skara Brae, home for fishermen and cattle breeders for something like 500 years, but there are many others, from Maeshowe in Orkney, to Puna Water in Shetland. Only evocative ruins now, with the wind wailing through shattered stonework, but once home to people who knew the beat of the sea and the bite of salted wind.

The Bronze Age brought new technology and new people, with forgotten traders shipping Irish gold northward along the Atlantic fringe, but it was another thousand years before the Celts burst into the esoteric islands of Britain. By then the climate had deteriorated becoming cooler, wetter, and the atmosphere altered as chieftains in wickerwork chariots brought iron weapons and a love for ostentatious display. This was the time of the crannog, those artificial islands whose remains merge with the silt-bed of a hundred lochs, and of the spectacular brochs that loom across the northern seas. Some 500 brochs stand in Scotland and they might well have been built as a defence against the half-legendary Formorians who swooped down on the northern coasts of Scotland, or perhaps the Formorians built them as pirate dens. Possibly Bronze Age natives erected them as protection against raiding Celts from the south; the mute mystery of history leaves only theories and the chill austerity of enduring stone.

Far to the south, in Broughter in Ireland, there is a model of a first century Celtic boat. Open to the elements, this vessel was around 50 feet long, had eight pairs of oars and a single central mast. The oars have blades, unlike the slim pattern currently used on Irish curraghs, and it appears that the hull of the boat was of leather. The technique of stretching hides onto a wooden-framed boat was highly developed among the Celts, who used leather boats for long voyages and over a long period of time. The light weight of the curragh gave them the ability to ride the worst of any weather, and if the lack of a keel made them vulnerable to cross seas and crosswinds, it also gave them the ability to beach in places often inaccessible to later craft.

The Irish king Niall of the Nine Hostages used curraghs when he raided the southern British coasts in the Dark Ages and he was only one of the Celtic warriors to use seapower aggressively. Rome had attempted to restrain the Picts behind the Antonine Wall that rested on the Forth and Clyde, possibly with a naval base on either flank. As Roman power deteriorated, Pictish raids became bolder, forcing them to erect defensive forts on the coast of Cumbria and mount coastal patrols with vessels manned by specialists in maritime guerrilla warfare. Not all Celtic craft were leather; wooden vessels are mentioned in one version of the *Navigo Sancti Brendani Abbatis.*

In dark-age Ireland disputes for land were not uncommon and more powerful neighbours pressed hard on the tiny kingdom of Dalriada. Accustomed to crossing the stormy waters between the islands of Ireland and Britain, Fergus MacEirc put his curraghs to the waves and sailed east to Alba – now Scotland. There were said to be 150 men in the fleet and it is possible to imagine the small curraghs bobbing on the short passage, their sails straining, oars propelling these 5th century Pilgrim Fathers toward a harsher, pagan land. By a combination of diplomacy, marriage and force the Dalriadans thrived in the gentle rain and frequent storms of the Alban west, while their constant passages to the islands and to Ireland honed their nautical skills. From his capital at Dunadd King Aedan of Dalriada waged war with Antrim and Orkney and Man, and seapower was so important that the nobility provided oarsmen rather than soldiers. All this maritime expertise made sea travel routine among the Gaels.

While bravery was expected of the warriors, it was equally evident among the Christian monks who explored the seaways of the west, spreading the gospel or finding near inaccessible islets on which to worship the Lord. It took courage to face totally uncharted waters in boats of twigs and hide, but these monks had incredible faith. From their base on Iona they travelled extensively, sometimes to Ireland, sometimes to other Scottish islands or to the mainland. While Saint Columba visited Skye, Ardnamurchan and Inverness other monks explored further afield.

Iona was their base and Adomnan their recorder as Celtic holy men boarded their curraghs and carried the cross far into the North Atlantic. With their sails pushing them on, these strange, blunt nosed craft passed the terrible tide rips of Orkney and struggled through the Sumburgh Roost to Shetland. Amongst the most intrepid of the explorers was Cormac Ua Liathain, who not only explored the northern isles but also took his curragh a further 14 days into the unknown north. As Adomnan wrote: 'Such a voyage appeared to be beyond the range of human exploration, and one from which there could be no return'.

Cormac was a colleague of that other legendary wanderer, Brendan of Clonterf, who was possibly the most successful of these Celtic explorers. Even if the stories are only partially true his journeys were as weird as those of Sinbad and contain clues of his route that shine like sails on a sunlit sea. Brendan seems to have reached the Faeroe Islands, perhaps even Iceland, and he is remembered as Brendan the Navigator. The tales tell of him landing on an island of sheep, on the back of a whale and finding an island of sparkling crystal. There is little doubt that whales would be sighted in the North Atlantic, while the island of sheep could be the Faeroes. The crystal island must surely be an iceberg.

Knowing the ways of birds, the seamen might have followed the skeins of long-necked geese that winged their way northward. There are few more evocative sights and sounds in nature than migrating geese, their call as mournful and lonely as the cry of a whale and their passage north surely an invitation to any adventurous seaman. It was long after Brendan's time that an Irish monk named Dicuil wrote *World Geography* while he was at the Carolingian court. Dicuil had met a monk from the Faeroes, two days sail from 'the northernmost British Isles' that had been inhabited by Celtic priests since around 720. Other priests had visited Thule, probably Iceland, before being driven away by Viking attacks. Even more fascinating is Dicuil's knowledge of permanent pack ice north east of Iceland, revealing the range of penetration by the Celts. This range extends further when it is remembered that the Dark Age climate was warmer and the ice field correspondingly further north. However much a reputation the later Norse gained for their seamanship, in the eastern Atlantic they followed the route of Celtic monks.

When the Swede Gardar Svavarsson[1] sailed from Scandinavia to the Hebrides, it was said that an Atlantic storm blasted him to Iceland, where he made a landfall near Papey, a name derived from the Celtic priests who were already there. Yet however

---

[1] A Swedish seaman of the Dark Ages who explored part of the Icelandic coast.

brave and resourceful the Celtic monks had been, they had not colonised Iceland but had only used it as a retreat from the world. Gardar was a more efficient explorer, and sailed past the eastern Horn, past mountains of ice and the violent rivers of the Vatnajokul to the mournful coast of the south. He saw Faxafloi and the cone of Snaefellsjokul, until at last the longship rounded the North Cape and reached the fertile valleys of Hunafloi. Gardar overwintered at Skjafandi, continued his circumnavigation the following spring and returned to more hospitable shores.

While the Celtic priests had been searching for solitude, the Norsemen were raiders and colonists, but of all European people, they were most wedded to the sea. Their reputation as Viking warriors taints their memory as explorers, yet both images are true. The early Norse were pagan, worshipping hammer-wielding Thor who controlled the weather but they sailed in some of the most beautiful vessels that have ever existed.

Clinker-built, the longship was the end product of centuries of endeavour in the sheltered Norwegian fjords. With planks painstakingly adzed to perfection and restrained by iron rivets, they were vessels of great strength yet possessed a surprising flexibility that enabled them to survive the force of the Atlantic seas. Yet the shallow

"...of all European people (the Norse) were most wedded to the sea". Remains of a Norse ship from a cairn at Gokstad. Courtesy of the Billie Love Collection, Isle of Wight.

draught of these ships allowed them to penetrate far up coastal rivers so they were excellent for exploration. Prior to the 8th century Norse ships were still mainly oar-powered and lacked stability, but experience or inspired genius gave them the true keel, accurately determined strakes and ribs and deck in exact proportion to the hull. A superb surviving example is the *Gokstadt* ship, a copy of which crossed the Atlantic in 1893, but the *hafskip* or *knorr* surpassed even this. The *knorr* relied mainly on its single square sail, carried two ship's boats and a side rudder and was between 65 and 80 feet long. Given favourable weather such a ship could sail at up to 10 knots, travelling perhaps 100 miles in a good days' sailing.

Navigation in later Norse vessels was helped by the development of the sunstone, which contained calcite that helped to perform solar observations. By the 12th century the magnetic circle was divided into sixteenths, which enabled fairly accurate bearings to be taken while the stars, currents and behavioural patterns of birds would be well known.

Flokki Vilgerdarson followed the same route as Gardar Svavarsson when he attempted the first Norse colony in Iceland, but the Bay of Faxafloi was named after Faxi, a Hebridean of his crew. His settlement at Breidafjord was blighted by such a bitter winter that he named the island Iceland and attempted to leave, only to be stormbound into a second winter. When a more permanent settlement was made by Ingolfur Arnarson in the late 9th century, the geographical knowledge of the North Atlantic had not only been extended, but the maritime area was now associated with mainstream Europe. It was not so fortunate for others of Ingolfur's company however, for the ten thralls he had captured on his last Irish raid rebelled and Iceland was baptised with a mixture of Celtic and Norse blood. Notwithstanding this Celtic infusion, the settlement of Iceland was akin to a Norse saga, with high-prowed ships probing the ragged coasts, threading the fjords and laying the roots of homesteads. Whatever their faults, their innate blood-thirst, their pagan gods, their fractious quarrels, the Norsemen were professional mariners and at that stage in history only they could have thrived in these high latitude seas.

Iceland was one step further in the exploration of the North Atlantic and the next logical step was Greenland. It was a man named Gunnbjorn who was first to sight Greenland after being storm driven far to the west while voyaging from Norway to Iceland. He neither landed nor explored this new coast, but news of his sighting travelled widely until it reached one Eirik the Red. A family feud had forced the Norwegian Eirik to Iceland, where he found all the best land already occupied. Stuck on a small holding on the austere and icy coast near Hornbjarg, Eirik moved south to Haukadal, became involved in more violence and finally decided to find the land glimpsed by Gunnbjorn. Iceland was simply too small for him. With his knack of making friends as easily as enemies, Eirik collected a crew and left for the unknown west. In the early summer of 982, with easterly winds propelling him across the 450 miles to Greenland, Eirik must have thought that there were better prospects ahead. However, the east coast of Greenland is bleak, unsuitable for settlement and Eirik slid south by south-west with the icecap backing the iron shore to starboard and nothing to entice him to land. At the tip of the island Eirik would either brave Cape Farewell or, more likely, thread through Prins Christians Sund, to find the coast climbing north-west.

There were islands that thronged with birds, a sea shoaled with fish, splashing with seals and whales. There were also fjords whose shoreline was carpeted with grass, bright flowers and a scattering of willow, birch and juniper. Best of all, there were no people, no neighbours with whom to feud, and Eirik named his country Greenland. He had taken three years on his voyage, and had not lost a single man. In 986 he returned with 14 ships full of colonists and Greenland had joined the orbit of European civilisation.

With this Norse settlement in western Greenland, it is perhaps inevitable that the next step westward should be taken, but here history steps beyond the shadowy and into the legendary. The sagas state that in 986 one Bjarni Herjolfsson was thrown west by a storm into an area of thick fog. When the fog lifted Bjarni realised he was close to an unknown coast with dense woods and low hills; disregarding the wishes of his crew, he sailed north. Within two days Bjarni sighted another coast but did not land. Driven for three days by a south-westerly wind, he sighted a third unknown coast, complete with mountains and ice, before finally heading for Greenland.

It took 14 years for the Norse to pursue this latest discovery, and it was Leif Eiriksson, the son of Eirik the Red, who commanded the expedition. There were 35 men in this, possibly the most famous and controversial of all the Norse voyages, and Leif started at the northerly land where Herjolfsson had finished. The first land he sighted appeared barren, just rock backed by glaciers, so he named it Helluland, the land of flat stones. From this apparently useless place the Greenlanders sailed south until they arrived at the low, wooded land, with 'wide stretches of white sand' which they named Markland, the land of woods.

Continuing south and south-east, Eiriksson discovered a cape with an offshore island, and sailed west in the passage between the two. Next they found a salmon river, and overwintered on an inland lake. They were somewhere south of Greenland and even in the winter there was no frost, which detail hints at somewhere far more southerly than New England. When a German of the crew discovered vines, Eiriksson named the country Vinland and returned to Greenland with the spring.

It was Leif's brother Thorvald Eiriksson who was next to sail west and became the first known European to be killed by the native Americans. His memory was maintained in Krossanes – Crossness – but this misadventure did not deter others from following. A third Eiriksson brother, Thorstein, failed to reach Vinland, but one Thorfinn Karlsefni reached the vine-growing region, where he also found wheat. Women had not figured in any of these voyages, but now Freydis, Eirik's daughter, decided to visit this land that was like a second home to her family.

There were five other women among the 95 people on her two ships, but either Freydis fostered a dislike for the Icelandic brothers Helgi and Finnbogi who came with her, or they offended her in some way. For whatever reason, as she overwintered at her brother's old camp, Freydis, obviously an assertive woman, persuaded her husband to murder the Icelandic brothers and their followers. After that Freydis wanted the other women killed, and when her men refused, she borrowed an axe and murdered them herself. This bloody expedition seems to mark the last Vinland venture of the Norsemen, but it leaves the question of veracity wide open. How accurate were these Norse accounts of their discoveries?

Given that the Norse settlements in Greenland were factual, there is little reason to doubt their ability to cross the intervening sea to North America, but which area of the continent they discovered is open to speculation. Few accounts give details of the distances travelled, which is understandable as the sagas were a mixture of family history and entertainment rather than sailing directions, but the account of Bjarni Herjolfsson was an exception. A full day's sail on a Norse ship was approximately 100 miles, so if Bjarni's first landfall was in southern Labrador, his second would be 200 miles further up the Labrador coast and his third, at a stretch, would take him to the south-east of Baffin Island.

However, there are no vines in Labrador, or for a considerable distance further south. It is a possibility that Vinland does not signify vines, but is a derivation of *ven*, a grassy plain, and the stories of grapes are a later, literary addition. If the discovery of grapes is disregarded, the Norse descriptions of the topography, rocky land to the north, dense flat forest further south, would suit southern Labrador and north Newfoundland. It is also possible that the milder climate of the period allowed grapes to flourish at a higher latitude. As late as 1530 Jacques Cartier found grapes around the St Lawrence River. It would be nice to think that they did push further south, romantic to think of Norse longboats probing past Cape Cod or cruising in the Chesapeake, and perhaps they did. Maybe the sagas dealing with these voyages were lost, or archaeological evidence is still to be discovered. But as the exploits of these Norse mariners were ignored or confined to mythology, mainstream Europe would have to wait for discovery of the New World.

There is another question: if the Norse discovered fertile land in North America, why did they not settle there? Perhaps the prevailing weather conditions were influential. When the westerly winds fail to bring storms to these seas south-west of Cape Farewell, there are periods of dense fog. Later navigators suffered losses in these seas, and the Norse must have been similarly afflicted. Even the Greenland colonies sat insecurely on the periphery of European navigation, particularly when the climate began to deteriorate. Their history is one of slow degeneration as Iceland lost her independence and Scandinavia was torn by political disturbances. Interestingly, when an English friar sailed to Greenland in 1360, he mentioned clearings in the woods where trees were felled. As there are no woods in Greenland, his geography may be faulty and he might have visited Labrador. However, only nine years later the last known trading ship sailed to Greenland and thereafter the Norse colony vanished from European ken.

Interest in the far Western Ocean did not die with the Norse colonies in Greenland, and the Celts did not lose their nautical skills when the Dark Ages waned. It was in the late 12th century that a Welshman named Madoc became involved in a family dispute that necessitated him sailing away. According to the story Madoc found land far in the west and around 1170 he came back to Wales, recruited more colonists and again headed across the Atlantic. This time he did not return. In 1669 new credence was given to the legend when the Rev. Morgan Jones returned from North Carolina with a story of how his party was captured by Indians who threatened to kill them. When Jones turned to his companions and told them to prepare themselves for death the Indians were said to have understood his Welsh, welcomed them as cousins and set them free. Unfortunately for romance, most people today believe that the story of Madoc was a myth.

There is also the 14th century legend of the Venetian seaman named Nicolo Zeno who was driven ashore in the Faeroe Islands, where he met 'Zichmini', who may have been Henry Sinclair, Earl of Orkney. If the story is correct, Zeno joined Sinclair's fleet in an attack on Shetland, during which an opposing Norwegian fleet was driven back by a gale. Left in command of a Shetland fort, Zeno interviewed local fishermen who spoke of sighting land in the far west. When Sinclair and Zeno sailed west, they landed in a new country and spoke with new people. Interestingly, this account ties in with a Micmac[2] legend that mentions ancient European visitors. There are other hints of this expedition; stone carvings of a mediaeval knight in New England, a pre-Columban cannon found off Nova Scotia and, even more intriguingly, carvings of North American maize in Rosslyn Chapel near Edinburgh, which was owned by Sinclair.

However, even if mediaeval Europeans crossed the Atlantic their probes at best were tentative. For the overwhelming majority of Europeans, the Atlantic Ocean remained an appalling barrier that only a madman or a hero could overcome. Or perhaps a red-headed Genoese known as Columbus.

---

[2] The Micmac are a native American tribe of eastern Canada and belonged to what are now Nova Scotia, New Brunswick and Prince Edward Island.

Chapter 3

Admiral of the Ocean Sea

'Over the cloud bridge of illusion lies the path of human progress.'
Fridtjof Nansen, In Northern Mists

At the beginning of the 15th century Europeans were generally ignorant of most geography beyond their own continent. What they did know was little more than mythology; they believed that the sea boiled south of the equator, they had heard of Marco Polo's Chipangu (the name that he gave to Japan), and they knew that the Ocean Sea stretched westward into the forever. By the end of the century a hundred voyages had multiplied their knowledge and two seamen from the Italian peninsula had opened up the western world. One was John Cabot, a native of Genoa but a citizen of Venice who had long experience in the trade of the East. The other was Christopher Columbus, also from Genoa, but sailing on behalf of Castile. Yet the Italians were not the only people exploring the Atlantic.

When Henry the Navigator first instigated Portuguese exploration of the African coast there was a proverb 'He who would pass Cape Nam will not return'. When a daring mariner proved this wrong it was only to find that Cape Bojador was worse. Bojador is an extended rocky arm of Africa whose vicious currents and splintering seas bar the passage south, but the Portuguese persevered, gradually unlocking the secrets of the Atlantic coast of Africa.

There was a combination of reasons for this explosion of European exploration. There was the development of more efficient shipping, the Moslem capture of Constantinople and the discovery of the compass. Around 1200 the Arab navigational aid of magnets floating in a bowl of water began to filter through to European mariners, while later that century an Englishman known as Robert devised a method of calculating latitude, so taking away much of the fear of sailing out of sight of land. Northern

European mariners used a *rutter*, a book that described voyages and ports, soundings and tides, with the best master mariners improving their rutter with each new voyage. Following a Genoese prototype, charts became generally available, with a pilot laying his course along any of the spider's web of pre-drawn lines. When seamen ventured outside their normal confines, however, there could be neither chart nor rutter to help them.

But why sail south along the inhospitable shore of Africa or west and ever west where there was nothing save sea serpents, and storms that could shred the sails from a shattered ship? For trade, treasure and perhaps especially spices, for at a time before preservatives Europeans needed Eastern spices to disguise the taste of rancid food. Even after the capture of Constantinople by the Turks, galleys from Venice traversed the Mediterranean to bring spice to Europe, but many mariners wondered if an alternative route east could bypass the middle man. Others remembered the riches that Marco Polo had spoken of in Chipangu where there were 'so many precious stones that you only have to bend down and pick them up'. According to Polo, Chipangu was all of 1500 miles from the coast of China, a geographical miscalculation that was to influence the imagination of Columbus.

In the meantime the Portuguese continued to probe south and west. In 1418 Madeira was discovered, with the first Portuguese Madeirans christened Eve and Adam in a rebirth of humanity as significant as the ongoing European Renaissance. Many more vessels followed the African coast. Diego Gomez sailed south from Morocco in 1445, but his three caravels hardly passed Cape Verde when powerful currents convinced his crew that they had reached the end of the world. Rather than India, Gomez explored the Gambia. In the 1450s the Venetian Alvise Da Cadamosto pushed into the Atlantic, called at Madeira, continued to the Canary Islands and coasted along Africa until he too reached the Gambia River. The following year he sailed as far as Cape Blanco, where an offshore storm drove him to the Cape Verde Islands, 2000 sea miles from Portugal. These islands were an excellent staging post for the African gold trade that had proved a diversion from pure exploration. However, Cadamosto continued south, reaching Conakry before heading back to Portugal. Further explorers followed, pushing along the jungle-lined coast, discovering and naming coasts and headlands and islands. Even when Prince Henry the Navigator died his work continued under King John II until the southern tip of all Africa was reached and rounded and the wonders of the East were exposed for exploitation.

Although Portugal was the instigator of these explorations, there were many mariners from the Mediterranean sailing free in the Ocean Sea. One of them is known as Christopher Columbus.

Sometime between 25th August and 31st October 1451, Cristobal Colon, or Cristoforo Colombo or Christopher Columbus was born, probably in the city of Genoa. His father, a weaver and the son of a weaver, was to have four more children, but it was his eldest who changed history. Genoa was a historical maritime city with a trading network that extended from the Mediterranean to Africa, the Low Countries and possibly Iceland so a Genoese mariner could see a fair chunk of the known world. Columbus was such a mariner and in 1476, off the Portuguese coast, a French pirate attacked his ship. Columbus swam ashore, made his way to Lisbon and found work as a chartmaker with his brother Bartholomew. He also met and eventually married Felipa, daughter of the Portuguese Governor of Madeira, that most Atlantic of islands. While Columbus certainly spent time in the Azores there is a possibility he sailed to Iceland, and some legends say he listened to stories of ancient voyages before he let the world know of his dreams.

For years Columbus had collected tales of strange items and strange people that had been washed up on Atlantic beaches; now he broadcast his belief that he could sail westward to Asia. His proposition of sailing to the Canary Islands, catching the eastern trades and following latitude 28 degrees until he hit first the island of Antilla and then Chipangu was received with scepticism. Although his intention of founding an entrepôt at Chipangu was laudably far-sighted, his calculation of distance was totally mediaeval. He believed that Chipangu lay only 2,400 nautical miles from Europe. But that seemed to be part of the character of Columbus, he was a strange mixture of practical seaman and dreamer, an eccentric who hoped that royalty would back him.

Columbus was tall with a ruddy complexion, clear grey eyes and red hair that turned white when he was a comparatively young man. He must have been resolute, even stubborn and if he had not been a good seaman nobody would have accompanied him on his most famous voyage. It is known that his extensive reading included the works of Cardinal Pierre D'Ailly, who not only predicted that a French Revolution would occur around 1789, but also thought a man could sail to India from Spain 'in a few days with a good wind'.

Columbus presented King John II of Portugal with his idea, but a Board of Inquiry refused him either ships or finance. However King John was possibly less sceptical than his advisors, for he sent the experienced mariner Fermao Dulmo to search for Columbus' island of Antilla. Dulmo found nothing but an ocean of wild waves that battered his ships.

Perhaps Columbus would have been received with more respect if he had demanded less. Not content with being financed by the king, Columbus wanted to be 'Admiral of the Ocean Sea' with powers over all the islands and lands he discovered, plus an income of 10% of all the riches that might be there. It was the ransom of an egoist, an indication that Columbus coveted eminence in excess of his monarch, so King John could be excused his negative response. Columbus could not be considered to possess diplomacy as a major strength.

Disappointment was followed by grief as Felipa died. It is now impossible to tell how much this loss affected Columbus, but he certainly withdrew from both the sea and from Portugal as he entered a Spanish monastery. Perhaps his sorrow was eased by the presence of his son Diego, a permanent reminder of his wife. It was a monk of the monastery who, four years later, obtained him an audience with Ferdinand and Isabella of Castile, but even though Columbus offered them the opportunity of enriching him, the joint monarchs refused his request. It was 1486 and the Moorish wars of Granada were approaching their climax, so perhaps there were more important things to consider than the ideas of a reclusive Genoese. Of the two monarchs Isabella was either more sympathetic or more curious, for she sidestepped her husband and ordered a junta to consider a feasibility study. As the church-dominated junta deliberated, Columbus waited impatiently and the Atlantic tides beat on the shores of Iberia. The junta debated all the maritime information contained in the Psalms of David and the writings of Saint Paul, then discussed Saint Lactantius' doubts about a spherical world. After all, Lactantius wondered, could there be 'a place on earth where things are upside down, and where rain, hail and snow fall upward?' After five frustrating years the junta decided that Columbus' ideas were 'worthy only of rejection'. There were no Antipodes and, if there were, Columbus could never return.

The rejection must have been heart-breaking. Columbus was almost finished: poor, ragged, probably mentally and emotionally drained, he must have wondered at the pointlessness of his life. But as things seemed totally black, a spark of light came in the person of a seaman from Palos, Martin Alonso Pinzon. After years in the company of monks and princes and learned men, the presence of the practical, straightforward seaman must have been a blast of sanity. Helped by Juan Perez, Prior of La Rabida, Columbus again approached Queen Isabella. He was 40 years of age, not young by the standards of the time, but with Granada at last in Christian hands, the sovereigns could be diverted to other matters and Columbus gained his three-ship fleet.

It was now that Columbus made another miscalculation, based either on greed or on a hugely-inflated idea of his impact on the Queen. Again he made extravagant demands for titles, power and treasure. Probably stunned by the sheer nerve of this pauper sea captain, the sovereigns immediately withdrew their favour, and Columbus left the court. While he was riding away with his hopes in tatters and his future unknown, a messenger galloped after him; the sovereigns had again reversed their decision. On 17th April 1492 the Articles of Agreement were drawn up and then all that remained was for Columbus to sail into the unknown and discover Asia.

Perhaps it was understandable that Christopher Columbus found it difficult to scrape together crews for his ships. Professional seamen either scoffed at his notions, feared the voyage or wondered where the profit lay. Why should anybody volunteer to sail beyond the unknown when there were ships sailing to ports with guaranteed wine and women? Desperate, Columbus offered free pardons to criminals but it was Martin Pinzon who saved him. Pinzon's practical reputation helped the recruiting, his personal fortune helped finance the venture and his propaganda proved more efficient than the press-gang. If Columbus was the catalyst, it was Pinzon who made the expedition possible.

Today their names are famous, but back in 1492 they were merely another three small ships bobbing at anchor in Palos. The flagship was *Santa Maria*, commanded by Columbus, crewed by men from northern Spain and with her owner-master, Juan de la Cosa, always present. Supporting her was *Pinta*, commanded by Martin Pinzon, and

Nina, under Pinzon's brother Vincente. Both *Nina* and *Pinta* were caravels, a type of vessel that had been developed from a 14th century Mediterranean vessel. The earlier caravels had been two-masted and lateen-rigged, but experience of long ocean voyages resulted in the addition of a third mast, with a square rig on the forward masts and a lateen-rigged mizzen. This type of vessel was known as a *caravela rotunda*. *Pinta* was about 58 feet long and carried 18 men while *Nina* was 56 feet in length, 90 tons in weight and also held a crew of 18. Only *Nina* retained the Mediterranean lateen rig.

Although *Santa Maria* was designated a *nao*, she seems to have been similar in design to the caravels, but larger. She was around 95 feet long and 100 tons in weight, with a crew of perhaps 40. None of these vessels could be termed luxurious with only the captain and first officer having a cabin in the forecastle. The crew lived, worked and slept on the open deck, where they also ate their meals of salt meat, hard biscuits and dried peas. Of necessity they would be a hardy bunch, weather-beaten, tough and probably superstitious. Knowing the type of men who chose the sea, Columbus had brought enough wine to give each man two litres daily for four weeks.

Towards the evening of 2nd August 1492 Columbus commanded that everybody confess their sins and take Communion, and on next morning's ebb tide the three ships slipped down the Rio Tinto toward the Atlantic. It is unlikely if anybody gathered to watch the ships sailing out, but Columbus must have felt excitement as his dreams became reality. His decision to sail for Asia was bold, but he was not foolish enough to sail direct. The familiar seven-day voyage to Las Palmas in the Canary Islands revealed some defects in the ships, for *Pinta* broke her rudder and *Nina's* lateen rig was found unsuitable for the Atlantic. With a lateen sail, the tremendous length of the yard, combined with the necessity to lower the sail while tacking, wasted time and effort so *Nina* was re-rigged with square sails on her forward two masts 'so that she might follow the other vessels with more tranquillity and less danger'. At last, with the ships readied and an unseasonable calm endured, Columbus led out his flotilla. It was 6th September and as the western rim of the known world disappeared astern surely even he must have wondered if he was doing the right thing.

Each morning as the sun rose in their wake and familiar shores slipped further astern, the ship's boy blessed the day while the rest of the crew intoned the Lord's Prayer and the Ave Maria. Only then did the day's work commence, pushing the squadron westward into the Atlantic, towards their destiny, towards Asia. At sunset Columbus had the binnacle lamp lit as the ship's boy sang:

> *'God give us a good night and good sailing,*
> *May our ship make a good passage,*
> *Sir Captain and Master and good company.'*

Again the men intoned the Lord's Prayer, the Creed and the Ave Maria, but as the familiar, nostalgic words faded, they must have thought of home. There was beauty around them, the flickering binnacle lamps reflecting in the long Atlantic rollers, the sound of water surging beneath the prow, the slow glimmer of stars above, but what horrors lay ahead? The regular prayer for protection 'from the waterspout' and the tempest every time the hour-glass was turned may have given comfort to some, or perhaps it only served as a reminder of the precariousness of their position.

For ten days the weather remained quiet, light winds caressing the sails of the three ships, dolphins playing beneath the bows of *Santa Maria* and always they pushed gently west. Around them was only the empty horizon, neither monsters nor danger, so that Columbus could write that 'there is nothing lacking save the sound of nightingales'. Even the omens were propitious for on 15th September the superstitious among the crew were heartened when a fireball 'fell from the sky into the sea four or five leagues away'. But Columbus did not sit back and enjoy the voyage. Each day he wrote his log and each day he inserted false mileage. When *Santa Maria* travelled 55 leagues, Columbus wrote 48; when she travelled 25 leagues, Columbus wrote 22. His idea was to have a margin of error so the crew did not know how far they had travelled. In a voyage of a few days such small deceptions would make little difference, but with each entry the difference would increase.

By 16th September the crew were already looking for signs of land in seabirds and floating vegetation, but although Columbus was prepared to believe in Atlantic islands, he did not yet expect to sight Asia – 'I take the mainland to be somewhat further on' he recorded. The tension of uncertainty must have affected him, for the very next day he wrote, 'I trust the high God, in whose hands are all victories, will very soon give us land'. His trust seemed to be realised when Martin Pinzon witnessed a cloud of birds heading to the west, thought to be a sure sign of land. There was further hope on the 19th when boobies were sighted, for this was a species of bird 'not accustomed to fly more than twenty leagues from land'. Perhaps these boobies flew by different rules, for no land broke the heaving horizon of never-ending sea.

Much more disconcerting than the lack of land was the behaviour of the compass needle, which swung alarmingly west of the Pole. It was not surprising that this phenomenon frightened the seamen, as all their lives depended on the captain's navigation. When some murmured that nature surely changed this far west and they must all die, Columbus' skilled navigation replaced his prophetic dreaming. Taking sightings at dawn, when there was no variation, he calmed the crew with a mixture of sound practicality and scientific theory that either convinced them of his leadership or baffled them into silence.

The flotilla floated on, ever westward, with the sea slopping beneath the curved stems and the daily routine of the ships unchanging, as familiar as if they were sailing in the homely waters of the Mediterranean. These were European seamen, used to gales and storms and the constant threat of shipwreck and piracy, and their sea was green or blue or heaving, hissing grey. Then overnight, this sole constant in a world of variables had altered; the sea had turned *yellow*. The water beneath their hulls had sprouted vegetation. Nothing could have prepared them for this and there was near panic among the superstitious. Even Columbus must have been perturbed but as *Santa Maria* sailed on, apparently unhampered, with *Nina* and *Pinta* close and unimpeded, the crew's fears diminished. They realised that they would not be trapped forever in a tangle of treacherous weed. Columbus had encountered the Sargasso Sea. At that time this gulfweed flourished across vast expanses of the Atlantic, and its appearance was always surprising for the uninitiated. It is this surprise that gives credence to the claim that Columbus was first to cross at least this section of the Atlantic, for if others had preceded him the presence of the Sargasso Sea would have been known.

By 23rd September the very ease of their trades-assisted passage troubled the crew. How would they return in the teeth of this constant wind? Columbus smoothed this difficulty over with his usual combination of cunning and charm. When the sea rose despite a lack of wind, Columbus used religion to dispel the fears of his crew. 'I was in great need of these high seas' he said, adding that 'nothing like this had occurred since the time of the Jews, when the Egyptians came out against Moses who was leading them out of captivity'. Perhaps Columbus was searching for a sign, hoping for divine guidance in his search for Asia. If sincere religious faith sounds strange in our technological age, it was expected in the 15th century, before doubt seeped into Christianity. Columbus certainly did not conceive himself as a second Moses, leading Europeans to a land more flowing with milk and honey than Israel ever was. Nonetheless, the New World was to prove a melting pot for the divided peoples of the Old, a place of spiritual hope, physical rejuvenation and a self-assured democracy that turned established ideas upside down. Perhaps some divine agent used Columbus to enable the world to recognise its full potential. Yet whatever his inspiration, Columbus still referred to a chart created by people who had never sailed these waters. Towards the end of September Martin Pinzon and Columbus debated islands placed on this fanciful chart and worried over details drawn from a cartographer's imagination until Pinzon saw land. It must have been a tremendous moment, with Europeans having sailed directly to Asia across the western ocean. Marco Polo's Chipangu was just in front of them.

Within minutes men were scampering up the rigging of all three vessels, exchanging excited comments as they pointed to this unknown landfall. There was no mistake – land rose before them like a dark cliff. Columbus prayed his thanks to a munificent God, Martin Pinzon led his men in a heartfelt rendering of *Gloria in Exelsis Deo*, and then the ships hove to for the night. No doubt Columbus spent the night preparing for the diplomacy of the following day; for the first time representatives from Europe were to meet men of Chipangu.

Rather than diplomacy there was intense disappointment as the promised land proved an illusion. There was only the sea, its customary immensity stretching to a cruelly-unbroken horizon. Seventeen days at sea lay behind them, and how many lay in front? Nobody could know the answer to that as they sailed on into increasing warmth and fear of a boiling sea, fear of lurking sea monsters, fear that this ocean might never end. As the voyage continued Columbus stood alone on the forecastle, staring west, gazing at the stars, a man obsessed with his dream.

OPPOSITE: *A late 19th century map of the Atlantic illustrating the position of the Sargasso Sea.*

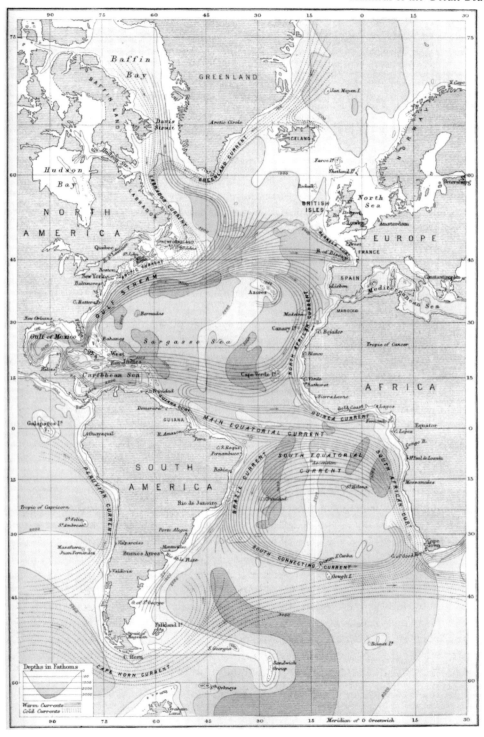

Across the Pond

Rather than use the speedy *Pinta* as a scouting vessel, Columbus kept his vessels together. The crew would feel more secure with friendly ships visible on the calm sea by day, would be reassured by the glimmer of lanterns across the dark sea by night. And still Columbus entered false mileage in his log; 24 leagues sailed on 29th September, and only 21 written down. As September passed into October the weather held fair and Columbus hoped for the charted islands to appear. But only flying fish rose from the sea, glittered momentarily in the brilliant air and disappeared beneath the waves. Now even Martin Pinzon revealed some doubt – on the 6th he advised that Columbus should steer south-west in case they missed Chipangu. Columbus, Admiral of the Ocean Sea, ignored him and the ships continued to sail into the unknown west.

Only when he saw a flight of birds flying from north to south-east did Columbus change his mind and course, but the horizon remained unbroken by land. *Santa Maria* sailed serenely, sometimes making eight knots, usually less but with the crew becoming increasingly restless. On 10th October a deputation approached Columbus with complaints about the length of the voyage, but Columbus rejected their demands; there would be no return until they had reached Chipangu. When the crew spoke of mutiny Columbus was nonplussed and Martin Pinzon saved the situation by bringing *Pinta* alongside *Santa Maria* and advising Columbus to hang half a dozen of the mutineers. The realisation that Columbus might just do that, augmented by his promise of sighting land within two days, calmed the crew.

Next day it seemed that Columbus was correct as for the first time in weeks there were signs of land – just green leaves and red berries on a floating branch, wood with unusual carvings and a floating plank, but enough for the crew to be 'rejoiced'. Another 27 leagues were covered before sunset and at ten in the evening what appeared to be a light gleamed ahead. With the caution taught by previous false alarms, the crew waited to see what morning brought.

Morning brought fleeting fame to a seaman named Rodrigo Bermajo. Perhaps others had crossed the Atlantic in the dim past, but if so their knowledge had been hazed by time. Rodrigo Bermajo made the first undisputed sighting of land in the western hemisphere by a European. Although the joint sovereigns of Spain had promised a pension for life to the first man to sight such land, Bermajo did not get a penny of it. Columbus, Admiral of the Ocean Sea, kept all the money for himself, an example of pettiness that diminishes his memory. This theft embittered Bermajo to such an extent that he left Spain for Africa and abandoned Christianity for Islam. The first sighting of the Americas had brought great expectations and resulted in disillusionment.

That dawn of 12th October 1492 found *Santa Maria* off a tiny Bahamian island that the natives knew as Guanahani, but which was quickly named San Salvador as Europe began its cultural imposition on the indigenous natives. At the sight of land, the crew of *Santa Maria* forgot their previous worries and clustered around Columbus, kissing his hand, asking his forgiveness and generally acting as men may do when they have survived imagined perils.

Columbus and the Pinzon brothers launched their ship's boats, hoisted the gallant banner of Castile and were rowed round the southern cape, through a gap in the coral reef to the curve of a quiet bay. When their boats slid onto the beach the captains and officers disembarked, knelt to kiss the soft sand, cried elated tears and thanked their God. As Columbus took possession of the island in the name of the monarchs of Castile, the captains and crewmen would watch, few understanding just how important this discovery was. It would make an interesting picture; the strong sun reflecting from armour and swords as the Europeans clustered on this first idyllic island of a New World. If the discovery of the Americas was to alter the world for Europeans, it was to completely shatter that of the naked, copper coloured natives who witnessed the landing.

Chapter 4

Unknown Coasts

'There will come men wearing clothes, who will dominate us and kill us.'
prophecy of the Arawak Indians, centuries before Columbus.

With no notion of property, the Arawak people of Guanahani neither cared nor understood when Columbus took possession of their island. To them, Columbus and his fellows were strange beings that had arrived in winged chariots, and when they could not answer his questions about Chipangu, Columbus up-anchored and sailed away. But instead of heading west, which would have brought him to the North American mainland, he sailed south, through the scattered Bahamas and on to Cuba, where rather than an oriental potentate he found tobacco. Still believing he was on the fringes of China, Columbus sailed on, to be astonished by the beauty of Hispaniola. It was now that *Pinta* slid away on a solo journey so *Santa Maria* had just *Nina* as a consort.

Columbus found the Arawak people free of vice, ignorant of the art of killing and willing to give away what little they had. But if he thought them 'the most loving people', he also observed that 'all the inhabitants of San Salvador could be taken away to Castile or held as slaves on the island'. On 20th December, after a leisurely cruise among the wonders of this gentle paradise, Columbus anchored in a Haitian bay he named Puerto Santo Tomas. Perhaps word of their arrival had spread, for hundreds of canoes surrounded the European ships and many of the indigenous people clambered on board. *Santa Maria* sailed for three more days but on the 24th, with Columbus and Juan de la Cosa cloistered in their cabins, the helmsman handed control of the ship to a young boy. Not surprisingly, *Santa Maria* ran onto a reef, the first known European shipwreck in the Americas.

Leaving the crew of *Santa Maria* with the gentle Arawaks, Columbus returned to Europe, and perhaps his messianic foresight guided him north-east to pick up the

Trades. Three weeks of fair winds may have lulled the explorers into thinking they had conquered the Atlantic, but the intensity of the inevitable storm removed forever any Columban sense of divinity. Meteorologists claim that Columbus' ships struggled through three separate weather fronts, but the seamen only knew about mast-high waves and a shrieking wind. This was sailoring as they knew it, fighting heavy seas with skill and a prayer while bare spars gyrated against a sky of ripped clouds. Columbus was so certain that he would lose his ship, and Castile would lose this wonderful new route to Asia, that he wrote a letter describing his discoveries to the joint sovereigns, put it in a sealed cask and consigned it to the gods of the sea.

His caution was unjustified for *Nina* reached the Azores, only to be buffeted by more bad weather on the passage to Spain. It was the familiar Portuguese Tagus that welcomed Columbus back to Europe, but the return destination scarcely mattered as he completed the most historic voyage in history. His was the first definitely recorded double crossing of the Atlantic and a voyage that saw Neptune relinquish control of his Atlantic trident to Spain.

Although it is Columbus' first voyage that has been best remembered, he did not rest on his laurels. In September 1493 he sailed from Cadiz with 17 sail and 1200 sanguine colonists. Again Columbus caught the trade winds and on Sunday, 3rd November made a fine landfall at the volcanic peaks of Dominica. Sailing northward he named many of the Leeward Islands, from St. Croix, with its cannibal Caribs, to the Virgin Islands and Puerto Rico, but when he reached Hispaniola the previous settlement had been eradicated. Stubborn in his optimism, Columbus guided the fleet to a new site on the north coast of the island. Although they had come to farm, many of the colonists were infected by the insidious side of the New World, the lure of the quick buck. Rather than labouring on the land they hunted for nuggets of gold while disease dropped men in droves.

Columbus sent most of his ships home, left the settlement in the charge of a council and took *Nina* and two other caravels on a five-month cruise that discovered Jamaica. Returning to subdue the native population of Hispaniola, Columbus sent 500 native slaves across the Atlantic and sailed to Spain in a voyage made terrible by contrary winds and possible cannibalism. On his third voyage in 1498 he touched on Trinidad and became the first known European to land on the South American continent. Only when he found the Orinoco, the largest river yet seen by Europeans, did Columbus finally realise that this was a New World, although he stubbornly believed that it lay somewhere to the south of continental Asia.

When the Hispaniola colony collapsed in chaos, the joint monarchs placed Francisco de Bobadilla in charge and Columbus came home in irons. After Bobadilla came Nicolas de Ovando, who treated his settlers with a calculated savagery that paled only beside his conduct to the Indians. In the meantime Columbus set out on his fourth and final voyage. When Ovando refused him permission to shelter from an approaching hurricane, Columbus the seaman rode out the storm that sank 29 ships in the Mona Passage. He sailed to the Gulf of Mexico and from August 1502 until January 1503 searched for the second sea of which the Indians spoke. An attempt to found a colony failed under local pressure, shipworm riddled his ships until, storm-battered, hungry and defeated, Columbus limped into Jamaica. It was nine months before Ovando sent a relief ship and when he eventually reached Spain Columbus had only 18 months to live.

By then a papal bull, the *Inter Caetera* had slashed a line right down the Atlantic and presented Spain with everything to the west. The later *Dudum Siquidem* went even further, handing to the joint monarchs 'all islands and mainlands whatever, found or to be found ... in sailing or travelling toward the west and south, whether they be in regions occidental or meridional and oriental and of India'. When the Treaty of Tordesillas pushed the line some 270 leagues further west, Portugal gained the eastern shoulder of South America and the trade route to India. But while clerics and courtiers argued over imaginary lines on inaccurate maps the secrets of the Americas were unveiled by a succession of gifted mariners. In any other age these men would surely be remembered as national heroes but so many jostled in Columbus' wake that they crowd each other out.

Vespucci sailed along the Venezuelan coast. Courtesy of the Billie Love Collection, Isle of Wight.

As early as 1499, Vincente Pinzon, formerly of *Nina*, took four caravels to Cape St. Agostinho in Brazil and cruised as far as Guiana, perhaps discovering the Amazon estuary. That same year Alonso de Ojeda and Amerigo Vespucci sailed along the Venezuelan coast between Margarita and Maracaibo, but rather than a passage to Asia or a shipload of treasure they picked up a cargo of brazilwood. The following year they traced the coast south to around the 35° meridian, where the estuary of the River Plate would appear to be the elusive strait to Asia. Ironically, while Ojeda is barely remembered, his companion left an indelible impression on the New World map. Amerigo Vespucci was a Florentine contractor who had worked with Columbus in 1492, had sailed under the Portuguese flag, and who in 1505 became a naturalised Spaniard. Three years later Vespucci was appointed as *piloto mayor* – chief pilot – of Spain, but for all his exploits, his fame comes mainly from his name. Accounts of Vespucci's travels were the basis of the book *Four Voyages* by the German cartographer Martin Waldseemuller. Perhaps because of exaggeration or distortion Waldseemuller apparently believed that Vespucci preceded Columbus and suggested that the entire continent be named in his honour. With the Latin version of Amerigo being *Americus*, the New World had gained its name.

The Europeans were searching for treasure and trade and although Ojeda's first voyage had achieved neither, Nicolas Guerra followed in his wake and started a pearl fishery on the island of Cubagua. Around the same time the explorations of Juan de la Cosa, one time captain of *Santa Maria*, led to an abortive settlement in the Gulf of Darien. Towards the end of 1509 Ojeda sailed for Columbia. He took a thousand men strengthened with the enthusiasm of pilgrims and the paraphernalia of the Renaissance, but disease cared little for valour and poisoned arrows brought even the proudest to his grave.

A relief ship from Hispaniola brought reinforcements, including Balboa who not only took control of the colony's relocation to Darien, but also explored that area of Central America. If Columbus had been a messiah, Balboa was the first of a new breed – a conquistador who married a local woman, conquered much territory and fought the indigenous Indians with crossbows and dogs – but he is probably best remembered for looking at a unique view. It was a September day in Darien when a local guide pointed to at a prominent hill. 'Climb this' he was informed, 'and you will see the other sea.'

Sixty Spaniards struggled upward but the determined Balboa reached the summit first and stared at the great South Sea. Perhaps he was aware of being the first European to see both the Atlantic and Pacific Oceans, perhaps he did not care, but four days later, with banner uplifted and sword in hand, Balboa strode into St Miguel's Bay. It was St Michael's Day, 29th September 1513, and the Spaniards had crossed a continent from sea to shining sea. But not all Spanish were so fortunate - Juan de Valdivia and his crew completely disappeared somewhere off Jamaica.

Yet Central America was nearly incidental to Spain's yearning for the Orient although Portugal got there first. While Balboa was clambering up a hill in Darien, Portuguese vessels had navigated the complexity of the Spice Islands to drop their anchors in the Moluccas. In 1519 when Magellan sailed through the Strait that bears his name, he finally proved that Columbus had discovered an entirely new continent and not merely an adjunct of Asia.

That same year Cortes brought 11 ships and just over 600 men to conquer Montezuma's Mexico, starting with the state of Tabasco. European harquebuses (matchlock guns)and the fearsome Spanish cavalry defeated the javelins, stones and manpower of Tabasco and, in so doing, the eight-year-old mystery of Valdivia was solved. Wrecked off Jamaica, he had navigated a boatload of men to the Yucatan Peninsula, where the natives proved unfriendly. In a scene straight from a horror movie, they ripped the hearts from Valdivia and three of his men, ate them raw and kept the other Spaniards captive. When Cortes came to the rescue there were only two Spanish survivors.

Horror and beauty also co-existed in Montezuma's capital of Tenochtitlan. In the shadow of the sacrificial pyramid were lovely houses with courtyards refreshed by splashing fountains, where featherwork hangings dappled the heat of the sun and men and women enjoyed the products of numerous vegetable gardens. Aztec civilisation of the New World was complex and complete and if their religion appeared barbaric, then so was the European practice of burning so-called heretics at the stake. Nonetheless, European and Aztec fraternised until Cortes banned human sacrifice and fighting broke out. When the Spaniards took casualties the Aztecs realised that these were men, not gods, and forced them out of the city by sheer numbers. Only when Cortes returned with Spanish and native reinforcements was Tenochtitlan captured, to become the power base for an expanding Spanish American empire.

The north-east coastline of America presented different, but equally formidable problems to explorers. Here there were foggy seas, icebergs and winters of unbelievable

...he soon emigrated to Venice...

harshness, but the reward of a sea where the fish supply was seemingly inexhaustible. Giovanni Caboto was another of the ubiquitous Italian mariners, probably born in Genoa around 1450, although he soon emigrated to Venice. As a merchant seaman, Cabot visited Mecca and was astonished at the variety of silks and spices in the market. After making enquiries, he discovered that these treasures were carried from the East on camels and wondered if it would not be possible to sail there directly by sailing west across the globe.

Like Columbus, Cabot searched for a financial backer and when the courts of continental Europe turned him down, he moved to England with his sons Sebastian, Ludovicio and Sancio. As Bristol mariners sailed regularly to destinations such as Madeira and Iceland, it is not surprising that Cabot convinced some to head for Cathay across the Western Ocean. Bristol merchants made one proviso; any expedition had to sail by way of the islands of Hy Brazil and the Island of the Seven Cities which were clearly marked on all the most reliable charts. Indeed, it was only four years since one John Jay had left Bristol in an abortive search for Hy Brazil.

Only when news came that Columbus had beaten Bristol across the Atlantic did the merchants drop their demands for island hopping. In March 1496 Henry VII of England granted Letters Patent to his 'well-beloved John Cabot ... to seeke out, discover and finde whatsoever isles, countries, regions or provinces of the heathen and infidels which before this time have been unknown to all Christians'. In May 1497 Cabot slipped down the Severn in a ship named *Matthew* and a crew of 18 men. The crossing was virtually trouble-free and in only 52 days a lookout on *Matthew* sighted land somewhere in North America. Nobody is exactly sure where Cabot arrived, but it may have been Newfoundland or Cape Breton Island, and Cabot could have cruised along the coast of Nova Scotia. Like Columbus, Cabot claimed the land for a foreign monarch, so King Henry became the dubiously legal owner of a long section of the Canadian coast. Possibly more important in the short term, when Cabot passed over the Grand Banks his men lowered baskets into the sea and hauled up great quantities of fish.

By the beginning of August *Matthew* was back in Bristol, where Cabot was praised for his discovery of the 'new island' which he thought was somewhere off Cathay. He was granted £10 'to have a good time with', an annual pension and the promise of six ships for another voyage to set up trading contacts in Chipangu and thus make London the greatest entrepôt in Europe. In actuality the King provided one ship, but Bristol and London merchants added another four and in May 1498 Cabot and 300 men sailed from the Severn. Neither Cabot nor his ships were positively seen again, but the Spanish sighted a mysterious squadron travelling south into the Caribbean.

During the course of the 16th century the Hanseatic League muscled into the Icelandic trade. Perhaps the English left willingly for there were fresher coasts to exploit, new waters where the fishing was so extensive that the wild waters of Iceland were not really worth the trouble. Fishermen from Brittany and Normandy, Portugal and Biscay and La Rochelle joined Englishmen off the Grand Banks of Newfoundland so as the

century progressed, European experience and knowledge of Atlantic conditions and currents increased. From exploiting the sea it became natural to spend summers in and around the gulf of St Lawrence and to trade with the natives for furs.

In the meantime the exploration of the American coastline continued with the historically-neglected Florentine Giovanni Da Verrazzano. While in his early twenties Verrazzano moved to Dieppe and, like Cabot, he sailed to the Levant. Perhaps it is true that Magellan infused him with enthusiasm for exploration but in 1523 Francis I of France provided a ship for a voyage to the Pacific while Florentine bankers gave financial support. With the 100-ton *Dauphine* and the even smaller *Normandie,* Verrazzano sailed to Madeira, where *Normandie* left him. *Dauphine* crossed to Cape Fear and coasted the outer Banks of Carolina and past Cape Hatteras. When they saw Pamlico Sound the crew celebrated, believing they had found the Pacific, but Verrazzano continued northward, becoming the first of the thousands of Europeans to cast his anchor in the narrows between Staten Island and Long Island. He called in at Narragansett Bay where today the town of Newport sits behind a cloud of white-sailed yachts, weathered curving Cape Cod and came at last to Newfoundland, from where he sailed quietly back to Dieppe.

Although Verrazzano believed that the coasts he had explored did not belong to Asia, his voyage had not proved profitable enough to encourage either crown or banker to sponsor another. It was three years before he sailed again, looking for a north-west passage to Asia, but his crew grumbled and he only managed to touch on Brazil, pick up a load of logwood and return to France. Although he had achieved nothing geographically, the logwood produced a profit and in 1528 Verrazzano was back at sea. Once again he hoped to find a passage to the East, but this time he did not even reach the mainland coast. Island hopping down the Antillean chain, he came to one of the larger islands, possibly Guadeloupe, and rowed ashore in a small boat. There was a small body of natives waiting and, perhaps remembering the friendly people of the North American mainland, Verrazzano stepped ashore. But these were cannibal Caribs, and they butchered Verrazzano and ate him. This was a blow to European exploration but there were too many ships for a single death, or a hundred, to affect the overall picture. Verrazzano deserves to be better remembered; he was not only the first known mariner to sail up the coast of America but also the first to realise that this was a single continuous coast.

Although the Pope's line was intended to keep all but Iberians from possessing land beyond the Atlantic, not all European monarchs acquiesced. The King of France in particular believed that what one Pope proclaimed, another may palliate. He married his son Henry to Catherine de Medici, the niece of Pope Clement VII, and conferred with his infallible kinsmen. They decided that the Bull of Demarcation referred only to already-discovered territories; now it was open season in North America.

OPPOSITE: *In May 1497 Cabot slipped down the Severn in a ship named* Matthew. *Reproduction of the* Matthew *at Bristol.* Courtesy of the Matthew Project.

On 20th April 1534 Jacques Cartier left St Malo with two ships and 61 men, hoping to find the north-western passage to Asia. Unimpressed by the bleak beauty of Belle Isle Strait, he turned southward, explored western Newfoundland and the island of Anticosti before cruising around the Gulf of St Lawrence to New Brunswick. This was better; Prince Edward Island was enchanting, Chaleur Bay had fine tall trees and the entire area was fertile, the Micmac Indians friendly and willing to trade their furs. If that was not enough, the water abounded with fish.

By the end of August Cartier was back in St Malo, hopeful that the St Lawrence led eastward. Next year he commanded three royal ships, over 100 men and had orders to sail beyond Newfoundland and discover 'certain distant lands'. Again he visited Anticosti Island, named his anchorage the Bay of St Lawrence and pushed up the Hochelaga River to search for the kingdom of Saguenay that lay beyond. There were walruses and snapping turtles, friendly Indians and fast currents. There was also a Huron Indian chief named Donnaconna who attempted to prevent Cartier travelling further, first by bribery with his niece and two boys, then with the warnings of three ferocious medicine men in canoes. Strong in his faith, Cartier sailed a 40-ton pinnace upriver, towing two longboats in his wake and enjoying the bracing Canadian weather and the magnificent scenery. It was the beginning of October when he arrived at the town of Hochelaga (which was later to become Quebec); some 50 buildings surrounded by a wooden palisade, and Cartier scrambled up a prominent hill to gaze westward towards Asia. But there was no Asia, only a series of vicious rapids that prevented any further passage. The disappointed Cartier named the hill Mount Royal (which later became Montreal) and returned to overwinter at Donnaconna's village. Regaled with tales of the riches of Saguenay, Cartier kidnapped Donnaconna and nine of his people before returning to France in the spring. European heroes have not always acted honourably in other lands, but Donnaconna had some revenge when he repeated his tales of Saguenay to the French court. This fabulous kingdom, he claimed, had not only priceless jewels but also spices and orchards and, he added to his naïve audience, men with wings.

In 1541 Cartier sailed on his third voyage, intending to settle this rich land and find the treasures of the mythical kingdom of Saguenay. Planting his settlers, with their associated convicts, at Quebec, he probed upstream until impassable rapids blocked his progress. With the once-friendly Hurons unhappy at his takeover bid, Cartier packed his ship with gold and diamonds before returning to St Malo. Although the gold was only iron pyrites and the diamonds only quartz, Cartier had still achieved a great deal; he had laid the foundations of Canada and opened up vast tracts of country. The Huron Indians had perhaps less reason to look fondly on him.

After Cartier the French concentrated on the Canadian interior, while others probed the iced waters of the north for a passage to the Pacific. There was Martin Frobisher, who also brought home a cargo of iron pyrites, and Bartholomew Gosnold, a forgotten seaman who sailed *Concord* across the Atlantic in the early 17th century, named Cape Cod and Martha's Vineyard and loaded his ship with furs. In 1607 he was back in

American waters with the Jamestown colonists. However, the voyages of John Davis were more significant.

Davis was from the great seafaring nursery of Devon and on 7th June 1585 he slipped out of Dartmouth with two ridiculously small vessels, the 50-ton *Sunshine* and 35-ton *Moonshine*, to search for the North-West Passage. Bad weather delayed them for a fortnight at the Scilly Islands and on the voyage across the Atlantic they fished for porpoises and ran into fog that concealed ice floes. Naming Greenland the Land of Desolation, Davis traded with the Inuit, hunted polar bears in Baffin Land and discovered a sound at a place that he feelingly named the Cape of God's Mercy. With

The Half Moon, *Henry Hudson's exploring vessel, 1609.* Courtesy of the Billie Love Collection, Isle of Wight.

deep water and a current from the west it seemed that they had found the passage to Asia, but there was no time to explore before winter closed in.

Next year Davis was back with four vessels headed by the 120 ton *Mermaid.* They arrived off Greenland in late June, but differences over religion strained their relations with the Inuit. When a barrier of ice halted his voyage north and the crew began to grumble, Davis chose some volunteers and continued in the small *Moonshine.* On 20th August, somewhere south-east of Baffin Island, Davis scrambled to the summit of a hill and looked west. There was only snow and ice; a dreary landscape with neither habitation nor a passage to Asia. Davis sailed south to Labrador, failed to penetrate the Hamilton Inlet and lost two men in a skirmish with 'the brutish people' who lived there. A storm sent them staggering back and on 11th September Davis returned to England.

Elizabethan seamen were remarkable for their tenacity and the following year Davis set out again. This time he had three vessels, *Sunshine, Elizabeth,* and the pinnace *Ellen.* The Atlantic voyage was unhappy, the crew wanted to exchange exploration for fishing and all the ships leaked. Davis persevered, again split his command and headed north up the Greenland coast with just one vessel. He reached a new furthest north of 72°12' but more importantly found 'a very great gulf, the water whirling and weaving as if it were the meeting of the tides'. This looked like the entrance to a strait, but the Arctic winter frustratingly forced him back to England. He never returned to the north.

The last of this generation of great North American explorers was Henry Hudson, who failed to find a north-eastern passage in the Barents Sea and persuaded his mutinous crew to accompany him to attempt an alternative route from North Virginia, possibly around the 40th parallel. His 150-mile voyage up the Hudson River in *Half Moon* failed to find the Pacific, but his interest had only been whetted and he re-crossed the Atlantic in 1610 with the 55-ton *Discovery.* Sailing up Hudson Strait, he thrust into Hudson Bay, remained there all summer and through the winter, despite his crew's discontent at the intense cold. There was mutiny in the summer of 1611, as Henry Greene left Hudson behind and sailed for home. While Greene died in a skirmish with the Inuit, Hudson's fate remains unknown. With his voyage, a remarkable period of exploration came to a full stop, but the exploitation and colonisation had scarcely begun.

Chapter 5

Treasure Seekers

'He who is master of the sea will be master of the land.'
Juan Maldonado Barnuevo, 1604

For a nation that clutched Neptune's trident with great tenacity, Spain lacked adequate harbours. To reach her northern ports, ships from the Indies had to hazard the coast of often-hostile Portugal, while southern Cadiz was not only exposed to Atlantic storms but also sat at the end of a rocky spit that was vulnerable to enemy attack. So from the beginning of the 16th century Seville, the main town of prosperous Andalucia, became the centre for colonial commerce. It was not ideal, being separated from the sea by the San Lucar sandbank and 50 tortuous miles of the Guadalquivir River, but perhaps its inaccessibility saved Seville from hostile raiding. Only eleven years after Columbus set out on his eccentric Atlantic voyage, the Spanish crown chose Seville to establish the *Casa de la Contratacion de las Indias,* that inspected the charts of westward bound ships. The *Casa* also recorded all the discoveries and explorations in the New World onto a master chart, the *Padron Real,* and licensed pilots for the New World. Its prestige was such that in 1508 the famous Amerigo Vespucci became the *Piloto Mayor* in charge of all other pilots.

The Americas had three significant harbours for the *carrera,* the transatlantic convoys. There was Vera Cruz, in the Gulf of Campeche, the island of San Juan de Ulua off Mexico and Nombre De Dios on the Darien coast. Neither was perfect; Vera Cruz could only offer an open roadway, while a bar made the river entrance hazardous. Given that summer hurricanes could turn any Gulf coast harbour into a howling nightmare and the unpredictable Northers could strike throughout the year, it is hardly surprising that many vessels sailed the 15 miles past Vera Cruz to the safer island of San Juan de Ulua.

Spain supplied just about everything to the early settlers, from building bricks to wine, tools to agricultural seeds, animals to flour and clothing. Spain was also the source of the human raw material who left their homes to hack out another life in the New World of Hispaniola, Yucatan or Cuba. In the 19th century the passage of the Atlantic became almost commonplace, but the first wave of colonists were a different breed. Those who were not adventurers or social outcasts were escaping the Inquisition, and for them the hardships of frontier life were probably no worse than everyday life in Europe. Yet, at a time when the Reformation scattered new ideas around Europe like leaves from a broken-spined Bible, there were also devout men who sailed to spread the Catholic faith. There were more Catholics at the end of the 16th century than there had been at the beginning because of Spanish missionaries. Although much of the land was conquered by force, Spanish military skills were severely tested against the flitting Caribs of the islands and the Chichimecas of the northern Mexican desert. Anglo-centric history books often neglect the perseverance of these Iberian settlers, but they were the colonial forerunners with no precedents to copy. Spain developed the ranching system, the agriculture and the mines of the Americas and the Spanish legacy cannot be forgotten, nor can Spanish courage be overstated. Between 1506 and 1600 an estimated 243,000 Spaniards crossed the Atlantic to settle their New World. As the overwhelming majority were young, male and healthy it was natural that they should look for wives among the indigenous peoples, so already a hybrid people was emerging, a blend of Europe and America.

In the early years individual ships were relatively safe from predators on the Atlantic seaway but, nonetheless, of the 70 vessels that left Spain in 1520, less than half that number returned. Some fell victim to shipworm or tropical damp, others were retained for colonial use or were simply wrecked. In 1563 alone seven vessels were driven onto the shore of Nombre de Dios while in 1587 six survived the crossing only to be thrust onto the San Lucar bar. In 1601 a northerly gale sank no less than 14 at Vera Cruz. Seamen suffered at a similar rate with the misunderstood silent killers of yellow fever and malaria.

War with France in 1521 ended the first phase of the New World adventure, as daring French seamen attacked solitary Spanish ships and isolated Spanish colonies. From the 1530s in particular the French ships prowled around the Azores and waited in the islands and cays of the Caribbean. In 1537 they flailed the mainland settlements of Honduras and snatched nine treasure ships in a devastating raid on the ill-protected Caribbean colonists. Six years later the French were back, leaving a pall of dirty smoke where Cubagua had sulked beneath the Venezuelan sun and emptying the western seas of Spanish shipping. In 1554 Santiago de Cuba was plundered and next year it was Havana's turn to suffer under the seaborne fury of the French.

Resilient as always, the Spanish responded with one of the most evocative breeds of ship ever seen. The Spanish galleon had actually been evolved in England and was simply an improvement on the three-masted carrack, square-rigged on the fore and mainmast and with a lateen-rigged mizzen. A warship of perhaps 500 tons, the galleon boasted fine lines for speed and an impressive broadside that could blow a lesser ship out of the water. Because she lacked a forecastle, she was more weatherly and more manoeuvrable than the carrack, and could better maintain her course to windward. Galleons were used to escort the convoys that Spain instituted in 1543 and which proved so reliable in frustrating privateers through the following decades. Convoys did not just deter attacks, they also ensured that the few skilled navigators could lead the merely average.

With its eight-galleon escort, the spring convoy, the *galeones*, left Seville in May, crossed the Atlantic and passed through the Mona Passage between eastern Hispaniola and Mona Island before splitting. The majority of ships sailed west, through the Yucatan Channel and the Gulf of Campeche to Vera Cruz; the others sailed to their respective island destinations. The Darien convoy slipped out of the Guadalquivir in August and although a few vessels sailed to the islands the majority remained in convoy for Nombre De Dios. There they loaded Peruvian silver before sailing for Cartagena to shelter during the hurricane season. As the century progressed the Spanish organisation tightened, with the lonely Manila galleon traversing the Pacific to Acapulco, to load her cargo onto mules for transportation to Vera Cruz and eventually to Spain.

In January the fleet headed north-west across the Caribbean, rounded Cuba's Cape San Antonio and anchored in Havana, where the Mexican *flota* joined them in March. Although Havana had the best location for sailing vessels, there were many hazards ahead. There were summer hurricanes, head winds in the Strait of Florida and pirates lurking in the Bahamian cays. Only when these were astern and the friendly westerly wind filled their sails could the Spanish relax, watch the powerful, silver-carrying galleons that escorted them and know that Spain was only a matter of weeks away. With perhaps 90 ships and ten escorts, the convoy was safe from any but the most daring of corsairs.

Although very few convoys fell to enemy attack they were expensive, ships could not be used to their full potential and the *aveira*, the duty that paid for the galleons, was crippling. There was also corruption, with galleons frequently smuggling American products to Spain and avoiding the taxes so essential to the Imperial economy; in one instance a ship was so packed with contraband that her lower gunports were under water. Those ships that travelled alone were vulnerable and in 1553 and 1554 privateers and pirates captured 25 Spanish vessels on the Atlantic. By the end of the decade about 65 Spanish vessels sailed westward each year, with rather less returning. The increase in their size necessitated the creation of dockyards nearer the sea than Seville, so passengers from the Indies landed at San Lucar de Barrameda, and transferred to smaller craft to ascend the Guadalquivir.

By now predatory seamen from just about every European maritime nation regarded Spanish shipping as fair game. A declaration that only Spanish ships could legally trade with their colonies was little more than a challenge for audacious men with little conscience and a talent for shattering whatever law they could not evade. With Spain so dominant, it was hard to imagine that other nations might someday acquire colonies, and implement their own strict mercantile controls. Free trade was as abnormal a concept as freedom from war, but when peace did break out in Europe there was seldom a truce across the Atlantic. By unspoken agreement anything south of the Tropic of Cancer was liable to attack.

In such a climate real seamen were required to command the Spanish *flota* and one of the best was Pedro Menendez de Aviles. Bred to the legends of Drake and Raleigh, few people in the English-speaking world know of Aviles, which is more than a shame. While Aviles spent 15 years as a privateer, Emperor Charles V was consolidating his rule over Spain, half of Europe and much of the Americas. Charles was undoubtedly the most powerful European of his time and in 1549 he sent Aviles to remove the French from the northern Spanish coasts, no easy task given the tenacity of French mariners, but one which Aviles completed very satisfactorily.

By 1555 Aviles was in command of the *flota*, despite the obstruction of less-than-honest merchants who had hoped for a less-than-honest man to turn a Nelsonian eye to their illicit trading practices. Under his firm control the *flota* arrived safely and with large profits, but Aviles refused to take the command again; fighting pirates was easier than coping with corrupt merchants. When another French war erupted in 1559 Aviles commanded the fleet that carried Phillip II from the Low Countries through the dangerous English Channel and past all the pirate ports of France to Spain. For the next two years he returned to control the *flota* but his honesty must have seriously disconcerted the merchants, and in 1563 he was imprisoned on false charges of corruption and smuggling.

Within two years he was returned to royal favour and heading west to found a colony in Florida. A Huguenot named Jean Ribault had already established the French, and despite the outbreak of peace he hoped to float French warships in the Florida Channel and block the route of the *flota*. Obviously this could not be allowed; Aviles built a fort at the Bay of St Augustine and within a few weeks had captured Ribault and some of his men. He left their bodies dangling from trees as a warning to any others who trod Spanish soil and drove the lesson home by adding the message 'Not as Frenchmen but as Lutherans'. There was little mercy beyond the line. It was three years before Dominique de Gourges retaliated for France when he overcame the fortress of Sao Mateo and executed the Spanish garrison. 'Not as Spaniards' his message said, 'but as murderers'. Perhaps de Gourges would have been less bold if Aviles had not already left Florida for Spain.

When Aviles later returned to command in the Caribbean he hoped for a large escort for the *flota*, augmented by naval patrols between the Azores and Andalucia, and a powerful naval presence in the Caribbean. Unfortunately Spain could not afford such an ambitious arrangement and, with so many predators in the Caribbean, Aviles had to neglect much of the coastline and islands to concentrate on essentials. He defended Havana, the treasure fleets and the Florida Channel. During his career Aviles captured perhaps 50 pirate vessels and, if parsimonious Spain had provided what he had required, piracy in the Atlantic and Caribbean might have been stamped on. As it was, the romantic bloody heydays of the filibusters were only beginning.

With seamen like Aviles in charge, the Spanish could not be shifted from their New World conquests. Nonetheless, predators could loot and burn, twist the Imperial Spanish tail and profit from the crumbs that dropped from the silver colonial platter. Northern European seamen swarmed across the Atlantic to act as parasites on the glittering Spanish host. Removed from Florida, the vengeful survivors of the Huguenots combined with the Protestant English. Raiding parties looted and burned along the Isthmus of Panama and punctured the peace of the Chagre River, attacked travellers on the highway to Panama and shipping on the sea around Nombre de Dios. By 1573 the Franco-English force had allied themselves with escaped black slaves, *cimarrones*, to harass the Spanish settlers. So persistent were the raids that the Spanish thought that the English were scouting out the land 'in order to come from England with more people to plunder and occupy it'. But even without Aviles, the Spanish could bite back. They routed John Oxenham's expedition in 1577, brought the *cimarrones* to heel and swept the French from the seas off Panama. The Spanish had shocked the French by using galleys, but mutiny and shipwreck dissipated their initial success and the French were again free to spread devastation around the Caribbean.

In far less than a century the Caribbean had become an important strategic target for nautical campaigns, and the transatlantic crossing was just an introduction. Although the constant dream of these campaigns was the capture of the *flota,* Drake's 1585 expedition, like so many others, only managed to devastate the shore settlements. When the English bickered among themselves, their opportunity of capturing Havana disappeared. Spain combined fast frigates and stout fortifications to maintain her hold on the treasure routes and although her control of the Main wavered for a while, Spain defeated Drake at Puerto Rico and drove him from Panama. Despite half a century of violent assault, Spanish hegemony in the New World was as complete as ever.

At sea the situation was more fluid as interlopers hovered from Havana to Honduras and plundered from the Gulf to Guiana. Most of these corsairs are forgotten, shadowy seamen from a past considered colourful by people living without the constant dread of English topsails puncturing the serene horizon. These were the Vikings of their day, spreading terror to the peoples of the coastal settlements, killing, raping, torturing, and burning. Spain sent armadas to cleanse the Caribbean and soldiers in steel morion and breastplate drove smugglers from their island bases. Human corpses sun-dried at a dozen gallows while fast Spanish ships seized smuggling craft, and all the time the slow convoys carried silver from the New World to the Old.

Men such as Drake and Raleigh made their names by butchery and plunder in the colonial ports, but with the death of Elizabeth and the placing of James on the throne of the United Kingdom of Scotland and England, peacetime piracies were not viewed with the same leniency. James abruptly extinguished the golden era of English privateering, and within four years peace between the United Netherlands and Spain eased the pressure on Spanish America. But official policy cannot change the habits of generations and the lure of gold continued to attract the wild men of the sea.

Elizabethan freebooters were, at best, violent patriots and although they damaged Spanish trade and marred the lives of thousands of comparatively innocent people, they achieved few major victories. Despite their pinpricking raids, all other Europeans in the Americas subsisted in the shadow of Spain. The Spanish were the original explorers, the original colonists, and possessed the bulk of an entire continent. Their ships traded between the islands and between Europe and the Americas; these were home waters for the colonial Spanish seamen. Spain retained her hold of Neptune's trident.

Peace, however, was a rare commodity and renewed war saw the Dutch and French swooping onto Spanish slave-trading posts on the west African coast. Losses of revenue from this source were augmented by the inflation that huge imports of American silver helped created, so Spain debased her coinage with copper. On the other hand, the increase of capital in the European financial system enabled private stock companies to exploit the expanded world. Entrepreneurs exploded out of Europe, traders at sea with a pistol in one hand, a ledger in the other and hard greed in their eyes. Spanish crossings to the Indies steadily fell as the Dutch West India Company declared that its aim was 'above all in humbling the pride and might of Spain'. Doughty seamen though they were, the Dutch lacked the glamour of the French or the ruthlessness of the English as their ships raked salt from the Venezuela lagoons, traded for tobacco or bartered for Hispaniolan hides. They were fast becoming the commercial carriers of the ocean.

The methods had changed but economic assault was still national warfare. Spain retaliated by stopping tobacco planting on the Venezuelan coast and cleared sections of Hispaniola to prevent the Dutch from trading. In a return to more traditional tactics Pieter Heyn brought a squadron through the Florida Channel, ambushed the *flota* off the north Cuba coast and chased them onto the Matanzas shore. It was the first time the *flota* had failed to get through and the West India Company purred at the bonus of 15,000,000 guilders it had earned. Pieter Heyn would feel sweet revenge, for he had learned to hate while chained naked to the bench of a Spanish galley. Spain's hold on the trident slipped in September 1637 when Admiral Marten Tromp defeated a Spanish fleet, but there was worse to come.

Raiding, looting and trading was bad enough but now the northern Europeans began to settle. The French grabbed Guadeloupe and Martinique, the Dutch took Curacao and Saba while the English showed an early proclivity for colonies by claiming St Christopher and Barbados, Montserrat and Nevis and Antigua. The Spanish riposte was swift, retaking Nevis and St Christopher, but the surviving colonists relocated to Hispaniola. Although this had been amongst the earliest of all the American colonies there were still wild open spaces for the incomers. Transposed colonists merged with sundry shipwrecked survivors, nautical wanderers, runaway slaves and others from the periphery of an already fringe society to form their own culture in this hectic New World. They created a masculine community known as the Brethren of the Coast, where men bonded with a trusted matelot and trouble-making women were forbidden.

Neglecting religion, they also scorned individual possessions, carried long-barrelled muskets to hunt the pigs and cattle that had escaped from Spanish farms, and lived by selling smoked meat to passing ships. In the 1630s the going price was three pieces of eight for 100 pounds of smoked meat, and because they smoked their kill on a *bukan*, the Carib word for a grill, the Brethren earned the name of buccaneers. It was a name that the Spaniards learned to fear.

At first the buccaneers were relatively harmless, but the Spanish moved against them, attacking the hunters with mounted lancers and, in a precursor of the later Indian wars, massacring the wild cattle. Bereft of their reason for existence, the buccaneers slipped over to the island of Tortuga, off the north-west coast of Hispaniola. For a while Levasseur governed them, but when he took one of the trouble-making women as a mistress he was promptly murdered. No longer able to live by hunting on land, the Brethren of the Coast learned to sail the local one-masted piraguas against their persecutors. In the beginning, buccaneers were merely another irritant in already perilous seas, but Spain took notice when a Frenchman named Pierre led less than 30 men in an attack on a vice-admiral's galleon. Cold steel in the dark, Spanish officers surprised over brandy and cards and Pierre sailed westward to Dieppe, retired on his fortune and doubtless relished his nickname of Pierre le Grand.

The Brethren built their boats from cedar, jammed the rudders of Spanish ships and boarded over the taffrail; the sleeping Spaniards were surprised by a horde of screaming buccaneers with musket, pistol and cutlass. As always the Spaniards devised new defences such as nails in the hull to tear the hands of clambering men and grease and tacks on the decks, but still they lost ship after ship to the Brethren who struck swiftly, killed with hot malice and tortured with exquisite enjoyment. Although some remained on Tortuga others used the raw colonies of non-Spanish European powers, and the vulnerable scattering of green islands embraced the Brethren as an unruly bodyguard that kept mighty Spain at bay.

In 1665 there were changes in Tortuga when Bertrand d'Ogeron introduced 150 French women, and if legend says they were prostitutes and women of no morality, then they were possibly better off with the reckless buccaneers than walking the streets of Paris. There was a sudden rash of weddings in Tortuga, and while some of the Brethren were manacled by marriage, others found their tumultuous independence restrained under the guise of legal privateers.

Equally riotous were the buccaneers of Port Royal. In 1655 a Cromwellian expedition against the Spanish Indies had failed in all its main objectives, but had snapped up the Spanish island of St Jago as a consolation prize. As the Arawak name was Xaymaca, the English naturally miscalled it Jamaica, but the colony struggled to survive until the English chapter of the restless Brethren swarmed over the horizon. Men such as Morgan made Port Royal the 'wickedest city in the world' and used it as their base for raids on the Main that brought in a plethora of pieces of eight. No longer content with simple *piraguas*, Henry Morgan took three dozen buccaneer ships to sack Panama – a Welshman commanding an English armada to threaten Spanish hegemony in the Americas. Too stubborn to submit, Spain built extra forts and increased the cannon power of the *flota* to negotiate a wary peace. When the 1670 Treaty of Madrid agreed that England could keep all she had clutched in the Caribbean, it seemed there might be peace in the Americas. The buccaneers had outlived their usefulness. As the English establishment realised their nation had grown past the stage of brawling youth into a *de facto* colonial power their perception of piracy altered. Legitimacy had replaced loot as the basis for wealth, respectability was more important than raiding, and in 1683 the Jamaica Assembly condemned the shocking practice of buccaneering. It was not quite the end of the old song, for 14 years later another European war had spread to the Americas and a mixed Anglo-French force of freebooters looted Cartagena. English and French fell out over their share of the booty and a squadron of the English navy moved in to cut out the French. As an incident it was minor, but it was a portent of the future for in that year of 1697 the Treaty of Ryswick formally confirmed that other European nations could own territory in the New World and ended forever the semi-legal era of the buccaneers. The perpetually proscribed pirates, however, continued to haunt the Caribbean, for pirating paid better than working for a pittance in some coast-slogging vessel in the storms and chill of European waters.

Further north, the natives of North America were about to experience the next onslaught of European expansion.

Chapter 6

The Colonists

*'They fell upon their knees and blessed the God of Heaven
who had brought them over the vast and furious ocean.'*
William Bradford, History Of Plymouth Plantation.

Until 1562 the French had provided the main opposition to Spanish America, but that year came a foretaste of a phenomenon that influenced the maritime world for centuries: the English were coming. Although nothing concrete came of a combined English and Huguenot plan for a North American colony, within a dozen years John Hawkins of Plymouth was sailing boldly where no Englishman had gone before. Hawkins broke into the slave trade in an age when slavery was honourable, but in doing so he created a rift with Spain that led to decades of declared and undeclared war.

For centuries the English had sought to control and conquer their neighbours. English armies had superficially subdued Wales, had invaded Scotland, contested France and were even then engaged in a bitter struggle across the Irish Sea. Perhaps it was a long stride from Ireland to America but the experience of Irish colonisation was invaluable and every Atlantic voyage added to maritime knowledge. The English were experienced in Caribbean raid and ravage, but not in the long-term, grinding business of settlement across thousands of miles of ocean, consequently their approach to North America was naïve.

Like many of the finest English seamen, Humphrey Gilbert was a West Countryman from Compton, near Dartmouth, and Queen Elizabeth granted him a charter to explore for a route to the East and set up a colony. His first expedition was scattered by the Spanish but his second, funded partly by 'selling the clothes off my wife's back' saw four ships cross the Atlantic in the summer of 1583. Claiming Newfoundland for England, Gilbert watched hopelessly as his colony splintered into squabbling factions. Sending the most mutinous men home in *Swallow*, he boarded the ten-ton *Squirrel*, waited until the remaining colonists had embarked on the other two ships and explored the coast to the south. When *Delight* ran aground Gilbert decided that enough was enough and a couple of days later both *Golden Hind* and *Squirrel* were heading for home. Scorning the Atlantic storms, Gilbert sat in the stern of *Squirrel* to read a book. 'We are near to heaven by sea as by land' he is reported as saying, but by morning *Squirrel* had sunk, taking Gilbert with her.

Walter Raleigh was next to attempt to settle in the Americas. In an age noted for flamboyant ruthlessness, Raleigh's Irish exploits had left him with an unenviable reputation for pitiless violence. So he was just the sort of ruffian that Queen Elizabeth most favoured, whether or not he placed his cloak over a puddle to protect her dainty shoes. When he renewed Gilbert's licence for a New World colony, Raleigh probably had little intent to grub for crops, and the all-male composition of his initial expedition was not promising for long-term settlement. There were two vessels and an Azores pilot named Simon Fernandez who had sailed with Gilbert.

Heading south to the Canaries, the Trade winds eased them to the Spanish Indies, and they bought supplies before sailing north to Roanoke Island in the Carolina Banks. Without doubt they had found a beautiful land, where sweet-scented cedar woodlands were populated by myriad birds, and deer and rabbits ran free. The indigenous Indians, led by a chief named Wingina, traded skins and fruit for axes and pots in an orgy of friendliness that ended with the Englishmen's clothes and feet being washed. If this was not paradise, it was not far short, marred only by the recurrent wars between the 'most gentle, loving, and faithful' people who inhabited this place that seemed perfect for a colony. Three years later Richard Grenville in *Tiger* led out the seven ships of Raleigh's colonising fleet. Losing only a pinnace in a Biscayan storm, they arrived at the island of St John off Puerto Rico.

Hiding their distaste under a veneer of diplomacy, English visitor and Spanish resident treated each other with wary politeness but when the English fleet left St John it snapped up a couple of unwary Spanish ships. When Grenville eventually sailed for Roanoke the entire fleet ran aground on the Carolina banks. Amidst arguments and frustration, over 100 settlers remained on Roanoke Island while the ships returned to England for supplies, capturing a Spanish ship en route. The settlers, under the soldier Ralph Lane and an artist named John White, explored the local surroundings and brawled with the Indians. By the time Francis Drake's relief expedition arrived there was open warfare and the colonists left with alacrity. So much for paradise.

Raleigh tried again. In May 1587 three ships left Plymouth with the redoubtable Fernandez as master and John White as intended governor. White, who hoped for an agricultural colony, clashed with the near-piratical Fernandez, and rather than land on the selected site on Chesapeake Bay, they settled again at Roanoke. The colonists rebuilt their old fort and if they lost a man to Indian arrows, they were cheered by the birth of

OPPOSITE: *16th centruy warfare: English attention was diverted to the Armada.* Courtesy of the Billie Love Collection, Isle of Wight.

White's daughter Virginia Dare on 18th August. After a month White returned to England; his wife and daughter were among the 86 men, 17 women and 11 children he left behind.

White hoped for a speedy return but his first choice of captain turned pirate and then English attention was diverted from Roanoke to the Armada. In early 1590 another intended relief expedition was distracted by Caribbean piracy and when White finally arrived at the infant colony the fort was empty, with swift vegetation thrusting through abandoned huts and only the screech of birds to answer the hopeful hails. The fate of the settlers remains a mystery.

The English failure at Roanoke did not discourage the French who attempted a convict settlement in 1598 at Sable Island, 110 miles east of Nova Scotia. That same year the English government decided that beggars could be shipped abroad as a punishment for their poverty, which highlights the reluctance of decent people to leave their homeland; the unwanted were required to perform the hard pioneering work. In 1603 the Sable Island colony collapsed in predictable mutiny, but it was the precursor of permanent settlement as the French shone the lamp of European civilisation on the supposed darkness of North America.

When Samuel de Champlain sailed to Canada as the agent of Seigneur de Chastes, who owned the monopoly for the fur trade, he spent as much time in exploring as in trading. He charted the Canadian coasts in a methodical search for a settlement site, until he sailed up the St Lawrence in 1608 to establish and name the city of Quebec. Friendly Indians guided Champlain to the lake that bears his name but European rivalries soon spread to North America and tribes fought each other for the right to supply furs for European fashion. Champlain, the son of a seaman, was elevated to Governor of the New France he had founded, but still he dreamed of finding the elusive passage to Asia.

In 1607 King James of the United Kingdom charted the Virginia Company with the specific intention of colonising the New World. While some of the 100 men who endured a stormy passage of the Atlantic expected their Chesapeake settlement to produce exotic fruits and naval stores, others hoped for a passage to Asia. Neither of these hopes was immediately realised. There was no technology to transport American timber across the ocean and although the settlers selected a river that flowed from the east, there were thousands of miles of unknown but undisputedly solid land between the Chesapeake and the western shore of North America. Naming their river the James, the Englishmen built their Jamestown but survived only with the support of the local Pamunkey Indians and the iron control of the ex-mercenary soldier Captain John Smith. Even through their friendliness, the Indians could foresee future events 'We hear you are come from under the World' one said in 1608 'to take our World from us'.

This seemed unlikely when Smith returned to England and the colony suffered the 'starving time' of the 1609–10 winter. Barely 60 survived into the spring, with one man reputedly eating his wife, and things remained tough for years. As the Virginia colony did not endear itself to established, prosperous people, many of the colonists were nonconformists and malcontents from the sediment of society. Others were plain unfortunate as a dredge of the backstreets of London had hauled in uncomprehending and probably complaining youths who were sent to Virginia as servants. Not surprisingly they did not make the best workers; indeed in 1610 Sir Thomas Dale thought them 'full of mutenie and treasonable intendments'. Some Virginians slipped south to join the Spanish, others became pirates or were assimilated by the local Indians. When an Englishwoman named Jane Dickenson was released from ten months as an Indian slave, she claimed the experience had been no worse than her life as an indentured servant, which is surely an indictment against European-style society. Their Irish experience had taught the English something about life in a colony where potentially hostile natives hovered just beyond the pale, and the Virginians introduced a form of martial law called the *Lawes Divine, Morall and Martiall*. A new rule that allowed 50 acres to anybody who would come to the colony, augmented with the growth of tobacco and the grabbing of Indian lands finally put the Virginia colony on a more secure footing.

The formation of New England was entirely different. In early 17th century England any deviation from established theology invited harsh persecution and from 1607 groups of dissenters, known as Separatists or Puritans, crossed to the Netherlands. When they realised that their children were becoming more Dutch than English the Separatists decided to sail to a new land 'devoyd of all civill inhabitants' where they could retain both their religion and culture. Interestingly, North America was not their first choice. Only after considering Guiana and other 'wild coasts' did they fix on Northern Virginia, now New England. On 22nd July 1620 in the small *Speedwell*, the Separatists sailed from the Maas, but only as far as Southampton, where they berthed beside the larger *Mayflower*. On 5th August 1620 the two ships hoisted sail, but the Atlantic soon revealed that *Speedwell* was 'open and leakie as a sieve' and they put into Dartmouth for repairs. On 23rd August the ships again sailed, but as *Speedwell* was still leaking they put into Plymouth. It was obvious that *Speedwell* would not last the crossing so while those Puritans who still desired to leave boarded *Mayflower*; those who had changed their minds remained behind with *Speedwell*.

Crossing in the 180-ton *Mayflower* would have been a constantly heaving, constantly creaking, constantly wet and, with her 102 passengers, incredibly crowded experience. While Christopher Jones captained the ship, William Bradford was in command of the settlers, about half of whom were those pilgrim saints who were predestined for salvation and sailed 'for the glorie of God, and advancements of the Christian faith'. The residue were termed 'strangers' and were ordinary settlers but all suffered in the interminable voyage westward. As the seagull flies it is 2,800 nautical miles between Plymouth and Cape Cod, but as *Mayflower* would be unable to sail against the wind and current, Jones would probably have chosen a southerly route. *Mayflower* may have sailed to the Canary Islands in the hope of picking up the South-easterly Trade winds, or could have steered as far as the Azores and navigated straight to the westward.

The seasickness that affected the passengers during the fine early days must have increased when *Mayflower* ran into the storms that opened the deck seams and leaked cold seawater onto the crowded sleeping quarters beneath. They spent 65 days on the Atlantic, days of tossing discomfort and anxious prayer, but the single death was balanced by the birth of a boy to Elizabeth Hopkins. She named him Oceanus. Not surprisingly, they 'were not a little joyful' to make a landfall at the crooking finger of Cape Cod that beckons the weary folk of Europe to the hardships and favours of a New World. However on that November day in 1620 Cape Cod did not appear welcoming and *Mayflower* hauled south, only to find the sea savage and the coast unfriendly. Back north again, to sail into what became Provincetown under Cape Cod's fingernail.

Shortly after landing, some of the strangers announced that 'when they were ashore they would use their own libertie; for none had power to command them ...'. They were legally correct, for *Mayflower* had landed outwith the area where they had permission to settle. However the leaders of the expedition retaliated by drawing up the Mayflower contract, where the settlers agreed to accept the laws created by elected leaders. This unique document marked the first beginnings of that consensual government style that marked the democracy of the New World.

New England was not sympathetic to inexperienced settlers. William Bradford thought it 'a hidious & desolate wildernes, full of wild beasts & wild men'. Even with the help of a Wampanoag Indian named Squanto, around half the settlers died during that first unbelievably harsh winter and the next hungry year. In the autumn of 1621 the Wampanoags joined the survivors in a thanksgiving feast, using American food and creating an American tradition as the culture of England began to merge with that of the New World. More colonists crossed the Atlantic and ships with names such as *Fortune, Charity* and *Handmaid* landed their quota of hopeful families on the wooded coast of North America. The unwelcome were returned to England, while those who could not take the severe climate or the severe religion relocated southward to Virginia. Yet if the land was ill to farm the sea was prolific and a combination of fishing and trading helped establish the Plymouth colony by 1630.

In March of that same year John Winthrop of Suffolk boarded the 350-ton *Arabella* in Southampton. Winthrop was a highly motivated man who, with others of the Massachusetts Bay Company, hoped to establish a religious community in America. As this company intended their colony to be self-governing they took the royal charter with them; there was to be a complete break with England. Most of the 700 East Anglian or London emigrants paid £5 for the passage, with another £4 for every ton of goods they transported. Contrasting with the Chesapeake settlers, many were fairly prosperous farmers or artisans and most travelled in family groups. Their onboard rations were fairly generous and typically English; each passenger was allowed half a gallon of beer a day, with one pint of water plus salted meat, biscuit, peas, oatmeal and butter.

A couple of days after leaving Southampton, eight unfamiliar vessels approached the four emigrant ships. Afraid of Dunkirk privateers, *Arabella* cleared for action, 25 passengers waited with loaded muskets and probably racing pulses while the ship's company prayed for divine help. Perhaps the prayers worked, for the strangers were neither privateers nor French. Such religious practices were a feature of the voyage as

Reverend George Phillps preached on Sundays and catechised his congregation on Tuesdays and Wednesdays. As he also ordered prolonged fasting in times of fog and storm, the seamen, weak from lack of food, would hope for divine help to maintain their grasp on slippery yards.

Contrary winds delayed *Arabella* at the Isle of Wight for 17 days before she could finally head west, but it was another three days before the Lizard faded astern. A week into the Atlantic a storm separated *Talbot* from the fleet but Captain Milborne sailed *Arabella* south to the latitude for Maine, then headed due west, passing the Grand Banks, sliding south of Sable Island and searching for Cape Sable in Nova Scotia. There was plenty of opportunity for fasting as they were whipped with westerly winds, hammered by high seas and soaked with lashing rain. When the fleet scattered in fog, Captain Milborne sailed *Arabella* to Mount Desert Island off Maine then southward to Salem harbour where the thankful, probably apprehensive, emigrants heard their anchor plunge into American water.

Arrival in Massachusetts was barely the beginning of their troubles. There were difficulties with religion and delicate negotiations with earlier colonists and the indigenous Indians, while Governor Winthrop's son was only one of 200 people that died that first year. A similar number returned to England, but others persevered. Winthrop sent a ship to Bristol for supplies, the inevitable disease ultimately burned itself out and a heavy harvest eased the food worry. Within a couple of years this English foothold in North America was tenuous but tenaciously established. It is significant that during this initial period of struggle Winthrop built and launched the 30-ton sloop *Blessing of the Bay;* already Massachusetts was groping toward a maritime future.

Ships from Massachusetts were soon carrying timber, furs and fish to England or Jamaica, returning with household goods, sugar or molasses. As the colonies spread along the coast of the continent, they were connected by land but separated by government; for instance Connecticut levied tolls on vessels from other colonies as they pushed up the Connecticut river. Rather than a unified American culture, back country provincialism characterised many isolated settlements that fretted over witches or believed that the earth was central to the universe. Unique characters emerged, such as the Bostonian Roger Williams who challenged the king's right to grant a land title in the colonies and believed that colonial magistrates could rule on theological affairs. The New World was breeding its own brand of people, and when Williams was expelled from the colony he hacked his way through virgin forest to the Mooshassuc River to found his own settlement that evolved into Rhode Island.

Nations other than the French or English also wished for New World colonies. There were Scots traders who muscled in to the English colonies during the 1650s until the restoration of Charles II led to parliamentary Acts that barred Scottish shipping. The Scots were not yet natural colonists. Among the numerous attempts was that of William Alexander whose dreams of a New Scotland failed in the face of reluctance to try the unbroken ground of North America, the capricious behaviour of Charles I and the French reluctance to relinquish their land. Alexander's legacy remains in the name of Nova Scotia and the strange fact that the esplanade of Edinburgh Castle has dual Scottish-Canadian nationality. Probably better remembered is the attempt to create an entrepôt at Darien. It was a heroic effort that failed, partly due to disease, partly to Spanish opposition and partly to bad management. Possibly the best thing to come from the Darien Scheme was the memory of sincere friendship between the Scots and the indigenous natives, and rumours of a red-headed Indian tribe in the Isthmus.

Between English success and Scottish failure was Dutch practicality. In 1609 Henry Hudson explored what is today the Hudson River. The river did not extend to China, but a cask of brandy helped establish friendly relations with the local Mohawks and in 1614 the Dutch established fur trading posts on Manhattan Island and at Fort Orange which later became Albany. It was ten years before the Dutch West India Company began to settle, but in 1626 Governor Peter Minuit made his bargain purchase of Manhattan, and New Amsterdam was born as a fur trading settlement. An attempt to transport feudal Europe to the Americas failed, and although the Dutch continued to trade, New Amsterdam survived rather than thrived.

In 1638 a Dutch renegade led a Swedish expedition to the supposed riches of the Delaware. When they found a convenient settlement site at a stream named Minquas, they bought land from the Indians, renamed the stream Christina and founded the town of Wilmington. Among the settlers in New Sweden were some Finnish Lapps, who built the sturdy log cabins that were native to their home and which were to become such a characteristic feature of European settlement in North America.

There were skirmishes as Swedes and Dutch competed for the fur trade; houses were burned and Governor Printz of New Sweden extracted tolls from ships using the Delaware. When Peter Stuyvesant, known by the modest title of 'High Mightiness', became governor of the Dutch colony, he literally drummed up recruits in the Netherlands, gathered a small fleet and attacked the mighty Swedish colony with its less than 400 settlers. Almost immediately the Swedes abandoned any pretence of aggression and concentrated on farming and trading. Ten years later an English fleet snapped up New Amsterdam while the wooden-legged Stuyvesant fumed in frustration at the apathy of his garrison. English terms were generous, allowing the Dutch soldiers to remain and farm 50 acres of free land, but New Amsterdam was renamed New York in honour of James, Duke of York and Lord High Admiral.

The Quakers were possibly the most likeable of the non-conformists of the period with their desire to return to the simple beliefs of the early Christians, to abolish slavery and to reform prisons. However their rejection of the Trinity was more questionable, their refusal to remove their hats eccentric and their occasional stark naked appearance in public surely offensive. Nonetheless, their non-payment of taxes was possibly more irritating to the government, who attempted to reform them with banishment, public floggings and executions. William Penn considered that a new start in the New World would be an ideal solution.

King Charles owed Penn's father £16,000 and Penn persuaded the king to pay his debts in land rather than cash. Charles agreed and handed over 55,000 square miles of some of the most fertile land in North America, much of it recently snatched from the Dutch. As sole proprietor, Penn had an economic advantage denied to most other colonists, and in October 1682 his *Welcome* took 70 colonists across the Atlantic and into the Delaware. Within a year 50 ships had arrived and Penn's planned town of Philadelphia had 80 brick-built houses while hundreds of farms spread into the surrounding countryside. Amazingly, Pennsylvania had no Indian wars for the first 70 years, probably because Penn's holy experiment attempted a new method of dealing with Indians: he kept his word to them. His colony was an example of what colonial America should have been like - a colony renowned for liberalism, religious toleration and humanity.

Pennsylvania proved to be a genuine American melting pot. There were Dutch and Swedes from the original colony of New Sweden; a community of Welsh; Germans of many religious persuasions, such as Zion's Breuder, Mountain Men and the intriguingly-named Society of the Women in the Wilderness. There were Lutherans and Presbyterian Scots-Irish from Ulster who moved to the frontier with their usual hardy, self-contained, quarrelsome characters. These were true frontier folk by blood and instinct, moving from the Scots-English frontier to the Irish and now the American.

Penn's Philadelphia was arguably the finest town in North America, with its planned layout, its solidly-built State House and Pennsylvania Hospital. It is easy to imagine the weathered Pennsylvanians sitting outside the Blue Anchor tavern as they watched the bustle of ships that traded to the West Indies, while the smell of tar pervaded the atmosphere and small boats swarmed on the water. Penn had created an idea of toleration that shone across the Atlantic like the torch of a later lady of liberty. His ideals were an example, not only to Americans, but also to the entire world.

Chapter 7

'This Stinking Smoke'

The Americas produced much that Europe wanted: timber and sugar, rum and molasses, nautical stores and indigo, but by the end of the 16th century tobacco was rapidly increasing in importance. The indigenous natives believed that this plant had unusual properties, for while they chewed tobacco, they believed they could be visited by the sun god if they smoked it. There was more: tobacco could calm a storm merely by being thrown onto water, buried tobacco would charm the earth god, and there were few symbols more potent than a pipe of peace. The growing European demand for this amazing plant encouraged illicit English trade with Spanish America, until peace allowed Spain to snuff out the smuggling and the English had to find alternative suppliers. For a while there was desultory trade with the Indians from the Guiana coast to the Amazon, but the introduction of commercial tobacco cultivation moved the centre of the industry to tidewater Virginia.

When Europeans disliked the local Chesapeake tobacco, *nicotiana rustica*, John Rolfe experimented with the sweeter, milder South American *nicotiana tabacum* and achieved immediate popularity. It is ironic that Rolfe should be better remembered for marrying the legendary Pocahontas than for his connection with one of North America's major industries, but perhaps people prefer romance to commercial reality. Initially Rolfe produced tobacco solely for his own use but when it became apparent that the colony was struggling, he exported a shipload to England. Selling at just over five shillings a pound, Virginia tobacco proved immensely profitable, and the rising demand from England multiplied the acreage under cultivation.

As the Virginia Company had hoped their colony would produce silk, gold, tar and hemp for England, the unforeseen popularity of this new crop alarmed the authorities. Augmented by protests from the English government, the company ordered the settlers to concentrate on producing food and creating industries that would benefit the home country, but the colonials thumbed their collective nose and planted tobacco. They had created a demand that appeared insatiable and now worked on the supply in an early example of the American genius for chasing profit. If there was land available, the colonists used it for tobacco, but when they planted the crop behind the wooden palisades of the fort and in the main thoroughfare of Jamestown, King James was compelled to compose his *Counterblast to Tobacco*. However, even royalty's opinion that smoking tobacco was 'loathsome to the eye, harmfull to the braine, dangerous to the lungs, and ... resembling the horrible stygian smoke of the pit...' failed to prevent the colony from producing the plant. Once across the Atlantic, it seemed, people felt free to dare the wrath of kings.

With even emigrant artisans becoming tobacco planters, the Governor of Virginia took legal steps, decreeing that people could only grow tobacco once they had planted two fields of corn, but this law could also be seen as permission to plant and tobacco continued to spread. Obviously unable to chop this new weed at its roots, King James decided to go for profit instead and hit it with a thumping duty of 5s 10d a pound. Money clattered into the king's coffers as England was wafted through the 17th century in a haze of Virginia smoke. By 1614 it seemed that every street corner in London held a tobacco shop and within a decade the tobacco crop had an estimated worth of £500,000. New shop signs intrigued country visitors to the cities, for tobacco sellers displayed their products under either the symbol of a 'carrote' – a carrot-shaped roll of leaf – or the more exotic Indian head surmounted by tobacco leaves.

The initial tobacco plantations were around Chesapeake Bay, that invitingly attractive gouge that nature has bitten out of the east coast of central North America. With the indigenous people either obligingly docile or evicted by force, there was a plethora of land on which to plant, for although a 200- or 400-acre plantation seemed large in comparison with an English farm, the scale of the country was unbelievably huge. Tobacco not only provided the colony with economic stability; it also influenced the pattern of settlement as plantations were founded along the rivers to facilitate crop transportation. Nevertheless, there were problems. The plantation system was labour intensive and North America had a perennial shortage of labourers, partly due to the truculent nature of the settlers, partly to the unhealthy climate. In order to provide a continual flow of workers, the colonies introduced a system of indentured service.

By this arrangement, people crossed the Atlantic on the understanding that they would work for a specified master for five or seven years, after which they received their freedom and all the opportunities of the New World. The servant gained by having his or her passage paid, plus board and keep, while the master achieved a guaranteed and hopefully compliant workforce. There was the added advantage to the master of the *headright*, which granted 50 acres of land to whoever financed the passage of a servant. Those men with the funds to transport dozens of indentured servants obtained vast territories in North America.

Although many indentured servants travelled of their own free will, exchanging years of personal freedom for the possibility of an enhanced future, others had no choice in the matter. Shortly after he had accepted the throne of both Scotland and England, King James set his mind to clearing up the chaos of the border between the two realms. For centuries this area had been the battleground where rival armies met, and naturally it had bred a violent strain of people. James tamed them with a mixture of 'Jeddart justice' – hang first, trial later – and wholesale banishment to either Ireland or the wars of the Low Countries. The idea of banishing criminals was a natural progression and in 1619 James transported 100 prisoners to the Virginia colony.

Transportation had a dual purpose; it removed the unwanted from Scotland and England and provided much needed labourers for the American tobacco plantations. The idea seemed so rational that a subsequent Act of Parliament ordained that certain types of criminals could be pardoned execution if they accepted a sentence of transportation. Usually transportation was for seven or 14 years, but the more hardened offender and political prisoners could be exiled for life. During the civil wars of the mid-17th century, and the ensuing religious troubles, transportation became an accepted method of dealing with troublesome prisoners of war. Many thousands of men were herded into vessels that were often unseaworthy, frequently to die of disease long before they sighted American shores. As the system became established, contractors rounded up these 'transports', shipped them to Virginia, Maryland or the Caribbean and disposed of them in the slave markets. Initially the contractors received £5 a head for the transports but when this price dropped profit depended on the price paid on the open market.

Whether voluntarily or by Government order, the indentured servants crossed the Atlantic by the thousand, and by the thousand they died. Living conditions were shockingly unhealthy, with mosquitoes breeding in the same stagnant water that the colonists drank from, so dysentery joined the malaria, yellow fever, and scurvy that killed eight out of every ten hopeful arrivals. Even when the death rate fell with improved hygiene and the introduction of a liquid derived from quinine (then termed Peruvian bark), indentured servants were still annually imported as a previous consignment completed their servitude. When demand exceeded supply, the unscrupulous developed kid-nabbing, when youths were knocked on the head in ports such as London or Bristol, or grabbed from their homes in rural Ireland, to be shackled in the hold of an America-bound ship. Some servants were African, kept on the same terms as their European companions in misery, and with an equal chance of obtaining freedom and land once their allotted time was completed.

The majority of servants were in their late teens or early twenties, young men who were committed to serve for five years 'honestly and diligently' with a promise not to 'neglect his Master's business night nor day except in the case of sickness or leave'. Those that survived five years of labouring were given a substantial supply of grain, new clothes and a musket. The lucky also received 50 acres of land. By hard work and after he had cleared his land, a single man could grow up to 1200 pounds of tobacco in a year, giving him a profit of perhaps £20, although falling tobacco prices reduced this as the century advanced. While Virginia continued as the chief producer, Maryland also grew tobacco and their combined total gradually increased from about 300 tons in 1635 to a staggering 80,000 tons in 1735. As with most commodities there were periods of slump: the re-introduction of the Navigation Act in 1660 restricted colonial trade to English ports, creating an excess that lasted until around 1680 when overstocked merchants flooded the European market. Perhaps the bargain prices ensured that the initial profit was low, but the creation of a demand made England into a vast entrepôt, although many of the colonial planters struggled to make a profit. Nonetheless, a steady reduction in production and transportation costs ensured an increasing acreage under tobacco.

Although tobacco ships could dock virtually anywhere in England, London and Bristol were the main tobacco ports and a regular system developed for the trade. The ships crossed the Atlantic in autumn, loaded up through the winter and returned in spring. At this time most of the plantations were along the riverside, allowing tobacco ships to load at their personal wharf. The number of tobacco ships increased, so by the end of the 17th century there were up to 200 sailing annually.

After 1707 English ports encountered opposition from their Scottish partners in the newly-united Great Britain. For the first few years Glasgow, a riverside town in the west of Scotland, chartered English ships but in 1718 the first Glasgow-owned vessel crossed the Atlantic. Once started, the expansion of the Scottish-American tobacco trade was startling, so by 1735 over 20 Glasgow ships regularly sailed to the Americas. With the Clyde so shallow at Glasgow, these vessels had to use Port Glasgow on the Firth of Clyde but by the 1750s Glasgow controlled half the British tobacco traffic and the merchants were demanding a more efficient system. It was decided to deepen the Clyde so that the tobacco ships could unload directly into the city. After a couple of abortive attempts, an Englishman named John Golborne succeeded by constructing groynes that directed and therefore strengthened the force of the current to scour a deeper channel. Virginian tobacco had financed the development of Glasgow, which was to be one of the great cities of the 19th century.

There were various reasons why Glasgow merchants were successful in capturing so much of the tobacco trade. Location was crucial; ships from the Clyde were often able to cross the Atlantic two or three weeks faster than those from further south which, in turn, meant less wages to pay and less storm damage to the ships. Faster passages frequently allowed Glasgow vessels to make an extra journey each year and with only three successful round trips enough to make an ordinary merchant wealthy, this single voyage could make an appreciable difference. The contrast in crossing times was appreciated by the novelist and spy Daniel Defoe, who said that 'Glasgow vessels are no sooner out of the Firth of Clyde, but they stretch away to the north-west, are out of the road of the privateers immediately, and are often at the capes of Virginia before the London ships get clear of the Channel'.

These privateers were a continuous hazard of warfare, but particularly in the early decades of the 18th century, the northern routes across the Atlantic were safer than the southern. While ships sailing from England had to travel in convoy or chance the voracious French privateers, Glasgow vessels could sail singly in relative safety. As the century advanced, however, the French wised up to Scottish trade and hovered off the Clyde. Between the wars, Glasgow had the additional advantage of having a monopoly to supply tobacco to France. Perhaps this was a distant echo of the auld alliance, more likely because the Glasgow tobacco lords could obtain and supply large quantities at a modest price.

As the volume of tobacco diverted from English to Scottish ports increased, English merchants muttered about Scottish underhanded methods as the bitter reality gradually sunk in that Union could be exploitative in either direction. Most of the ships were fairly small and on the outward voyage they carried glass and leather articles, iron tools for the colonials, clothing and cloth and thread. Many of these vessels, such as *Argyle,* and the 100-ton *Lillie* were New England-built, for although much of the tobacco money passed to British merchants, the New Englanders were quick to recognise an opportunity. Although there were brigantines and brigs in the trade, possibly the most common was the snow. This rig had the mizzen, with a fore-and-aft spanker, close behind the mainmast to balance the headsails on the long bowsprit. The snow rig created less strain for the mainmast which, in turn, lessened the stress on the hull, which kept the ship more watertight and ensured that the hogsheads of tobacco arrived in better condition.

For all that the Atlantic crossing was common, it could still be dangerous. There was the case of *Good Intent* that spent 24 weeks at sea, arriving in New England in January 1752 with the captain and most of the crew dead and the few surviving passengers starving. She was not alone, *Love and Unity* sailed from Rotterdam with 150 people on board, but a prolonged passage meant that the 34 survivors had to buy water to drink and rats to eat. *Sea Flower* of Belfast had an equally horrific four-month voyage during which 46 people died out of 106 and the survivors spoke darkly of cannibalism. Yet despite the hazards of the Atlantic, the tobacco industry continued to grow, with the vast bulk crossing from Virginia to Britain, and over 50% of that being re-exported to Europe.

By this period black slaves had replaced the indentured servants. As early as 1619 a Dutch slave trader had sold the first consignment of Africans in Virginia, but the supply was intermittent until the British captured the Dutch West African trading posts. Once the Dutch were removed as trading rivals, the number of African slaves rapidly increased. Controversially, some people, including William Eddis, an Englishman who was the surveyor of customs at Annapolis in 1770, believed that the Africans were luckier than the indentured white servants, 'over whom the rigid planter exercises an inflexible severity'. Whereas the African slaves were apparently cared for as a long-lasting investment, the indentured servants were 'strained to the utmost'. Others, of course, disagreed, pointing out that the Europeans were frequently assigned to lighter labour in Virginia. It must also, and always, be remembered that the Africans were neither convicts nor volunteers; they were ordinary people kidnapped against their

As early as 1619 a Dutch slave trader had sold the first consignment of Africans in Virginia.
Courtesy of the Billie Love Collection, Isle of Wight.

will and subject to life imprisonment with hard labour. Probably worse, they worked with the knowledge that their descendants faced a similar doom. The sheer horror of that sentence is hard to stomach.

Different areas of the Chesapeake sold their produce to particular British ports. The areas around the James, York, Potomac and Rappahannock Rivers traded with Bristol merchants who sold the mild, sweet tobacco within Britain. Traders from Liverpool, London and Glasgow purchased the darker Oronoco variety that was mainly grown in Maryland and the Virginia backcountry, and re-exported it to Europe. But any variety of tobacco exhausted the Chesapeake soil within about three years, so the tobacco country had a permanently shifting frontier with the working plantations presenting islands of cultivation amidst a vast expanse of raw and secondary growth. Although the image of southern life is of vast wealth and hundreds of slaves, the majority of plantations contained only eight, with the master frequently working at their side. There were some mansions, lime-washed and with front and back doors to allow in a cooling breeze, but the majority of planters inhabited rough-hewn log cabins little better, and frequently not as grand, as an English cottage. They lived by the seasons, with the first rain of summer causing a frantic dash to transplant delicate tobacco seedlings to the prepared raised beds.

Around the end of August when the leaves began to yellow, the tobacco plants were cut and the stalks stored in a 'tobacco house' until they were ready for packing. Barefooted slaves trod down the tobacco into hogsheads, with two hogsheads making a tun, which weighed around half a ton. As transportation by road was nearly impossible in the backcountry, Reverend Robert Rose's invention of a tobacco raft for the rivers was a godsend. Little more than a simple platform positioned on two canoes, this raft proved extremely manoeuvrable and was able to hold up to nine hogsheads. American ingenuity had solved a problem unique to American conditions.

Despite the overwhelming significance of trade to the Chesapeake, it was a long time before a merchant class evolved. Primarily this was because planters possessing their own private wharf could deal direct with a British merchant with no need for a middleman. Yet few planters benefited from this arrangement, for by providing credit for the following year's supply of tobacco, British merchants often placed the planters permanently in debt.

As the plantations exhausted the land around tidewater Virginia and withdrew inland, direct purchase replaced the consignment trade system. This meant that rather than the planters owning the tobacco until it was sold in Britain, the merchants used local merchants or, more commonly, factors, to purchase the leaf in the colonies. Interestingly local laws encouraged the use of factors – the Tobacco Inspection Acts of Virginia in 1730 and Maryland in 1747 ordered that tobacco be gathered in warehouses rather than scattered throughout the colony. Somebody had to organise the procedure for the British merchants, so resident factors were introduced.

When settlement expanded there was a tendency for the larger planters to become merchants in their own right, but many British merchants preferred to deal with the smaller planters of the interior. By using credit from company stores in an area lacking competition, British merchants could set their own prices, and if credit was welcome the colonists were often tied to a single merchant. The store system allowed Glasgow merchants to order shiploads of tobacco in advance, so reducing the time ships had to remain in the colony and cut out some freight costs. Stores were invariably managed by the British as the colonials tended to be outdoor people, unwilling to work long hours indoors. Equally invariably, relations between the indoor British clerk and outdoor colonial settler were often tense; the Virginians blamed their perennial lack of coin on the British government's refusal to let them trade with anybody save Britain. In a sense the relations between storekeeper and settler were a microcosm of the developing rift between the colonials as a body and the British crown and government. Scottish merchants were particularly unpopular, with the radical colonial William Lee stating that 'a North Briton is something like the stinking and troublesome weed we call in Virginia wild onion... it is extremely difficult to eradicate them, and they can poison the ground so that no wholesome plant can thrive'.

Although most of the major British merchants had served an apprenticeship as a storekeeper or factor in the Chesapeake backcountry, most apprentices were merely indentured servants. Very few indentured apprentices would rise high enough to gain a share in a tobacco company because the price of at least £1000 was far beyond their reach. For those who did the rewards could be huge. The Glasgow merchant Alexander Speirs had a fortune of £153,000 while William Cunninghame had a Glasgow town house valued at £10,000. Much of this money came from credit with John Glassford, probably the greatest tobacco lord of them all, estimating that in 1778 Scottish merchants were owed £1 million by the planters.

Invariably the trade routes were more elaborate than a simple double Atlantic crossing. As the colonials demanded other than just British goods, merchants developed new routes to satisfy their prime Virginian customers. Ships of the tobacco merchants traded for Russian flax and Caribbean molasses to fill the Virginian stores and so developed a triangular route from the Clyde to the Caribbean and the Chesapeake. The North American taste for rum appeared as insatiable as Britain's for tobacco. Neil Jamieson, the head colonial representative for John Glassford, traded in wine and timber, shipbuilding and shipping, salt and slaves. Glassford owned around 25 vessels and traded around £500,000 through his two companies and associations with another four. Lack of capital had led to this peculiarly Scottish system of mutual dependence for a single merchant, or at most a partnership of two or three, usually controlled the tobacco companies of Bristol, Liverpool or London.

Throughout the 17th and 18th centuries tobacco was the most valuable export from North America with nearly £1 million worth being exported in 1775, but when 13 of the colonies rebelled the entire commercial picture altered. As it became obvious that grumbling discontent would escalate into real trouble, the merchants ran themselves ragged chasing tobacco to fill their ships. For once the planters had the advantage and demanded payment in hard cash. By August 1775 demand for shipping space was so great that tobacco replaced staves and barrel hoops on decks of eastward-bound shipping.

The Atlantic was a highway for the United States privateers, who poured eastward to the rich pickings in British waters. Glasgow tobacco ships were particularly vulnerable on the unescorted passage between the Clyde and the convoy assembly point at Cork. In 1776 there were five known United States privateers in Irish waters, a number that increased to eight the following year. Naturally the Glasgow merchants retaliated by arming the tobacco ships, with *Jupiter* carrying 24 cannon and six anti-personnel swivel guns. However, such weapons were inadequate against the other threat to tobacco trade seamen; the Royal Naval press-gangs that were active in the Firth of Clyde and off Ireland. Despite the war many tobacco merchants attempted to maintain their trading links, with some Scottish merchants swearing to remain neutral and abstain from activities detrimental to the newborn United States. Representatives of the tobacco interest in Glasgow also petitioned the British government to be more understanding towards the republic, while the city was the only Scottish burgh not to send loyal greetings to the king.

Many Scots actually in America kept a low profile or remained in the backcountry, but some swore loyalty to Congress or took on neutral Danish citizenship. Such actions were necessary as the state of Virginia passed an Act in 1778 claiming all 'lands, slaves, stocks and implements' owned by British subjects. Stunned by a succession of retrogressive commercial blows, some companies switched to trading for Canadian timber and fish, or smuggled past the Royal and Continental Navy, but more dealt with Dutch or Danish islands in the Caribbean who, in turn, traded with the United States. To evade the Royal Naval blockade, the tobacco merchants used fast vessels known as runners, and were so successful that they owned much property in St Eustatius even before the British captured that island in 1781. Not every tobacco company indulged in smuggling; others leased their ships to the government or purchased letters of marque in order to convert them into privateers.

Although the Glasgow merchants resumed their Atlantic connections after 1783, there was no place for monopolistic men such as John Glassford. Clydeside ships sailed as much to the Caribbean as to the Chesapeake and the resulting diversification was probably healthier for Glasgow than the earlier dependence on a single commodity. Simultaneously, the United States exported their own tobacco in their own vessels, bypassing Britain to trade directly with Europe. Tobacco had been the first product to bring some prosperity to the colonies, but with the shackles of colonialism released, United States traders were about to challenge the world.

Chapter 8

Form Line of Battle

'You have done your duty in pointing out to me the danger;
now lay me alongside the enemy's flagship.'
Admiral Sir Edward Hawke to his ship's master who pointed out dangerous
rocks during the battle of Quiberon Bay on 20th November 1759.

Spain's maritime dominion had slipped away to more northern powers and despite
the flowering of the Netherlands, by the 18th century it was France and Britain who
wrestled for control of Neptune's trident. Dynastic and territorial disputes created
near continuous European warfare which expanded into the Atlantic, so fleets of
battleships exchanged broadsides from Cuba to Cape St Vincent.

Each battle had its own character, each its own incidents. At the battle of Barfleur
in May 1692, an Anglo-Dutch naval force attempted to eclipse the ascending sun of
Louis XIV of France. This was a typical naval engagement of the late 17th century -
scrappy, protracted and homicidal. It began early on 19th May but both fleets anchored
when fading winds and then fog made fighting impossible. When the French withdrew
next morning, adverse winds and tides frustrated the allied pursuit, so by late afternoon
of 21st May some French vessels had retreated into the Bay of La Hogue and the allies
were anchored just outside. They moved in the next morning, brave colours flapping
above the bulky battleships and sweating men working their cannon so the dense white
powder smoke added to the confusion of battle. Sir Clowdisley Shovel, commanding
the British Red Squadron, was wounded, fire ships flared and sparked while seamen
in ships' boats clashed with French cavalrymen riding saddle-deep into the bay. After
the smoke had cleared and the screaming wounded were carried to the cockpit, the
result was a conclusive victory for the allies. Dutch and English hands clasped together
in uncomfortable amicability on the hilt of Neptune's trident.

The War of the Spanish Succession, Queen Anne's War in North America, broke
out in 1701 and set the scene for the century. On one side were Austria, England

(joined by Scotland after the Scottish-English Union that created Great Britain in 1707) and the Netherlands. On the other was an alliance of France and Spain that threatened to dominate both the Old World and the New. In 1702 a Franco-Spanish fleet had escorted the Spanish treasure fleet from the Caribbean, only for Sir George Rooke's Anglo-Dutch fleet to spring upon them in Vigo harbour, north-west Spain. When HMS *Torbay* became ensnared while attempting to break through the defending boom, the French Admiral Chateau-Renault sent in an ex-merchantman hastily converted to a fire ship. As Captain Charles Hopsonn frantically battled the flames on *Torbay*, the fire ship blew up, smashing the boom and throwing her cargo of snuff into the sky. A dark mantle descended on the bay, dousing the fire on *Torbay* and drenching the decks of the French warships, so dozens of French seamen leaped into the sea to ease the agony of lungs burning with vast quantities of snuff. During the confusion, Rooke thrust the Anglo-Dutch fleet through the shattered boom. He captured 13 enemy vessels in the ensuing brawl, and when the Spanish gold was later turned into English coins each one was stamped *Vigo* as a reminder of the first naval victory of the century.

The war continued with the Duke of Marlborough's victories in Europe, bitter Indian fighting along the New England frontier and confused conflict between Spaniard, Frenchman, Indian and colonist in the Carolinas. In 1710 the Royal Navy carried colonial militia to victory at Port Royal, but a later scheme to attack New France went badly wrong when many British ships were wrecked on the shores of the St Lawrence. With the Peace of Utrecht, the sun set on Louis XIV's dream of a united French-Spanish dynasty and dawned on an enlarged British empire that now included Gibraltar, Newfoundland, Hudson Bay and Acadia. As a sordid sideline, Britain gained the *Asiento*, the sole right to supply African slaves to the Spanish colonies for the next three decades.

Despite the European peace, Britain seemed intent on antagonising Spain. In 1726 Francis Hosier was given 16 ships and the impossible orders to prevent the Spanish treasure fleet from crossing the Atlantic but without starting a war. Hosier did his best by blockading Porto Bello in the Isthmus of Darien in Central America, but yellow fever spread through his squadron and killed him and another 4000 British seamen. Nonetheless, the British continued to increase Spanish suspicions by founding the colony of Georgia that seemed to threaten Florida. It was almost inevitable that Spain should retaliate by agreeing to the Bourbon family pact, whereby France would support her should Britain attack her colonies.

Yet the Spanish were perhaps not entirely blameless; they employed small vessels known as *guarda-costas* to prevent smuggling and, according to Captain Robert Jenkins, in 1731 the crew of one *guarda-costa* boarded his brig *Rebecca*, looted the cargo and sliced off one of his ears. At the time the story elicited little interest but seven years later Jenkins appeared in front of a House of Commons committee and showed them his detached ear. Although some claimed that Jenkins lost that particular ear after being placed in a pillory for drunkenness, the resulting war became known as the War of Jenkins Ear. There were, however, many other examples of *guarda-costas* interfering with British shipping. Within a few years this private squabble merged with the greater War of the Austrian Succession.

In 1739 Admiral Vernon commanded a naval expedition against the Spanish Caribbean colonies, again with a contingent of colonials on board. Although the British captured Porto Bello, they were repulsed at Cartagena, repelled from Santiago de Cuba and ravaged by disease. More successful was the joint Royal Navy and New England militia attack on the French fortress of Louisburg on Cape Breton Island. There were also fleet actions in the Atlantic, with one of the most notable fought 70 miles west of Cape Finisterre in Spain. It was 9.30 in the morning of 3rd May 1747 that a lookout of Admiral Anson's British fleet of 14 ships sighted the topsails of a French fleet of 38 mixed warships and transports. The French intended to separate into two squadrons, one hoping to recover Cape Breton Island, the other sailing to attack British bases on the Coromandel Coast. By noon, nine of the French had formed a line of battle to cover the withdrawal of the others, and at three in the afternoon the fleets were close enough for Anson to signal a general chase. This entailed the British ships closing on the nearest suitable Frenchman. It was a long afternoon of thick powder smoke and falling spars, wounded seamen and the Union flag flapping triumphantly over six captured French ships. There was £300,000 of prize money paid out for that bloody afternoon's work, and Anson became a peer.

Cape Finisterre was a classic use of the Royal Navy for destroying the warships of an enemy to protect British merchantmen while capturing the merchant shipping of the enemy. At this period the Royal Navy's tactics were still based on the 21 Fighting Instructions that had been laid down in the early 1650s. Central to the Instructions was the Line of Battle, where rival fleets would form a long line of battleships and slug it out broadside to broadside, with the commanding admiral choosing either the windward or leeward position. The windward fleet had better manoeuvrability and the wind would clear gunsmoke away, while the leeward fleet could withdraw more easily, damaged ships could be driven clear of the enemy and the lower gunports could be kept open longer, giving a greater weight of fire. As the navy's scope increased it became obvious that more flexibility was required and admirals such as Vernon and Hawke added innovations such as the general chase, where individual ships could make all sail to attack the first available enemy. Later in the century developments in signalling further relaxed the rigidity of fleet actions, but most major battles were still fought at half musket shot, around 100 yards or less. It is horrifying to picture the effects of a broadside of 12- or 18-pound cannon firing at that range into a wooden vessel packed full of men.

The War of the Austrian Succession – or King George's War – ended with the Treaty of Aix-la-Chapelle in 1748. Louisburg was returned to France, the main differences were unresolved and the Spanish retained all their colonies. In North America, Briton, Frenchman and colonial glowered at each other across ill-defined boundaries, various Indian tribes sharpened their scalping knives as settlers spread slowly towards the Appalachian Ridge while Atlantic waves surged heedlessly over the shattered timbers of half a thousand ships.

By the 1750s, Atlantic trade was as important to Britain as any success in Europe, while France had secured her position in Quebec, Louisburg and New Orleans. Although the British colonials numbered many times the population of New France, there was more to colonial power than demographics. The French claim to a huge arc of territory from the Great Lakes to the Gulf restricted the British colonists to the eastern seaboard and frustrated their expansionist dreams. In 1754 friction sparked into colonial conflict and redcoat and militiaman exchanged musketry with French-influenced frontier Indians.

By 1755 the French were preparing to reinforce their garrisons in Canada. Although Britain and France were still officially at peace, Edward Boscawen, nicknamed 'Wry-necked Dick' as the result of an injury at Cape Finisterre that gave his head a permanent twist, was ordered to prevent the French from crossing the Atlantic. Boscawen caught the French off the Canadian coast and, in an action made more confused by thick fog, captured two transports together with £80,000 that had been intended to pay the French garrison of Canada. As Hardwicke, the Lord Chancellor said, this was 'too little or too much'. The loss of two ships would be too little to affect the French position, but the action was too much to be ignored. In earlier wars Britain had neglected her North American colonies but this time she took them seriously, pouring money, men and munitions across the Atlantic, while motivated Indian allies backed the strong French military presence. In the initial stages, British and colonials attacked where the French were strongest, the Navy was scattered throughout the globe and the French seemed triumphant. Not until William Pitt organised the British war effort was an effective strategy formulated and, in 1758, Admiral Boscawen, General Jeffrey Amherst and Colonel James Wolfe sailed from Halifax with 157 vessels to besiege Louisburg. Despite 100 boats capsizing in the Cape Breton surf, Louisburg was captured on 26th July and the St Lawrence was open to an invasion.

Realising the increasing importance of North America, a French minister wrote that '... it is possessions in America that will in the future form the balance of power in Europe ...' adding that British domination there will '... usurp the commerce of the nations ...', and the British seemed determined to prove him right. In 1759, a fleet of 250 ships, including around 50 warships, thrust up the St Lawrence towards Quebec. For weeks it seemed that the French fortress was too strong to attack until Captain Simon Fraser noticed that washerwomen used a small path up the Quebec cliffs. When some 4800 British and colonial troops negotiated the path in the pre-dawn dim of a Canadian morning, they formed up on the Plains of Abraham and swept away the French by volleys of musketry and a Highland charge of flashing broadswords and screaming Gaelic slogans. This was one of the crucial battles of North American history which decided that the bulk of North America would be English-speaking, and it was only possible because of the Royal Navy's control of the Atlantic. The capture of Montreal in the autumn of 1760 removed the final French power base in North America.

Meanwhile, Admiral Rodney swept through the Caribbean capturing Martinique, St Vincent, St Lucia, Grenada and the major Spanish island of Cuba while the French

West Indies squadron remained uselessly at anchor at Cap Francais, wasted away by hunger and disease. British victories in India and the Philippines only emphasised their obvious superiority in the colonial war game.

Admiral Hawke won possibly the most important battle of the eastern Atlantic at Quiberon Bay in 1759. After months of blockade, a November gale forced Hawke's fleet from their station off Brest, allowing the French Admiral Conflans to slip out. Hastily replacing damaged spars and sails in Torbay, Hawke emerged for revenge, found the French and signalled for a General Chase. The British pursued the French to Quiberon Bay, used the French ships to pilot them around the dangerous rocks and attacked as the early dusk fell. Scattered, the French could offer no cohesive defence and lost half a dozen battleships in a confused melee as flickering flames reflected off the darkening water and splintered wreckage surged on the tide. The remainder of the French retreated to the Charente and Vilaine Rivers, where most foundered in the shallows. Hawke lost only two ships.

The Peace of Paris in 1763 confirmed British power from Hudson Bay to Florida and from the Mississippi to the Atlantic. Of her former North American colonies, France retained only Guadeloupe and Martinique in the Caribbean and a couple of minor islands in the Gulf of St Lawrence. The British American colonies gained freedom from the threat of France and the opportunity to consider their position. Back in 1754 Benjamin Franklin's Plan of Union had been scoffed from sight, but now as Britain demanded taxes in payment for protection that was no longer required, and imposed restrictive laws on an expansive people, the colonials began to feel less British and more American. As rebellion stirred on the western shores of the Atlantic, embittered France waited her chance for revenge.

In 1776 the trouble in North America came to a head and the British colonial bloc split, with 13 of the colonies declaring themselves free from British rule. For a time only United States privateers carried the war beyond North America, but when Britain did not immediately crush the rebellion other European nations declared war on her - France in 1778, Spain in 1779 and the Netherlands in 1780. By the early 1780s Britain stood alone against virtually every maritime power of Europe, plus much of the North American population. In this period the French navy was probably at its peak, while Spanish ships were superior in design and firepower to anything the thinly-stretched Royal Navy possessed. More concerned with maintaining her lines of communication with the army in North America, Britain temporarily lost her naval superiority in the Caribbean and even in home waters struggled to cope with the depredations of United States and French privateers.

Among the best of the French Admirals was the Comte de Grasse, a veteran of both the War of the Austrian Succession and the Seven Years War. By 1778 he was a commodore, commanding the battleship *Robuste* in the drawn battle of Ushant. Three years later he was commander-in-chief of the French Atlantic fleet and encountered a British fleet under Admiral Graves which was attempting to relieve Yorktown, then under siege by a combined United States-French army.

Graves' 19 battleships were laden with supplies for Cornwallis' army when they sailed into Chesapeake Bay, only to find de Grasse with 24 ships at anchor. In the early afternoon de Grasse eased out on the ebbing tide to meet the British. The fleets fought about 12 miles east of Cape Henry but the angle of Graves' approach kept his rear watching in impotent frustration while his vanguard and centre were engaged. Rigid conformity to the Fighting Instructions prevented the British ships from singling out an individual enemy thereby contributing to the loss of the battle and the loss of the North American continent. After a couple of hours fighting the fleets broke contact and spent the next four days watching each other, with Graves seemingly unwilling to attack an enemy of superior power and de Grasse apparently satisfied to prevent the relief of Yorktown without a battle. When the British withdrew to New York, Cornwallis, bereft of his desperately-needed supplies, surrendered. It was 18th September 1781 and the independence of the United States was virtually assured. If sea power had gained Britain an Atlantic empire, a temporary lull in that power had contributed hugely to its loss. It was Britain's misfortune, but possibly the world's good fortune, that Graves and not a fighting seaman such as Admiral Rodney had opposed de Grasse off Yorktown.

At the beginning of 1780 Admiral Sir George Rodney had been escorting a convoy to the western Mediterranean when HMS *Bedford* sighted a Spanish fleet of 11 battleships off Cape St Vincent. Rodney launched his 18 ships in a General Chase, ordering them to take the lee gauge so the Spanish could not retreat to a secure port. The fighting started around four in the afternoon and continued through a gusty night of foul weather, with ship after Spanish ship lowering her flag. At two in the morning a brilliant moon illuminated a sea where only two Spanish battleships and two frigates remained under their own flag.

Two years later Rodney commanded the fleet in what was to prove the last major action of the war. As Admiral of the West Indies fleet he commanded 36 battleships and was opposed by the same de Grasse who had bested Graves in the Chesapeake. De Grasse had 30 ships and met Rodney at the Saints, a collection of small islets between Dominica and Guadeloupe. At seven o'clock on the 12th the opposing fleets passed each other, but two hours later a shift of the wind enabled Rodney to lead five ships through the French line. When Sir Samuel Hood's rear division followed, the British gained the weather gauge. A French attempt to reform a line of battle resulted in the loss of four ships to the British, and just before 6.30 de Grasse's 104-gun flagship *Ville de Paris* surrendered to Hood's *Barfleur*. Rodney did not follow as the battered French fleet retreated to join the convoy it was guarding, but de Grasse never commanded a French naval ship again.

A combination of North American tenacity and European naval and military support had lost Britain 13 of her North American colonies and shaken her command of the sea. However, France had spent more than she could afford in supporting a republican revolution and now her people murmured against their own king. The French Revolution proclaimed liberty, fraternity and equality while the baskets beneath

Madame Guillotine filled with the heads of priests, peasants and aristocrats. Even those Britons who at first supported the red-capped revolutionaries realised that tyranny had been replaced by terror. When the inevitable war erupted there were some differences from the navy of the previous war: carronades, a type of cannon with a large calibre but a short range, squatted in many broadsides and improvements to signalling had finally consigned the Fighting Instructions to history. They had been effective in their time but, based on battle experiences of a century before, were scarcely practical in the new flexible age. It was also to prove a more ruthless and efficient age; Rodney's comment after the Saints 'Come, we have done very handsomely' would be replaced by Nelson's 'England expects'. Victory was not just expected, it was demanded, and the enemy had to be crushed.

The first major test of maritime strength was the Battle of the Glorious First of June 1794, when Admiral Lord Howe waylaid a French convoy of grain ships from the United States. The fleets were even – 25 British against 26 French – but the British broke the French line to capture six ships and sink another. This was despite the French standing order that any officer who surrendered without his ship being 'in danger of sinking' could be guillotined. It appeared that the British were tactically superior at sea. The French, however, could claim a strategic victory as the much-needed grain convoy reached France.

After a couple of frustratingly minor victories in the Mediterranean, the addition of the Spanish to Britain's French and Dutch enemies caused a temporary withdrawal from that sea. The appointment of Sir John Jervis as commander-in-chief of the Lisbon-based fleet was the beginning of a major turnaround. As a result of messing with the warrant officers while a midshipman, Jervis had a tremendous knowledge of the workings of the ship, and the minds of his men. Perhaps his discipline was strict, but he installed 19th century efficiency into the 18th century fleet and on 14th February 1797 his methods were tested. With only 15 ships, Jervis faced the 27 Spanish battleships of Admiral Don Jose de Cordova off Cape St Vincent. De Cordova intended to combine with a Franco-Dutch fleet to gain control of the Channel preliminary to an invasion of Britain.

Although greatly outnumbered Jervis knew he had created probably the most efficient naval force in the world, while Atlantic gales had scattered his opponents into two ill-defined squadrons. Jervis thrust his ships between the Spanish squadrons, and when the Spanish weather division (those ships closest to the direction of the wind) attempted to sneak past him without fighting, Horatio Nelson in HMS *Captain* and Cuthbert Collingwood in HMS *Excellent* sailed across their bows. Nelson positioned *Captain* alongside *San Nicolas*, captured her and followed on by boarding and seizing the 112-gun *San Josef*. As the Spanish lee division was about to join battle, Jervis brought his ships into line astern formation and the two fleets parted, Spanish for Cadiz, British for Lagos. The results of the battle were far greater than just the four captured Spaniards, for while British morale rose, Spanish slumped. Jervis became Earl St Vincent and Nelson was knighted and became a public hero.

That same year the Royal Navy suffered mutiny at Spithead and the Nore, but still managed another victory when Admiral Duncan destroyed a Dutch fleet at Camperdown. A French attempt to threaten India by attacking Egypt saw the Royal Navy thrust into the Mediterranean, where Nelson won the battle of the Nile. Next came a British strike against the northern alliance, which ended with Parker and Nelson's victory at Copenhagen on 2nd April 1801.

After an uneasy peace in 1802, the following year's conflict was dignified by the title of the Napoleonic War. Once again Napoleon decided to invade Britain, after luring the Royal Navy away with a supposed threat to the West Indies. The idea was for Admiral Ganteaume to break free from Brest with 21 battleships, drive the British from Ferrol and release the blockaded Spanish fleet. Simultaneously Admiral Villeneuve would leave Toulon, join his squadron to that of Cadiz and cross to the Caribbean, meeting Ganteaume at Martinique. The British would counter this threat to the Caribbean with the Channel fleet, but while they were crossing the Atlantic from east to west, the French would cross from west to east and escort an invasion fleet across the undefended Channel.

The first part of the plan was successful, with Villeneuve raising the blockade of Cadiz and sailing a combined fleet of 18 ships to Martinique, trailing Nelson in his wake. However, Admiral Gardner had prevented Ganteaume from reaching the open Atlantic, and Nelson decided that 'some cause … has made them resolve to proceed direct for Europe'. Lord Barham, in charge of the Admiralty, spread a net for Villeneuve, so that Sir Robert Calder encountered him and took two Spanish prizes. Although outnumbered, Calder was heavily criticised for failing to press home his attack, something that could not be said of Nelson when his 27 ships met Villeneuve's 33 off Cape Trafalgar. With veteran professional seamen led by experts opposed to untried conscripts who had spent much of the war blockaded in port, the issue was never really in doubt. Nelson died in this battle that broke French sea power and for the next century the Atlantic saw a respite from major warfare. Tactics and technology would be vastly changed when national navies again contested the Atlantic seaways. In the meantime Neptune could hand his trident to the safe care of Britannia and retire for a century or so; there was no real remaining opposition.

*Admiral Duncan destroyed a Dutch fleet at Camperdown…*Photograph by author.

Chapter 9

The Slavers

It was in sweet Senegal, That my foes did me enthral,
For the lands of Virginia-ginia, O!
Torn from that lovely shore And must never see it more,
And alas! I am weary, weary, O!'
Robert Burns

When the Portuguese reached Cape Blanco in their slow unfolding of coastal Africa's mysteries, they encountered slave merchants and quickly established a slave station on Arguin Island. Trading first with local dealers, then with the caravans that trekked from the north, the Portuguese initially exported African slaves to the sugar industry of Madeira, but soon added Sao Tome in the Gulf of Guinea to their islands of slave labour. In 1531 the Spanish initiated the carriage of Africans to the Americas by transporting a shipload of slaves from Sao Tome to Santo Domingo, and by 1550 Sao Tome became a staging post for slaves on their sorrowful journey to the New World. By the end of the century Portuguese Brazil was the world's largest importer of slaves.

The Atlantic islands proved a prototype for the later large-scale export of Africans to the Spanish Americas. Already by 1600 an estimated 125,000 Africans had suffered the appalling middle passage, always unwillingly, often in chains. If the statistics are nauseous, consider the sheer human misery; each one of these thousands was a thinking, feeling human being, man, woman or child. When even one example of cruelty is unjustifiable, the thought of millions of such individual tragedies should be enough to ensure that such practices, where they exist today, should be utterly eradicated.

In 1562, when the English first became involved, the Atlantic slave trade was hardly viewed as immoral. It is an interesting indictment of national morality that John Hawkins, England's first dealer in African slaves, should still be viewed as something of a hero, but also a reminder that something acceptable in one age is reprehensible in another. In October 1562 Hawkins sailed from England with three vessels, *Solomon* of 120 tons, *Swallow* of 30 tons and *Jonas* of 40 tons, together holding around 100 seamen. Helped by a Spanish pilot, Hawkins collected 300 people from West Africa, some by trade and others by blatant kidnapping, crossed the Atlantic to Hispaniola and exchanged them for precious metal, pearls, sugar and ginger. The trip was not entirely trouble-free, for the Spanish authorities in Cadiz snatched a ship Hawkins had chartered in Hispaniola, but overall the expedition was profitable.

It is encouraging to learn that Queen Elizabeth of England stated slaving was detestable, but her belief failed to prevent her buying shares in Hawkins' second voyage. The parsimonious queen always had an eye for profit, but much of human greed appears to correlate with human degradation, so the mental and spiritual health of the slavers was enslaved by the attraction of wealth. Possibly it is easier to negate the suffering of others if they are unseen or of a different culture. When the Spaniard Bartoleme de Alborney spoke against the trade in 1573 his was a single voice in an ocean of assent; the institution of slavery was to pervade Atlantic society for centuries.

Hawkins took four vessels out of Plymouth in October 1564 and this time he made no pretence at legitimate trade. Starting at Sambula Island off present-day Sierra Leone, Hawkins raided unsuspecting villages for slaves and if he lost a few men when the inhabitants of Bymba fought back, he probably thought the profit was worth the pain. Seamen were easier to obtain than slaves and the 400 Africans Hawkins collected should have made him a fine profit. For four weeks his ships were becalmed in the Atlantic and when they reached Venezuela it was to learn that foreign vessels were forbidden to trade with Spanish America. However, by the same combination of force and stealth with which he had obtained them, Hawkins sold off his captives and returned to England. He had set a precedent and made a profit, and now the English could compete with Spaniards and Portuguese for the trade in transporting unwilling Africans to America.

European slavers created a bizarre coalition of cruelty and piety as they plundered Africa of her people. On one voyage Hawkins forced his crew to a religious ceremony, before combining with some African chiefs to drive some 7000 people into the sea at low tide. Picking 500 for slaves, Hawkins left the others to drown in the rising tide. Although the Europeans were the instigators, they could have achieved nothing without the co-operation of equally callous men from Africa.

No sooner had the English entered the trade than they were elbowed aside by the Dutch. By the end of the 16th century the Dutch were the rising maritime nation of northern Europe, replacing and frequently displacing the German Hanseatic League. Their progress continued as they became the main sea carriers of north Europe, with innovative ideas in ship design, from the herring buss to the grain boier. In 1606 they entered the Atlantic slave trade and within a couple of decades the newly-formed Dutch West India Company had torn much of the Atlantic trade from the Iberian nations and was heavily engaged in slaving.

The Dutch West India Company permitted each patroon – a farming member of that company – twelve 'black men and women out of the Prizes in which Negroes should be found'. Although the Dutch dominated the trade they did have colonial competition. Built in Marblehead in the late 1630s, *Desire* was only the first of many New England slavers, and in 1640 she 'brought some cotton and tobaccos and negroes etc.' from the West Indies. The callous reference to human beings as just another commodity is typical of the period. Already the infamous triangular trade had begun, with ships from the North American colonies exchanging rum for West African people who were carried to the West Indies, traded for molasses that was made into rum in New England. As time passed and the plantation system spread, the southern colonies of the eastern seaboard became prime destinations for the slave ships. At any one time up to 100 could be crossing the middle passage, creating fierce competition among the slavers, or rum-men as they disarmingly called themselves.

In 1660 the Duke of York gave a charter to the splendidly titled Company of Royal Adventurers of England, but it is unlikely that the slaves appreciated the ducal connections of the letters DY that were branded into their shoulder. Their initial remit was to supply the English North American colonies with 300 slaves, but despite the guinea coin that King Charles issued to help finance them, the Royal Adventurers failed. In 1672 the Royal African Company took their place and proved far more successful at ousting the Dutch from the Atlantic slave trade.

By the 1680s the English were prominent slave traders by which time perhaps 2 million Africans had already been torn from their homes and carried to lifelong slavery in the Americas. There was a single shaft of humanity as Massachusetts outlawed slavery, but there were too many alternative markets to concern the scores of traders that infested the West African coast. Each trader filled their barracoons (a barracks where slaves were held temporarily) with people, who were later herded into the airless interior of the ships that rocked on the unfamiliar sea. Shackled in long rows, the terrified and beaten Africans lay in the stink and gloom of the slaver amongst heartless men from an alien culture. It was a nightmare worse than any horror story could conceive and the wonder is that any retained their sanity, yet alone attempted to maintain some of their culture. The fact that some did both is testimony to their tremendous resilience.

When the ships were filled with captives they headed west in a voyage that could take two weeks or two months, and by the time they crossed the Atlantic an average of 6.5% of slaves had died, and 11% of seamen. The disparity in percentages is not surprising as slaves were reckoned to be more valuable than seamen, with the captain obtaining around 4% of the selling value of each slave. So why did men work in such a disgusting and dangerous job, with disease guaranteed and slave mutinies always a possibility? Money: a slaveship seaman could earn six guineas a month which was around twice the pay of an ordinary merchant mariner.

On the plantations the white slaves and indentured servants accepted the black slaves as equals. Perhaps the idea of racial superiority is only a variety of social superiority, the feeling that somebody must be an inferior because of their lack of social standing, not because of the colour of their skin. In those early days black and white slaves had sexual relations, genuine friendship and frequently combined in conspiracies against their masters.

After the Treaty of Utrecht in 1713 Great Britain controlled the Guinea coast of West Africa from the Congo to Gambia. By grabbing the *Asiento*, the contract for slaves to the Spanish colonies, Britain became the chief European slaving power. First Bristol, then Liverpool became the major slaving port, with their ships carrying their sorrowful cargo for sale at £30 a head in Jamaica or Barbados, while vessels from the North American colonies controlled their own trade. With about 70,000 people annually transported across the Atlantic, African middlemen ensured a steady supply of raw material which alleviated the need to fight along the foetid African swamps or on the beautiful, surf-battered beaches. Slavers cruised the Guinea coast trading their gunpowder, beads, kettles and rum for a 'bar' or 'ackey', the local slave currency, whereby a number of 'bars' purchased a slave.

This was a golden time for the rum men, with ships queuing at the barracoons, most sections of society approving of the trade, and when a cargo of healthy Yorubas or Mandingos could make a man wealthy. It was a time when even small ports in Atlantic France, Britain and North America had their quota of slavers and African chiefs earned prestige and power by their participation in the trade. During the 18th century British slavers carried an estimated 2½ million Africans across the Atlantic out of an estimated total of 6 million. By the end of the century more than 700,000 slaves laboured in the United States alone.

Nonetheless there were signs that public opinion was shifting against the trade. In 1783 a Quaker protest reached Parliament and in 1788, after John Newton published his *Thoughts upon the African Slave Trade*, Parliament ordered that all slave ships should carry a qualified surgeon. A small sign of the pricking of parliamentary conscience, but it was the beginning of a gradual erosion of slaving. For 19 years William Wilberforce struggled to abolish the trade. He pointed out that male slaves on the middle passage were squeezed into a space 6 feet by only 16 inches, while boys had 5 feet by 14 inches and girls only 4 feet 6 inches by 12 inches. They lay like this, spooned against each other for perhaps 20 hours a day for the entire voyage. By this time Parliament was satisfied with a death rate of 2%.

If the death rate was constantly declining, this was due to commercialism and not compassion. Slaves were becoming expensive to purchase, even in Africa. The price of slaves in Africa rose to around £25 in trade goods, from gold-laced hats to knives and looking-glasses, but with some prime slaves fetching as much as £80 in the slave markets of the Americas, there was still profit to be made. Nevertheless, pressure from Wilberforce, Newton and the Quakers influenced the House of Commons' decision to end the trade by 1796, ignoring despairing protests by the Bristol Society of Merchant Adventurers and the City of Liverpool. It looked like success, but the outbreak of the French Revolution distracted Parliament from abolition and the sinister ships continued to slip across the sea.

Despite the war, the abolitionists continued their Christian struggle. In 1802 Denmark was first to abolish the trade, and five years later the British Abolition Act declared the slave trade illegal. On 27th July 1807 the last official British slaver, *Kitty's*

Amelia, sailed from the Mersey and from that year a slaver could not legally fly the Union flag. The following year the United States made the slave trade illegal and in 1811 the Royal Navy, already overstretched in blockading Napoleon's European empire and guarding British trade routes, released five ships for anti-slavery duties. The greatest trading nation was making the first tentative steps towards becoming the greatest anti-slavery nation. Britannia's tarnished trident began to regain some of its lustre.

The Netherlands joined the abolitionists in 1814 and although Spain followed in 1817, Spanish slaving south of the equator remained legal until 1820. Yet despite all the good intentions of the abolitionists and the hard work of the anti-slavery squadrons, there was a massive gap between what appeared possible in Parliament and what was physically possible at sea. Although the number of countries banning slave trading rose, with the significant addition of Brazil in 1826, slave ships continued to cross the Atlantic. In 1833 Britain abolished all slavery within the empire, but as the United States spurned any prospect of an anti-slavery treaty and Royal Navy vessels were prohibited from searching American shipping, the Stars and Stripes proved an invaluable refuge for illegal slaving. Not until the arrival of United States warships off West Africa in 1840 were these slavers liable to capture, and when United States and Royal Naval ships worked in conjunction from 1842 there was major progress. Until then the Royal Navy struggled against repulsive people and shocking odds. 'Here we are in the most miserable station in the world', said one anti-slavery seaman, 'attempting the impossible'. And with a ponderous Royal Navy brig it frequently was impossible to catch a fleet Baltimore clipper or New York sloop, yet alone schooners such as *Wanderer*, owned by a syndicate from Georgia. *Wanderer* wore the New York Yacht Club pennant and once entertained officers of the Royal Navy on board, then sailed across the Atlantic with a cargo of 750 slaves. Such specialised vessels could sail circles around the Navy's all-purpose, all-weather floating gun platforms. Although by 1842 there were five steam ships in the squadron, sailing craft provided the backbone. The humid wooden ships were quickly infested with vermin in the tropical climate and crewed by men who were sick and sticky, hot-tempered and frustrated. The anti-slavery patrols were perhaps the Last Hurragh of the old Navy before technological progress removed forever the free power of wind and muscle and the superb skills of the old-time mariner.

By 1816 the French wars were finished, Bonaparte was safely ensconced in St Helena and the differences between Britain and the United States had been smoothed over. That year Captain Sir James Yeo was 'required and directed' to take HMS *Inconstant* to West Africa to search for slaving vessels. The Royal Navy had to patrol in excess of 2000 miles of coast, find and capture the slavers and bring their captain to a suitable port for trial. To complicate matters, the coast was riddled by mangrove swamp, penetrated by veiled creeks and defended by sudden shoals and savage surf. What few anchorages that did exist were unhealthy and often unfriendly. There were tortuous inlets in the north, sandy beaches between Cape Mesurado and Lagos, and the delta of the Niger. Here amidst the half-explored maze of creeks, islands and swamps were small kingdoms ruled by terrible people whose main income came from slavery. As if to compensate, the coastline is smooth after the Niger, but the climate remains as oppressive as the contrary wind. When breezes did break the long periods of calm, they came from the south or south-west to press the squadron against the African coast. Augmenting these difficulties was the ship's continual struggle to patrol against the eastward-flowing current. Even the landscape was frustrating with only Cape Mount or Cape Three Points breaking the dull green monotony.

Although in the 40 years after 1808 the West African anti-slavery patrols freed perhaps 14% of the slaves being transported, and cut down the Brazilian trade from 60,000 slaves a year in 1848 to 800 four years later, this was anything but a popular posting. West Africa offered nothing but disease, hardship and frustration, only occasionally sweetened by a success that freed a cargo of human beings from a living nightmare. As battleships were too slow to catch the slavers and too cumbersome to probe the creeks, the largest vessel on the West Africa station was usually a 40-gun frigate, supported by a couple of 28-gun frigates and a number of sloops and brigs.

Many actions involved even smaller craft, as in March 1821 when Midshipman Lyons navigated a local canoe manned by Kroo men and 30 seamen in the boats of

'…the largest vessel on the West Africa station was usually a 40-gun frigate…' HMS Unicorn, *a 46-gun frigate launched in 1824.* Photograph by the author.

HMS *Thistle* into a creek off the Bonny River in the Niger Delta. The objective was a Spanish slaving schooner, *Anna Maria*. It is easy to imagine the suppressed excitement, the creak of muffled oars, the mosquitoes and feeling of claustrophobia as the jungle closed around the ship's boats. Lyons led the attack and there was an exchange of pistol fire followed by a panicky rush off the schooner. Local tribesmen fled upstream in their canoes, hoping to alert any other slavers, while some female slaves on *Anna Maria* jumped overboard and were eaten by circling sharks. Altogether the Navy managed to carry 450 freed slaves to Freetown.

In April of that same year Lieutenant Mildmay led the boats of HMS *Iphigenia* and HMS *Myrmidon* up the Bonny River to clear up a group of seven Spanish and French slavers. With Union flags defiant against the musketry and grapeshot that churned the water around them, the boats sailed directly toward the slavers. For 20 minutes they endured the slavers' fire, but then the bluejackets unsheathed their cutlasses and boarded. Two men were killed and seven wounded but Mildmay captured five vessels and freed nearly 1500 slaves, despite the attempts of one slaver to blow up his ship together with its human cargo.

For the first few years the Navy had to catch the slave ships actually carrying slaves. Out of the 16 ships HMS *Myrmidon* searched in two months in 1822, she could arrest only one, and HMS *Pheasant* had to release all six Portuguese slavers she stopped at Badagry and Whydah. Not until 1824 did an equipment clause declare that even ships without slaves could be arrested if they contained any items, such as shackles, that appeared to be slaving accessories. The slavers retaliated with many subterfuges, from wearing false flags to carrying false papers, and the middle passage remained just as terrible for the slaves. With the Royal Navy on the hunt, slave prices rose even higher and slavers took extra care of their charges, but even so the bodies of slaves that died on the voyage were tossed carelessly overboard. If they were in danger of being caught by the Navy, slavers could dispose of live slaves the same way.

The small scale, inch by inch blockade and patrol work continued year by excruciating year. In 1852, with the trade in decline but still continuing, HMS *Sealark* probed around the Rio Grande in Portuguese Guinea, hoping to locate a suspected Spanish slaver. Both the resident chief and a Spanish groundnut dealer named Tadeo Vidul claimed ignorance, but Commander Sotheby of *Sealark* continued to search the local creeks. Only when he put forward a substantial reward did a local man volunteer to guide him to a hidden ship. *Sealark*'s boat pushed up a concealed creek, passing beneath overhanging branches that released their quota of irritating insects on the bluejackets below, but the result made the effort worthwhile. With her masts removed for camouflage, the slaver cowered behind a screen of mangroves, equipped for slaving and ready for the bluejackets to burn.

Their African guide showed Sotheby where the 'innocent' chief had stored shackles and muskets, and an ultimatum led to the release of 20 slaves. Vidul the groundnut dealer was the supercargo for the slaver, while the chief was notorious for selling his fellow Africans as slaves. While Sotheby carried the freed slaves to Freetown in Sierra

Leone, a city founded by the British specifically for released slaves, Vidul was sent for trial. There was nothing spectacular about this work that slowly ground out the West African slave trade.

When John Quincy Adams, United States Ambassador to Britain, was asked if he knew of a worse evil than the slave trade, he replied that it would be worse if any ship wearing the Stars and Stripes could be stopped by a British ship. He professed to believe that such an action would make slaves of the entire United States population. This mistrust was enhanced in 1841 when Africans on the slaver *Creole* mutinied and brought the vessel into British-owned Nassau, free soil. When the United States demanded the return of their property, the British authorities refused and the Africans remained free.

By 1853 the Brazilian slave market closed but with the United States still proclaiming their right not to be searched, fast American ships thumbed their noses at the toiling Royal Navy patrols. If the bruised pride of the bluejackets was irrelevant compared to the sufferings of the African cargo, there were mixed feelings in the United States about the British part in suppressing the trade. Although some United States citizens believed that abolition was a British ploy to quash American trade competition in West Africa, the United States' naval officers who participated in the suppression were as dedicated as the British. They could not be blamed for the political wrangling, and at a time when the United States was tearing itself apart over the question of slave and free states, perhaps there was some justification for their governmental caution. It is unlikely that the slaves would have agreed. Victory for the north in the United States Civil War ended most American participation in the slave trade and the Thirteenth Amendment freed the slaves, but it was not until the late 1860s that the closure of the Cuban slave market virtually killed the Atlantic slave trade.

Between the 16th and the late 19th century somewhere between 15 and 20 million people crossed the Atlantic as shackled slaves. Only in the latter decades of the 20th century did their descendants overturn centuries of oppression and degradation to finally become accepted as equals in their New World. Perhaps the ghosts of some of these manacled travellers will look fondly on their descendants who adapted to a new continent, a new culture and created a new sense of pride.

Chapter 10

The Privateers

'A covert and indirect form of war.'
Sebastien Vauban

Darkness was approaching that winter's day and Captain Jonathan Haraden of the Salem vessel *General Pickering* had already fought off one British attack. Now the London privateer *Golden Eagle* was hovering nearby hoping to capture her cargo of sugar. The swells of the Bay of Biscay rose around them as Haraden checked his ship. At 180 tons she was not large, but with a crew of 45 and 14 six-pound cannon she could deliver a powerful punch. It was 1780, the War of Independence was at its height and Haraden was never inclined to give in to a British ship. As the light faded, he brought *General Pickering* close to *Golden Eagle* and hailed the British privateer. 'Strike sir!' he may have shouted 'Or I'll sink you with a broadside!' When *Golden Eagle* refused, Haraden announced that he was a Continental frigate, and the British ship hauled down her colours. Within minutes a prize crew was clambering aboard and an American privateer had captured yet another British ship.

Jonathan Haraden was one of the most successful of many privateers that sailed from the port of Salem. A mariner from boyhood and a master mariner even before the War of Independence, his capture of *Golden Eagle* marked only the halfway stage in this particular action, for HMS *Achille*, a 40-gun London privateer sailed to challenge him. After recapturing *Golden Eagle*, *Achille* looked set to overpower the smaller Salem vessel. There was no rest for Haraden that night as he dressed in his smartest clothes and readied *General Pickering* for the impending battle. He inspected his cannon, ensured that the matches were burning and the crew knew their stations.

When the Biscayan dawn revealed both ships waiting for battle it seemed that half of Bilbao had assembled to watch, with Spanish fishing boats bobbing on the sea and interested spectators lining the shore. *Achille* approached steadily, hoping to use her superior manpower to board and capture the United States vessel, for a quick capture with little damage would bring more profit than a vessel battered by cannon fire. Haraden, however, was not inclined to be a victim. Knowing he had the more manoeuvrable vessel, he crossed the stern of *Achille,* raked her with his seven-cannon broadside, then recrossed and fired again. Fourteen iron cannonballs had travelled the entire length of the British ship – killing, maiming and destroying – and while *Achille* ran to lick her wounds Haraden calmly entered Bilbao to sell his cargo of sugar. Haraden was an experienced privateer commander who, in another encounter, captured all six vessels of a Halifax to New York convoy, but he was not unique. Nations with weak navies had long called upon private seamen to fight for them and even Great Britain, self-proclaimed mistress of the seas, utilised privateers in time of war.

If pirates were as old as seafaring, then privateering began when governments started to take an interest in sea warfare. From the 13th century ships' masters were licensed to attack any enemy of their king, so there was seldom peace at sea where anything floating was fair game. In May 1449 Robert Winnington and his Devon privateers encountered the hanseatic salt fleet, a mixed convoy of Flemish, Dutch and Hanseatic vessels that had been peacefully sailing on its own business. Winnington had no quarrel with the Hanse, and had indeed been hunting for Breton ships, but the Hanse ships had entered waters Winnington regarded as English. Boarding the leading vessel, he requested that they surrender in the king's name. The reply was perhaps understandable as Winnington claimed, with some indignation, that 'they bade me shit in the king's name of England'. If there had been no animosity before, that answer provided reason enough and Winnington snapped up the entire fleet. Life was hard at sea.

A century later privateering was a little more organised with the introduction of a system whereby private mariners were required to purchase a licence – a letter of marque – from a government official before they could go privateering. Normally directed against a national enemy, a letter of marque was occasionally issued to an individual with a personal grudge, as when the Barton family of Leith was licensed to attack Portuguese shipping in reprisal for previous Portuguese piracy.

But this system could lead to major repercussions; there was no war in 1545 when Robert Reneger of Southampton seized a Spanish treasure ship off Saint Vincent, and the Spanish retaliated by capturing a clutch of English ships. Reneger did not mind; he had netted nearly 30,000 ducats and had set an example to generations of loot-hungry privateers. Reneger's raid reveals just how intimate was the relationship between privateering and piracy.

By the close of the 17th century privateering seemed as regulated as any other form of warfare. By law, captured vessels were to be carried intact to a government-approved court, thus ensuring that the monarch gained his tithe, and the Admiralty their fifteenth, of the plunder. The ship owner gained half the loot and what remained was divided among the men who had actually done the dangerous work of capturing the vessel. While each seaman was entitled to a single share, the junior officers gained half as much again and senior officers twice that. The captain was allotted five shares while the ship's boys, the most abused people aboard, were allowed half a share. If the voyage failed to make a capture, well, the seamen had signed articles saying 'no purchase, no pay' so everybody came back empty-handed. It was little wonder that many privateers chose to disregard the rules once their topmasts dipped beyond the horizon.

These same articles detailed compensation for wounds, so that the loss of a right arm entitled the sufferer to 600 pieces of eight, a left arm 500, a right leg 500 and an eye or finger only 100. If the privateers-man died in battle, his widow or heirs were awarded 1000 pieces of eight. Possibly this fairly generous arrangement helped persuade many men to go privateering rather than join the Navy.

The incessant warfare of the 17th and 18th centuries was a boom time for privateers, particularly as a belligerent nation could issue a letter of marque to any ship owner who fancied a spot of licensed plunder. In a period when naval costs were soaring, private enterprise plugged the gaps in national defence with surprising ease. It must be remembered that there was no uniform for seamen, merchant ships appeared similar to warships and any merchant seaman could be scampering up the rigging one minute and standing behind the breech of a cannon the next. With technology in its infancy, cannon were relatively easy to operate and any untrained landsman could wield a boarding pike or a cutlass.

Towards the end of the War of the League of Augsberg it was obvious that France's naval forces were failing against the hostile alliance that encircled her. As an alternative, Sebastien Vauban, soldier, inventor of the socket bayonet and royal advisor, suggested that France should abandon traditional naval strategy and concentrate on privateering. Vauban pointed out that 'France possesses advantages for the waging of privateer warfare ...' with Marseilles and Toulon dominating the entrance to the Mediterranean and Dunkirk 'admirably suited' to raid the trade of the northern nations, plus shipping from either the East or West Indies. He believed that Brest was 'situated as though God had created it with the special purpose of being the destroyer of these country's trade'. According to Vauban, privateering was 'simple, cheap and safe'; a virtual panacea to cure all France's ills. Of all European countries it was perhaps France who most perfected the skills of privateering, but the lessons they taught were well learned by the seamen of the United States in their later wars with Britain.

One of the St Malo privateers was René Dugay-Trouin, whose 14-gun vessel ravaged allied shipping and left masters and merchants cursing from Ramsgate to Rotterdam. In 1691 his luck changed and he was captured and imprisoned in Plymouth, from where he could hear the seagulls cry their freedom above the Channel tides. With plausibility part of a privateer's armoury, Dugay-Trouin charmed a local girl to help him escape from his prison and back to his nautical home. Promoted to the command of a 48-gun privateer, Dugay-Trouin proved so successful that he was commissioned into the French navy, in which position he captured the bulk of an English convoy at the western approach to the Channel. Success followed success, with the one-time privateer commander capturing Rio de Janeiro and ending as a vice admiral.

Others found it easier to cross the ill-defined boundary between privateer and pirate. In 1703 John Quelch was a New England crewman on board the colonial privateer *Charles*, but he found the restrictions of an official hunter too confining. Instigating a mutiny, Quelch quite callously dropped the captain into the Atlantic before hauling down the Union flag. In its place he raised 'Old Roger', a flag with the motif of a skeleton holding an hourglass in one hand and a bloody spear in the other. A blatant and unashamed pirate, Quelch ran riot amongst the merchant shipping along the eastern seaboard of North America before entering Marblehead. Only when some of the crew bragged of their exploits did the authorities react, and Quelch ended his career hanging from a New England gallows. The local merchants continued to trade with less talkative pirates.

During the War of Jenkins Ear, George Walker made his name as one of the wiliest of privateers. By outfitting abroad, he kept his crew safe from the press-gangs that infested British ports, and while approaching an intended victim used dummy crewmen and false cannon to appear more powerful than he was. In a single cruise Walker captured over £20,000 of enemy shipping but, like many seamen, he was naïve on land – when his prize agent robbed him, Walker was thrown in a debtor's prison.

Captain Michael Driver of Salem, Massachusetts must have regretted that privateers had ever been invented. Early in 1759 Driver was commanding the schooner *Three Brothers,* trading from Salem to the West Indies with cargoes of fish and timber when a privateer approached him. Perhaps the Union flag fluttering from the forepeak deceived Driver into a sense of security, for he seems to have been surprised, captured and taken into Antigua as a prize. Later that same war Driver was commanding the schooner *Betsy* when a French privateer captured him and, as was quite common, released him to obtain a ransom. Sailing back to Boston, Driver was again captured, this time by *Revenge*, a British privateer. When an Admiralty court in the Bahamas ruled that he should be released, Driver might have thought his troubles were easing, but another Frenchman scooped him up on his homeward voyage. Only after months as a penniless castaway did Driver manage to return to Massachusetts.

Not surprisingly, privateers were interested in profit rather than patriotism, so they avoided the mid-Atlantic where ships were hard to locate, storms customary and horizons empty, and frequented those areas most used by enemy shipping. In all the wars of the 18th century privateers infested the approaches to the English Channel, the Irish Sea and the Florida Channel. Although only the most daring would approach an escorted convoy, preferring lone merchantmen, many lurked behind the convoys, hoping for stragglers or a storm that would scatter the ships.

As the 18th century progressed Britain became increasingly dependent on North America for her shipping. By 1730 around 16% of British shipping was built in North America, a figure that increased to around 30% by 1760. Not only complete ships, but masts and other stores were supplied by the colonies, and this contributed to the increasing volume of trade that crossed the Atlantic. Britannia's trident had a shaft of American pine and prongs that were securely controlled by the anchor cables of New

England. By the 1760s perhaps half of all British shipping operated on the Atlantic routes, sailing to and from any of the British colonies that stretched from Newfoundland to Florida and across the islands of the Caribbean. No single nation had been so dominant in the area since the years of Spanish hegemony. However, when 13 of these colonies declared their independence in 1776 the Atlantic became a battleground with a horde of vigorous United States' privateers loose among the shipping of the largest trading nation in the world.

Throughout this war Britain relied mainly on the Royal Navy while the brand new republic depended far more on privately-funded and privately-manned vessels. It is perhaps significant that the deciding naval battle in the Chesapeake was only possible because of French naval power, while American privateers disrupted British trade. In 1776 the Royal Navy had around 100 vessels in North American waters, but the seas were wide, British merchantmen were plentiful, there was a long coastline and a maritime-minded population to watch.

For generations the men of the north-eastern seaboard had looked to the sea rather than the land. The small coastal ports of Salem and Boston, New York and Baltimore with their narrow, often terraced streets, their gable-ended houses and scents of the sea were crammed with men longing for a crack at the British who had taxed them and whose Admiralty courts had curbed their smuggling. If the United States' privateers experienced no difficulty in obtaining a crew, their very success inhibited recruitment for the Continental Navy since there was less possibility of prize money. Eventually, and with supreme irony, the frustrated Continental Navy turned to methods very similar to the British press-gang.

Virtually any vessel could be a privateer, from frail cutters that hardly seemed worthy to leave the Hudson, to fine ships that could fight yardarm to yardarm with any undermanned British frigate. They were needed; in 1776 Congress could barely muster 31 warships. They sailed with high hopes and high courage, flaunting the Stars and Stripes of the republic in defiance of the massed broadsides of the British warships that pressed a blockade on the coast. If by 1782 only seven ships of the Continental Navy remained at sea, they were replaced twentyfold by predatory privateers and Britain, so often the hunter, found her ships hunted in their own element. Within two years of the outbreak of rebellion, United States vessels claimed that 700 British ships had been taken.

The privateers could snap up the supply ships for the British army in North America, or cross the Atlantic to scour the approaches to British ports. The Irish Sea was so infested that the numbers of unemployed in Liverpool multiplied and British merchants sent their goods in French shipping – until France joined the war. In September 1779 the privateer *Black Prince* hovered off Fishguard in Wales, captured a local ship and demanded a ransom of £500 for her return. As an afterthought *Black Prince* also asked for another £500 or she would bombard the town. When Fishguard called up the local Dewsland Volunteers, *Black Prince* opened fire, damaging some houses and wounding one woman, Mary Fenton. Only when a local smuggler returned fire did *Black Prince* withdraw; although she had acted against Britain, she had both Englishmen and Irishmen in her crew who were profiteering from the war.

The British returned to the convoy system, with the Admiralty deciding on a rendezvous where ships heading for a specific destination would gather. Once the convoy was assembled, the senior naval captain advised the merchant masters of the order of sailing and the signalling codes. With many independent-minded merchant masters paying scant heed to naval signals, and the Navy's resources strained by the expanding war, convoys were no guarantee against privateer attacks. One West India-bound convoy lost 35 vessels out of 60 and any ill-armed or undermanned merchantman could be cut out by a fast Yankee raider before the Royal Naval sloop or brig could intercept. In this period most British merchant seamen were barely educated and even the officers knew only the three Ls – lead, log and latitude. Physically they were unbelievably tough, but often cruel and so many were addicted to the bottle that Captain Frederick Marryat believed that more than half the shipwrecks and accidents at sea were the result of drink. An illiterate, drunken captain was no match for the superb seamen from New England.

Although 13 of the North American colonies declared themselves independent, other colonies remained loyal. One of these was Nova Scotia, the old Acadia of the French. A governor of Massachusetts had founded Halifax to provide protection for New England but now the town was destined to be a base for both the Royal Navy and loyalist privateers. Loyalty, however, could also mean danger, for it invited retaliation from the United States' privateers just a short sail to the south. The raiders' stock tactic was to threaten the destruction of some unprotected village unless a ransom of some thousands of dollars was paid. Naturally this aggression turned many previously neutral Nova Scotians into ardent patriots who supported the vengeful local privateers. This war between neighbours was often bitterly fought at sea.

With a letter of marque costing around £1500 in Britain, the Glasgow tobacco lords who fitted out 14 privateers hoped to recoup their losses from United States' merchantmen. Not all were successful, but only privateering saved hard-pressed Liverpool from financial collapse. As early as 1775 unpaid seamen rioted in the city, gaining control of the centre for three days before they were quelled. Despite the glamorous image, however, most privateers were lucky to make two or three captures a year, and few ships were crammed with gold and spices. Timber or hides, wheat or coal were the more prosaic reality. The crews too were unlikely to be stout patriots – privateers had a reputation for drunkenness and riotous behaviour.

Both sides suffered in this War of Independence; by 1783 the United States had lost an estimated 1000 ships, including nearly the entire New England fishing fleet. Thousands of New England seamen had migrated north to Nova Scotia, augmenting the already firm nautical base of that province. Although British losses had been less than in the War of the League of Augsberg, they had still lost over 3000 merchant ships, although nearly 500 had been recaptured and a similar number ransomed. In all, over a third of the British merchant fleet had been lost.

Barely a decade later Britain was fighting for her freedom against the military might of France. Again the privateers were called out, with the usual mixture of triumph and sorrow. Perhaps typical was the Leith privateer *Roselle*, who battled it out with Frenchmen and Spaniards and once caused panic in Peterhead by firing a cannon to announce her arrival. Fortune may favour the bold, but foolhardiness is never recommended at sea and *Roselle*'s career ended when she sailed too close to the broadside of a Spanish battleship.

When French and Spanish warships decimated the Greenock sugar trade, the town retaliated by sending out privateers. In 1807 Captain Frazer Smith of *Neptune* captured a prize of real value in *Charles Maurice*, homeward-bound from Mauritius and although *Neptune*'s owners pocketed the bulk of the £25,000 prize money, Smith and the crew would collect a handsome amount for themselves. However *Neptune* shared *Roselle*'s not-uncommon privateer fault of impudence and lost her fight with a brace of Spanish warships. Continuing her seafaring legacy, Bristol sent out more than 60 privateers that were fit to fight the French.

By 1812 the French wars had continued intermittently for nearly 20 years, and further trouble arose with the United States. Given the expansive nature of the republic, and the commitment of Britain struggling for her life against most of Europe, it is not altogether surprising that one faction in the United States wanted war with Britain. Partly there was a desire to add Canada to the republic, partly an objection against the impressment of American seamen and partly a protest against the searching of United States' ships for British deserters. However, the most maritime states of the Union were also the most opposed to any British war.

Impressment was a terrible procedure, kidnapping a merchant seaman and forcing him to join the Navy, subject to danger and harsh discipline. By 1812 as many as 60% of any crew could be pressed, so it is hardly surprising that many thousands deserted. However, the Royal Navy practice of stopping and searching American ships for runaway seamen created discord, particularly when they pressed American seamen. The situation was complicated by the proliferation of false certificates that stated the carrier to be a citizen of the United States. When one alleged deserter from the Royal Navy became captain of the American privateer *Young Teazer*, he was chased into Mahone Bay in Nova Scotia. Rather than be captured and hanged by the Royal Navy, this man threw a blazing torch into his own powder magazine.

Baltimore was the chief privateering port in this new war, and Captain Thomas Boyle commanded one of her 60 privateers. Fully as reckless as his British counterparts, Boyle announced a blockade of the entire British coastline with the 16 twelve-pound cannon and the 100 men of his single schooner *Chasseur*. Perhaps Boyle was a little over ambitious, but *Chasseur*'s capture of 18 ships in her initial cruise was surely successful. Other vessels were equally triumphant, with *Governor Tompkins* disposing of 14 British ships in the English Channel and *Harpy*, also of Baltimore, bringing home half a million dollars worth of ex-British goods.

Again the United States' privateers concentrated on British trade in the Irish Sea, the Channel and the North Sea. In these waters the majority of shipping was British and much was coastal, consisting of small craft with a crew of three or four, far too weak to resist the powerful privateers, some of which carried 30 guns and hundreds of men. It was a privateers' heaven, particularly as it was nearly impossible to arrange convoys for such small craft, and any naval patrols consisted of the small brigs of war, ill-armed, badly-designed and often undermanned by pressed, untrained and reluctant crews. There was no doubting the bravery of the Royal Navy, but they were attempting to dam a river of privateering with a very leaky sieve. Insurance rates rose higher in the war of 1812 than they had ever been during the French wars.

In a curious example of the nuisance value of the privateers, there was the incident of the United States' privateer *Leo*, which captured the British *Alexander* on passage from Livorno in Italy. There was nothing extraordinary about just one more privateering success, except that *Alexander* carried a marble memorial ordered by the Prussian government to commemorate their late Queen Louise. At that time the Congress of Vienna was in session, with half the statesmen of Europe attempting to settle a lasting peace for the continent, and this event diverted the Duke of Wellington from his statesmanship to issue an apology to the Prussians. Incidents such as this encouraged Britain to increase her blockade of the United States.

Once the French wars ended, the Royal Navy was at last free to cross the Atlantic in force and, when they did, the door was slammed shut on both privateering and American coastal trade. The northern section of Maine was occupied, Washington was burned and the New England states contemplated a separate peace with Britain. However, when United States' privateers refitted in neutral French ports, this brought bitter protests from the British government and with a Russian war not beyond the bounds of possibility, conflict with the republic was an irritation Britain could have done without.

United States' privateers claimed 1300 British prizes in the war, but British and Nova Scotian privateers were also out hunting. Liverpool was a Nova Scotian port with a privateering heritage and her famous privateer, *Liverpool Packet*, is alleged to have captured 100 New England vessels within the first year of the war. Another Nova Scotian privateer carried a cannon in her bows and, according to legend, its vivid blue colour gave the seamen of that province their epithet of 'blue noses'.

When the 1812 war ended with Canada firmly British and trade on both sides badly disrupted, privateering by developed countries was virtually finished. Nonetheless, it was not until the Paris Peace Conference of 1856 that its demise was made official. Most of the major maritime powers signed the document to ban privateering, and if the United States did not, perhaps the republic regretted its decision as Confederate raiders ravaged her shipping during the 1861–65 war. Yet it appears that the technology of modern warfare had marked the end of the privateer; the gulf between the modern warship and merchant ship is perhaps too large to bridge. But nothing is certain at sea; in 1999 a convoy of three armed ships left the port of Barrow-in-Furness, England. Rather than privateers, they were merchant ships carrying nuclear fuel and they were armed against possible terrorist or criminal attack. If some outlawed nation had decided to capture such a convoy, what better cover would there be than a seemingly-innocent merchant vessel? Privateers may be hovering just over history's horizon, waiting to return.

Chapter 11

The Emigrants

Ten families scraped a contented living along the glen of Lorgill until that summer day in 1830 when four policemen and the minister escorted in the sheriff officer. When the people gathered around, women nursing their babies, men fresh from toil and children chattering cheerfully, the sheriff officer ordered that they were to leave the glen at noon on 4th August 'with all your baggage but no stock'. The people were to travel to Loch Snizort, where Captain Morrison's *Midlothian* would carry them to a new life in Nova Scotia. Anybody refusing to leave would be 'immediately arrested and taken to prison' and everybody over 70 who lacked younger relatives to look after them would be placed in the poorhouse. As the people listened to their world collapse, the sheriff officer gave them a final warning. 'This order is final and no appeal to the government will be considered'. The presence of the minister ensured that neither could there be an appeal to the Lord. On their last day in Scotland, home of their blood, spirit and ancestors, the people gathered together, sang Psalm 100 and trekked to their destiny.

Decade after decade, similar scenes were enacted until the emigrant ship became an all-too-familiar sight throughout the Highlands and Hebrides. Crowds wept through their cheers as the sad ships departed and the pibroch, *Cha till mi tuille*, 'We shall return no more!' wailed forlornly to a nation whose soul was seeping away. But not only Scotland suffered from emigration. These sad, bitterly-hopeful vessels left from most ports of Europe as the Old World exported its unwanted and shipping lines founded their fortunes on the transatlantic trade in people.

To travel on an early emigrant ship was something worse than horrific. The Atlantic

New York harbour at the height of the emigrant boom.

crossing – and far more vessels sailed to North America than elsewhere – was a terrible ordeal as men, women and terrified children were jammed into the badly-ventilated, stinking, sodden holds and 'tweendeck. In fair weather the hatches were left open; in bad seas the hatches were battened down and it would be hell at sea in the dark, heaving foulness below. It was not unknown for women to scream for days at a time out of sheer fear, while seasickness was normal and hygiene facilities were at best primitive; emigrant ships were a bucking black hole of Calcutta. No wonder that when the hatches were opened after a day or a week of gales, the steam and stench from the packed bodies made even experienced seamen gag. Conditions on the early wooden vessels have been compared to those on a slaveship, except profit was an incentive to keep the slaves alive. In 1801 when *Sarah* sailed from Fort William to Pictou slave ship regulations would have kept the number of passengers to 489 but she carried 700 and 49 died on the voyage. Often officers and crew used brutality to control the passengers – harsh language was common and it was not unknown for a seaman to wield a rope's end at the slightest dissent.

In the 1840s, passage from Britain to North America cost around £3 10s, although compassionate shipowners frequently asked less from people fleeing the Irish potato famine. In 1848 the emigrant ship *Cradle*, sailing from Solva in Wales to New York, charged only £3, but the emigrants had to supply their own food. As the voyage could last for anything from four weeks to four months and space was restricted, hunger was virtually guaranteed. There were between 300 and 500 emigrants on board *Cradle*, crammed into the 150-foot long 'tweendeck and although an Act of 1817 had demanded headroom of at least 5½ feet in the hold, this was often disregarded. There were no bunks, only wooden shelves about 3 feet across and the spaces between were piled high with all the belongings the emigrants could carry. Most vessels did have a galley for the emigrants' use, but the poorest frequently had little to cook.

Even in the minority of emigrant vessels that carried a doctor, the onboard congestion encouraged an epidemic that could sweep away a high proportion of the passengers. Until the 1850s a 10% death rate was acceptable and 25% quite possible. Of the diseases, typhus was perhaps the most frequent, with cholera not unknown and various unrecognised fevers killing by the score. The years of the Irish famine were possibly the worst, with an average death rate of about 17% and 40 emigrant shipwrecks adding to the misery. Not until steam power combined with mid-century health and sanitary regulations did the mortality rates fall, but the emigrant crossing remained anything but pleasant. Nonetheless by the early 1860s the death rate had fallen to less than 1%.

In 1846 the Canadian authorities thought the arriving immigrants, despite onboard conditions, were 'clean and industrious, if poor' but the following year typhus ravaged the immigrants, with many deaths occurring in the quarantine station at Grosse Isle near Quebec. By 1851 the Irish flood to Canada had receded by around 20%, and perhaps it was their experience of extreme poverty in Connaught that persuaded them to seek a future in the cities rather than in agriculture. Not until the 1870s did Irish emigration again increase, and again it was the result of a potato crop failure. The statistics are frightening; in 1844 Ireland had a population of around 8 million, but by 1911 death and the emigration of over 4 million people had cut the population to only 4.4 million. These figures are a sad indictment on any government. Of the immigrants, the Catholic majority tended to choose the United States, but many Protestants were encouraged by the presence of the Orange Order to emigrate to Canada. Blood and culture obviously was as much a draw as the economic advantages of crossing the Atlantic.

Until mid-century, Britain produced many times more emigrants than the rest of Europe combined, but the Europeans were becoming aware of the possibilities that lay beyond the Atlantic. One crucial factor was the increasing use of steam power on land and sea. Prospective emigrants who hesitated to face a voyage of uncertain length aboard a sailing ship were less wary of the faster, steam-powered vessels. The replacement of sail by steam was a gradual process, with ships combining both power sources for years until sail was finally dropped. Not until 1884 did the Cunard Line's *Umbria* become the first steam passenger ship to cross the Atlantic without the insurance of auxiliary sails. These later emigrant ships carried three classes of passengers and by cramming as many emigrants as possible into steerage class, ship owners hoped that the poorest passengers would pay for the voyage, while first and second class passengers provided the profit. In the 1860s steerage emigrants paid around £5 10s for the privilege of subsidising their betters.

With European emigration gaining momentum, the United States preferred people from northern and western Europe who had a similar culture and, usually, religion to the settled population. When Scandinavian emigration began around 1840, the majority of emigrants headed straight for the United States. This was a different type of emigrant from the starving hordes of Irish or the sorrowful victims of the Highland Clearances, for they chose to cross the Atlantic to search for a more prosperous life. Land-hungry Norwegians and Swedes hoped for farms in the Canadian territories of Saskatchewan, Alberta and British Columbia, or Wisconsin in the United States. There were other reasons; after the Prussian-Danish war of 1864, many people from Schleswig decided to become United States' citizens rather than Prussian, while Baptists and Mormons emigrated for religious freedom. The companies that had constructed the railroads across the United States had been granted an incentive of millions of acres of land on the Great Plains. Now they sold that land to Europeans in emigration packages that included passage, railroad and farmland. Posters of a bronzed farmer ploughing up coins on a Great Plains farm showed an idyllic picture of life in the Great Plains as steamship companies touted for both business and emigrants right up to the First World War.

Most Scandinavian emigrants started their journey by travelling to one of the local ports, from where ships carried them to Hamburg in Germany, Copenhagen in Denmark or Hull in England. Both the Thingvalla Line in Copenhagen and the Hamburg-Amerika Line carried passengers directly to New York, but until the 20th century many emigrants crossed England from Hull to Liverpool before boarding a ship for North America. As time passed there were more single women among the emigrants, for the hard-working Danish women could earn more in a week as a New York housemaid than in four weeks at home.

The German states had always been second only to Britain in providing immigrants for the United States, and from 1820 numbers steadily increased. Even after German unification in 1871 emigration continued with the ports of Bremen and Hamburg a European mecca for tens of thousands of unsettled people from northern and eastern Europe. There was a continual and swelling drift from the Austro-Hungarian Empire, Sweden and Denmark to these German cities, a movement from east to west as Europe bid farewell to millions of her people. Further south, the Italian flood began as people of the peninsula journeyed to Naples, Genoa, or Trieste before embarking in the wake of so many Italian mariners. Mobile people from the Balkans also sailed from Trieste, while after 1900 Russians and Ukrainians left from Odessa. It was a massive population movement, from creaking Europe towards the Atlantic sunset, towards hope and opportunity and North America.

During the depressed 1880s, over 1¼ million Germans crossed the Atlantic, but towards the end of the decade emigration eased as industrialisation provided the security of reasonably paid jobs. Again the majority of emigrants were young and male but with an increasing number of single women among them, for women had a particularly bad time in Germany. Overseen by a man, they performed manual jobs in the fields and quarries, but earned perhaps half a man's wages. One appalled United States visitor commented '… it is a very serious thing to be a dog in Germany, or a cow, or a woman.' Determined to obtain fairer treatment, droves of women discarded their hoes and picks and tramped to the embarkation ports, dreaming of office occupation in the bustling American cities.

In the 1870s emigration fever spread to central Europe and people from Hungary, Austria and Bohemia left their homes to head west. The spread of a European railway network boosted emigration by easing travel to embarkation ports and by facilitating the spread of cheap North American grain that made marginal lands unprofitable to farm by bringing down prices. Once they crossed the Atlantic many central Europeans headed for the plains of Kansas and Nebraska, soon joined by hardy Croatians, Slovakians and Russians. The abolition of Russian serfdom freed thousands from bondage on the land, and these unemployed masses also swarmed west, like iron filings drawn toward the New World magnet. It seemed that all Europe was on the move, searching for something, somewhere, the mythical golden Atlantis at the end of the Atlantic rainbow.

Between Italian unification in 1871 and the outbreak of World War One around 5 million Italians crossed the Atlantic. People from the industrialised north of the country filled the railway carriages that took them to the German ports, and thence to Brazil and Argentina, although by the 1880s many were heading for the United States. Southerners preferred the direct three-week crossing from Naples to New York that was a boon for both genuine emigrants and the 'birds of passage' whose habit of pecking for employment in America before returning to their Italian nest annoyed the United States' citizens. The South American nations were culturally more suited for Italians, but the United States was easier to reach, had higher wages and a better choice of employment on the railroad or on construction gangs. It was quite normal for young Italian men to cross the Atlantic in spring, work in New York or another large city throughout the summer and return to Italy in winter. Yet until the last few years of the century more young Italians migrated seasonally within Europe than across the Atlantic.

Europeans had pursued seasonal working for centuries, chasing the harvest around the Continent, shifting from country to country as the jobs became available and returning home when the work finished or they had gathered sufficient money for their purposes. The United States, Argentina or Brazil merely provided an extension to this mobility so the steamships were busy both ways. Many Hungarians regarded the United States purely as a place for employment; one year working at United States' wage levels would gain them sufficient money to purchase a hectare of land or eight cattle which ensured moderate prosperity in Hungary. When the 1879 crop failure forced thousands of Slovaks to head west, many only intended to remain in North America until they were economically secure. Polish women and children continued to cross to eastern Germany for agricultural work in the sugar beet industry, Hebridean Scots headed east for the fishing, Irishmen sailed to Britain for farm work – crossing and recrossing the Atlantic was merely a larger step.

Despite the lure of freedom and the possibility of social and economic advancement offered by the New World, there had always been a reverse flow of people returning to Europe. Persecuted for their neutrality during the War of Independence, some Nantucket Island Quakers sailed eastward to Britain. Led by Samuel Starbuck, they had intended settling in Dartmouth as whalers but, with true colonial adaptability, they ended up as Welsh bakers, brewers and merchants instead. The Quakers' Yard in Milford Haven is the only memorial for these determined, quiet-living people. Nonetheless, the flow west was very much greater.

With the increasing number of people pouring across the Atlantic, the emigration lines bought larger, faster ships with more efficient engines and more frequent services. As early as 1858 the German Hamburg-Amerika Line and the Norddeutsche Lloyd Line started fortnightly crossings to New York, increasing that to weekly sailings in the late 1860s. By the mid-1870s German, British and French shipping lines were using ships of between 3000 and 5000 tons, carrying up to 1500 passengers on each trip. One of the best-remembered emigrant lines was the British White Star, who launched the 3708-ton *Oceanic* into the transatlantic run in 1871. *Oceanic* was one of the largest and certainly the most comfortable ship on the Atlantic, with a crew of 130 to care for her 200 passengers and the 1000 who travelled steerage. By the middle of the decade the White Star Line was only one of 17 shipping companies that carried the surplus of Europe across the Atlantic.

Immigrants to America could be running from hardship or unemployment in their own country, they could be attempting to escape conscription into a European army or one of the fierce *pogroms* that the Russian authorities ordered against the Jews. They could also be lured across the Atlantic by the promise of a better life. Europe teemed with recruiters attempting to entice people to the United States. United States' industries, railroad companies, state governments and the federal government all set up bureaux to encourage immigration. Many devices were used to entice immigrant labour; the seemingly limitless land was used as a bribe and in 1864 the United States Contract Labour Law authorised companies to pay for the passage of European workers. The prospect of owning a homestead enticed many Germans and Scandinavians to cross the Atlantic and if they were disappointed to find much of the Great Plains unsuitable for small-scale agriculture there were other opportunities in America. From the turn of the century it was the High Plains of Montana and North Dakota, together with the Canadian prairies that seemed a golden land to land-hungry Europeans, but by then the North American continent was seen as filling up and most people settled in the expanding cities.

On both sides of the Atlantic governments and companies constructed facilities to cope with the human surge. The Hamburg-Amerika Line had agents throughout eastern Europe, aiding the harassed Russian Jews, advising Mennonites of the farming opportunities in the United States and bringing in rural workers from Bohemia. In Hamburg itself the district of Veddel was thoroughly organised for the emigration trade, with cheap boarding houses and hostels for people waiting to board their ship, societies for the impoverished, hospitals and a host of porters and not-always-honest ticket agents.

Not surprisingly, the massive influx of often ill-educated people brought disease into the city and cholera killed almost 10,000 people in the winter of 1892. Superior sanitation kept the death count of equally-crowded Bremen down to only six. Two years later the Hamburg-Amerika Line improved its facilities by adding an area for disinfection and increasing the number of baths and sleeping quarters. Even spiritual comfort was provided for with both churches and synagogues for the intending emigrants, while new quarantine regulations ensured that disease did not travel with them. The Hamburg-Amerika Line already had superb ships, with the 7661-ton *Augusta Victoria* launched in 1889, and 8430-ton *Fuerst Bismarck* the following year. Either could cross to New York in only seven days but, not to be outdone, Norddeutsche Lloyd introduced *Kaiser Friedrich Der Grozze* to the Atlantic in 1897. Advertised as 'the ship of the decade', *Kaiser Friederich* was over 14,000 tons, but was soon dwarfed by others. White Star brought in *Olympic* and the ill-starred *Titanic* at 46,000 tons, Hamburg-Amerika responded with the 52,000-ton *Imperator* and in 1914 the 56,551-ton *Bismarck* was only one of the 442 ships the company then owned.

Overall these improvements in shipping ensured there was little loss of life while crossing the Atlantic. Regulations controlling health and space on board guaranteed that even steerage passengers had a tolerable, although scarcely enjoyable voyage. Out of the approximately 100,000 emigrants carried by the Hamburg-Amerika line, only 150 died – mostly the very young – a tremendous improvement on the early coffin ships. Inevitably there were some tragedies, the best known being the *Titanic* where the majority of the 1600 passengers that drowned were from the third, or emigrant class. The following year a chemical fire sunk SS *Volturno* which was sailing from Rotterdam to Halifax and New York. Gales hampered the rescue, but the tanker *Narragansett* spread oil to calm the sea and the Cunard ship *Carmania* was among those that sent over lifeboats. Over 500 people were rescued but over 130 were not.

By the turn of the century most families travelled together and many had relatives ready to receive them on arrival. With improved information people no longer travelled blind; many chose a particular destination where there was suitable work. Blood ties and politics were also important. In the 19th century most British emigrants had headed to the United States but after 1900 the outflow to Canada increased, particularly from Scotland. The Irish continued to pour into the Unites States, with many emigrant ships from the Clyde and Mersey picking up passengers at Londonderry, Cork or Galway. After the famine of the 1840s the status of Irish women had declined. Arranged marriages became the norm, dowries were fashionable, and some women labourers carried sacks of potatoes or broke rocks, but were still excluded from the pubs that provided a release for the men who worked beside them. So it was hardly surprising that from the 1870s more Irish women than men headed over the Atlantic, seeking the factories and offices of New York.

As the numbers increased so the ethnic origin altered as Jews and Italians, Czechs

'an uplifting beacon to the oppressed peoples...' Photograph courtesy William Donnelly,

and Croats, Russians, Poles and Greeks outnumbered the British and Irish, but all headed west in the largest popular migration in history. As they sailed into the vast harbour entrance of New York they would gape around them, but not until 1886 would they see Lady Liberty. The Statue of Liberty, a gift from France, was an uplifting beacon to the oppressed peoples of Europe. Here was the promise of freedom to people who had lived with the dread of persecution, the possibility of prosperity for the pauper, a New World in exchange for animosities that had poisoned European relations for millennia.

But first there were the immigration formalities that punctured the euphoria and brought the newcomer back to reality. Until 1890 immigrants were processed at Castle Garden receiving centre, a place of corruption, cruelty and crime. There were money changers who gave unbalanced rates of exchange, railroad agents with inflated ticket prices, baggage handlers who cheated and blackmailed. When Castle Garden closed the Bureau of Immigration created a spanking new centre on Ellis Island, a mile south of Manhattan and in full view of the Statue of Liberty.

Across the Pond

The first thing that immigrants would realise was the continuation of class. Perhaps this new republic had no native aristocracy, but while non-steerage passengers were pre-interviewed and permitted to walk directly from the ship to America, the steerage passengers had to be processed. The procedure was not pleasant as an array of officials alternatively probed, examined and interrogated the already disorientated and bewildered immigrants. Questioned about finance and religion, health and politics, the worried European wondered if he or she would be allowed to enter the land of opportunity. Perhaps 2% were rejected, the anarchists, the diseased, the criminal; for them there was no American dream. Some, who had names that sounded strange to the federal officials, were renamed, entering their new life with an unfamiliar appellation. Most walked through the gates of America.

Unscrupulous recruiters waited for them. While pretending to befriend the immigrants, the recruiters offered employment but claimed a percentage of their wages in an arrangement that might last for years. Many immigrants returned to work they had known in their native land, and entered communities of their ethnic origin. Rather than a melting pot, the great cities of the United States became a confusion of ethnic ghettos, with communities of Italians, Poles or Irish clinging to familiar accents and customs. The cities were huge, with dumb-bell tenements as unsanitary and tightly-populated as any early emigrant ship and a mortality rate comparable to the worst European slum.

Perhaps it was to be expected that there was a nativist response, as many established citizens of the United States resented this massive influx. Assumptions of superiority developed into the Wasp (White Anglo-Saxon Protestant) culture that evolved towards anti-Semitic or anti-Catholic societies; there were attacks on the incomers that presaged the later black/white race riots. Ironically, this behaviour would have the effect of banding the ethnic peoples together, making the process of assimilation more difficult. Even more ironical was that all the Wasps had descended from immigrants at some time. Despite the natural and imposed difficulties, many of the immigrants, and many more of their children, achieved greater success in the United States than they would have in Europe.

Between 1800 and 1914 perhaps 65 million Europeans emigrated to the Americas, of which about 15 million returned home when the New World either lost its appeal or had provided enough wealth. The fact that around 50 million remained in the United States reveals not only America's success in attracting such a diverse range of people but also the failure of Europe, then at the height of her power and prestige, to hang on to her population. European politicians had surely let their people down. In a mad century of folk wandering, overcrowded Europe had emptied into under-populated North America, and if both continents had gained something, perhaps the Atlantic shipping lines had profited most of all.

Chapter 12

Caribbean Sugar

'Sugar, sugar eh? All that sugar! How are the duties, eh Pitt?
How are the duties?'
George III's comment to William Pitt as he saw
the luxurious carriage of a West Indies merchant drive past him.

It was nearly a century after the discovery of the New World before Humphrey Gilbert suggested to Queen Elizabeth that England should muscle in on the Spanish Caribbean preserve. When Elizabeth, that cautious queen of duplicity, sent her mariners west and south in a series of rollicking forays, they enhanced England's prestige but failed to prise even a square inch of America from the steel gloves of Spain. Not only did Spain retain her island colonies, but she also consolidated her position in the New World and expanded into Central and South America. Any gains by other European nations in this area were either outside the Spanish sphere of interest or were mere fleabites of islands in the Spanish American hegemony. But these fleabites were to be considered the most financially important of all the European overseas possessions.

Realisation of the potential value of the Antilles occasioned a bewildering double century of acquisition, colonisation and conquest. Some islands retained their original coloniser; neither the English occupation of Barbuda, Antigua and Anguilla, nor the French colonisation of St Bartholemey and Marie Galante were challenged. Other islands were less fortunate such as Montserrat and St Christopher that passed between French and English, with the attendant assault and counter-assault by soldiers weakened by fever. The Dutch possession of St Eustatius, Saba and St Martin was sometimes disputed. Tobago was French until the 19th century when Britain took it over, while St Thomas was Danish. Of the larger islands, Cuba and Puerto Rico remained Spanish, Hispaniola was split between Spain and France while Britain possessed Jamaica from 1655.

Warfare over such small scraps of territory at so long a distance was only feasible if there was a profit, and in the Caribbean the profit came from sugar. Spices from the

East, sugar from the West; the merchant companies of Europe made their fortunes from luxuries rather than necessities and fleets of battleships faced each other in sordid slaughter so that English housewife or Dutch burgher could indulge their craving for sweetness. Desire for sugar created much of the turmoil in the New World.

Even the voyage to the islands could be eventful. In May 1631 Sir Henry Colt, a gentleman of Essex, sailed from Weymouth for the Caribbean plantation of St Christopher. English overseas settlement was in its infancy so the colonists were pioneers in an area that was regarded as a place for adventure and a quick profit, if sometimes an equally quick death. Unusually, Colt kept a journal of his voyage, and as he boarded *Alexander* 'riding in Portland road' there is a sense of excitement in his words, 'Now we are all met, our joy not to be expressed'. He recorded the mixed complement on *Alexander*, with the 'divers captaynes and gentlemen of note' being augmented by a sprinkling of women and children. *Alexander* was fairly large for the period, with a cargo capacity of 200 tons, but her 16 cannon were little enough protection in a Caribbean sea made hostile not only by dominant Spain but also by an appalling variety of predatory mariners from other nations. Obviously aware of the dangers, Captain Burch detailed 29 of his crew to man the guns, and created an instant militia of 60 musketeers from the passengers. It is difficult to assess the defensive potential of such a force but if *Alexander* was accosted at least they could make a brave show.

Around 90% of pioneers were male, most of them were single and many were indentured servants, subject to stringent rules and strict discipline as they performed the physical work of breaking in the wild islands for profitable agriculture. As *Alexander* set her bow to the sea the passengers settled into their novel life, finding their sea legs, learning to ignore the creaks and groans of shipboard life. They sailed a standard route, passing the Lizard and then south across the stormy Bay of Biscay, past Madeira and the Spanish Canary Islands and onward towards the Caribbean.

Even as they sailed towards tropical waters they ate broth and boiled biscuits, pudding and pepper, raisins and cheese. There was some meat, presumably salted, but no fresh fruit. It would be many years before the connection was made between the absence of fruit and the presence of scurvy. One cultural experience imported from the New World was the hammock, but when Colt tried sleeping in one he found it cold and constricting and reverted to his more familiar flock bed. However, the increasing warmth of the climate persuaded him to remove his quilted doublet. He still retained his sleeveless jerkin and knee breeches, his hose stockings and stomacher and, of course, the feathered hat that was a must for any English gentleman.

There were prayers three times a day, passengers and crew gathering to ask the Lord for his help in this new venture as they made their 500 miles a week. West of the Canaries *Alexander* caught the trade winds and headed south-westerly toward the Caribbean. Used to the brisk cool winds of the north, Colt thought the tropical breeze 'like the languishinge motions of a dyeing man' but when it strengthened, *Alexander* travelled an impressive 180 miles in a single day. Save for the weather, Colt found little to fill his diary on that uneventful Atlantic crossing, but *Alexander* was fortunate to have seen only three sails, and have not a single passenger sick. At last, in the dim early morning of 1st July, with Captain Burch tacking anxiously as he searched for the low silhouette of Barbados, the welcome cry of 'Land!' came from aloft. Although Colt peered ahead he could see nothing until improving light revealed the white batter of surf on the shores of a wooded island.

More passengers came aboard during their three-week stay in Barbados, while a cargo of dyewood and tobacco was packed into the hold. Colt noticed that African slave and English indentured servant toiled side by side on the island, and when some of the latter attempted to stow away on *Alexander* it was perhaps because the planters appeared more interested in drinking and squabbling than in tending to their plantations. Overall, Colt found the exotic vegetation and bird life more interesting. The settlers were fortunate that there had been no indigenous native inhabitants to remove, so no aftermath of bloody skirmishes and punitive raids. Within a decade, sugar was to spread to this most windward of the Caribbean islands and the planters would become among the most prosperous in the colonies, but *Alexander* and Sir Henry Colt were bound for St Christopher, 300 miles through the Caribbean.

As they sailed northwards past Guadeloupe a score of Spanish ships approached them. Too long odds for a merchantman to face, so Captain Burch ordered all sail hoisted and fled to the east. *Alexander* outdistanced all but two, which sailed close enough for Burch to clear for action. The preparations that had seemed so pointless in the broad Atlantic proved their worth now as the crew dismantled the wooden bulkheads that separated the cabins, threw the surplus cargo overboard to clear the gundeck and ran out the cannon. The ominous rumble of wheels on the wooden deck would sound across the water. Mustering the gunners and musketeers, Captain Burch encouraged them by passing around 'two great bottles of hot water' – presumably rum or some other fiery spirit. It would be a fine scene, spindrift arching from the bows and glinting in the sun, as the three ships sped over the tropical sea. The Spaniards fired first, with white smoke jetted from their broadsides, followed by the flat reports of cannon. There would be a tense wait aboard *Alexander* as Burch waited until the enemy closed before retaliating. Both ships would heel to their broadside, but while the Spaniard turned away *Alexander* continued, letting in water and off course but otherwise unhurt. Five days later she reached her destination.

Unlike Barbados, ownership of St Christopher was disputed, and with the British in the centre, the French at both ends and the Carib Indians likely to raid from nearby Dominica, it was necessary to organise a militia. Adding to the tension was the constant possibility of Spanish attack and discontent among the bonded servants, whose loyalty could not be relied on. When the Spanish had overwhelmed St Christopher and Nevis not long before, the servants had thrown away their muskets and rushed to greet them, shouting 'Liberty, joyful liberty!' To complete the turbulence there were fatalities from brawls and the suspicion that the Caribs who attacked unprotected planters were really naked Frenchmen in disguise. No wonder that sentinels with matchlock muskets were posted at night, and the constant unease caused Colt to think that 'all men are heer made subject to the power of this Infernall Spiritt'. English and French were to contest ownership of the island for the best part of a century.

In the meantime Sir Henry Colt had more prosaic matters to worry him. Clearing the tough jungle vegetation for planting was demanding physical work, particularly as he had brought only a single axe, so he eventually purchased a patch of ready-cleared land and planted wheat, potatoes and peas in the tropical soil. As he worked, *Alexander* ran into a tropical storm where a single bolt of lightning killed six of her crew, split the mainmast and tossed Captain Burch to the deck. Short-handed, Burch had to repair his vessel and recruit more seamen before he could return to England.

The 'Infernall Spiritt' of the Americas seemed to have already affected Colt as he planned to purchase a pinnace to sail to the Spanish Main on a mixed trading and Spanish taunting mission. He did not long enjoy his lands in St Christopher – within four years of his arrival he was dead. The Caribbean, that gave so much to Europe, demanded a heavy payment in human life, but it was men like Colt who pioneered the plantations.

As settlement spread through the islands Caribbean products such as molasses and rum became popular, but it was sugar that began to dominate; in the century after 1670 English consumption of sugar increased 25-fold. While Jamaica, Barbados and the Leeward Islands produced the coarse brown muscovado sugar, Barbados also produced the crude white, or clayed, sugar that was reckoned as being of finer quality than even St Kitts' muscovado, which was the best in the British West Indies.

Sugar was a labour-intensive industry, with African slaves gradually replacing the bonded servants in the gruelling work of cutting the cane in humid tropical heat. Once cut, the cane was squeezed between wooden rollers and the resulting juice was caught and boiled. The molasses was separated from the brown sticky muscovado, which was poured into barrels of North American oak. The full hogsheads weighed around 13 hundredweight, and were transported to the nearest port by cart or by drogher, one of the small coasting vessels that carried much of the produce around the islands.

Of the two types of British ships that sailed to the islands, the majority were 'established' vessels pre-chartered by a merchant to sail from Britain, collect an agreed cargo for an agreed freight rate, and return. Most established ships were British-owned and had been built specifically for the sugar trade. The second type of ship was known as a 'seeker'. As the name suggests, these ships actively sought out cargoes and they often carried African slaves. During wartime the seekers frequently became runners, ships that travelled independently of the convoys, depending on their speed to avoid hostile warships and carrying food to the island colonies.

By the 18th century most maritime nations of Europe had colonised some Caribbean island. While Spain had clung onto the vast bulk of land, Britain and France were powerful among the islands, but the Netherlands clung tenaciously to its colonies and even Denmark and Sweden were involved. The European ships sailed in on the trade winds, entered the Caribbean in the chain of the Lesser Antilles and headed north, west or south as their destination dictated. Those British ships returning from Jamaica could sail leeward by the Yucatan Channel and then, avoiding the adverse currents to the north of Cuba, use the more helpful current to pass through the Straits of Florida or the Bahamas Channel. Even here there was danger from August squalls, while an unwary captain could find his vessel pushed onto ragged reefs. The alternative was to attempt the Windward passage between Cuba and Haiti, where some vessels fought the trade winds for so long that they ran out of water. As if the trades were not enough, the French had doubled the hazards by building a fortress at Cape Nicholas, making this route nearly impassable in wartime. Shipping from the Windward Islands usually headed for Tortola before heading north and east to Britain.

The sugar trade was subject to the usual commercial frustrations, from delays by weather in the Caribbean, inefficient loading procedures and the constant threat of war. Even established ships often had to wait for hogsheads and barrels to be gathered from half a score of plantations, and in the summer such delays could mean the difference between a quiet passage home and the howling horror of a Caribbean hurricane. It is easy to imagine the captain's curses as the tardiness of a planter left his ship exposed to such danger. An example of such a delay occurred in 1773 when Foord and Delpratt, Jamaica agents for a Bristol sugar merchant, explained that it was a 'grand dispute' about freight charges that was detaining their vessel *Byron*. Apparently the planters hoped to receive 4s a hundredweight for their sugar while *Byron*'s captain was willing to pay only 3s 9d. As well as being seamen and warriors, ship's masters had also to be financial negotiators.

The years between 1748 and 1775 have been called the silver age of sugar planting, when established ships worked regular routes with known planters. Bristol merchants were known for their business acumen, frequently dividing their sugar between ships to increase the chance of some arriving for the early market and therefore obtaining the highest prices. Planters often divided their crop, sending it to a selection of British ports so that there was less chance of a glutted market. Yet although Bristol was a major player in the sugar trade, London was by far the greatest entrepôt with perhaps 75% of the trade. Liverpool was also important but the Clydeside ports hardly registered until late in the century. Within a decade of the first Greenock ship crossing the Atlantic around 1701, the port built itself a larger harbour to deal with the expected trade. Tobacco was important, but Greenock specialised in sugar and rum with the sugar refining industry surviving all the upheavals of the next two centuries.

Most sugar was carried in specifically-designed vessels known as West Indiamen. Usually ship-rigged, these were anything but fast yet were comparatively comfortable although, like most British ships of the period, they were both too narrow and too deep. The majority of British West Indiamen were between 200 and 500 tons and until around 1800 were normally built in London. After that date it was cheaper to build them elsewhere. Although the sugar trade was vital the Indiamen made only one voyage a year, leaving Britain in the autumn carrying foodstuffs, manufactured goods and, strangely, Christmas gifts for the slaves, and returning the following summer before the hurricane season increased insurance rates. The sugar ships had to arrive in Britain in time for part of their cargo to be re-exported to the Baltic in advance of the northern ice. In wartime West Indiamen sailed in convoy for, despite their valuable cargo, they had little protection against privateers. In peace or war they acted as passenger ships, carrying up to ten people of substance and position. In 1796 the West Indiaman *Lord Sheffield* boasted separate sleeping cabins with a mahogany waistcot, a pier glass and a sofa for the passengers, plus portholes for their private use. Every morning in the tropics the male passengers could enjoy a bath on deck, with the females presumably kept below to prevent them being scandalised, or amused. Possibly the women bathed in the privacy of their quarters, or else remained unbearably hot and sticky for the duration of the voyage.

Ships sailing westward often faced Atlantic storms, with the London vessels frequently tacking their way out of the choppy Channel for weeks. Frequently the Indiamen endured unsettled weather until they reached the latitude of Madeira and picked up the steady trade winds. There was little rest for the crew, for the captain often ordered them to clean up and paint his ship, or set up awnings for the comfort of the passengers. This stage of the voyage would be enjoyable for the passengers, who could watch the flying fish and relish the breeze that moderated the baking tropic heat. They might have been less comfortable as they crossed the tropic of Cancer, the infamous line of times past, when the captain mustered all hands and put the first-timers through a ceremony similar to that endured when crossing the equator. On every ship there must have been a thrill at the first sight of the Caribbean islands, with the passengers on deck, the hands in the rigging and the officers congratulating each other on their navigation.

Returning West Indiamen frequently carried the wives of planters, escorting their unsuspecting children from the pampered life on a plantation to the rigorous discipline of an English public school. Even when the ship caught the trade winds the crew was not allowed to relax, being employed in any of the myriad tasks on board from scrubbing the deck to re-caulking the seams. A good captain would have careened his ship to scrape off the weed, remove any of the terrible boring shipworm he could find and check his copper sheathing. On the return journey, however luxurious their quarters, neither passenger nor crew could escape the constant presence of sugar. Leakage from hogsheads created a pervading scent, augmented by a leaden film that covered every surface and rubbed off on the hands and clothes of even the most fastidious of travellers.

By 1774 there were over 230 ships in the West Indies trade with 76,600 casks of muscovado being carried across the Atlantic annually, together with more than 12,000 casks of rum. British trade to the Caribbean occupied five times the tonnage of shipping to Asia and 28 times the tonnage trading to Africa. But the sweetness of sugar profits disguised the reality of the plantations, where huge profit was based on the degradation of the African labour force. The estate house would be balconied, solid and cool, while the slaves existed in jerry-built shacks and under a regime that could vary from Christian charity to unbelievable cruelty. Often it was the planter's wife who took the final say in the treatment of the slaves, and if women of this period appear elegant with their flowing dresses and parasols, the slave at the whipping post or nailed by the ear to a tree might see things differently.

The start of the revolutionary war in 1776 saw a massive decline in profits as privateers played happy havoc with the sugar vessels. As in other wars, insurance rates rose with vessels trading to Jamaica particularly hard hit, presumably because of the longer voyage in more dangerous seas, and merchants had to pay higher wartime wages. Ships sailing to the Caribbean usually left in a single huge convoy that rendezvoused either at Cork or Spithead, but the worst danger was not encountered until they neared the sugar islands. Frenchmen from Guadeloupe or Martinique waited to windward of Barbados while Spaniards from Cuba hunted the Straits of Florida and the Bahama Channel. When they reached the British colonies, shipmasters needed diplomacy to negotiate with the island pilots, who may have been slaves but whose skilled seamanship gave them good reason to be arrogant. On one occasion the Kingston pilot was so resentful of being termed 'blackie' that he led a Royal Naval cutter through the Port Royal shoals.

Returning convoys sailed northward from the Caribbean to the 30° latitude line, from where they headed north-east until they were safe from the Newfoundland Banks before catching the westerly wind to Britain. While the convoy system provided some protection from privateers and stray foreign warships, the simultaneous arrival of an entire fleet of sugar ships invariably led to a glutted market. Daring runners that sped ahead of the convoy chanced the privateers but could obtain prime sugar prices.

Ultimately the sugar trade was about money, and there were fortunes for the fortunate. Some of the best Bristol merchants served their apprenticeship in the islands, learning about local conditions and making contacts that would be invaluable in later life. One merchant named Henry Bright left £50,000 when he died while Michael Atkins left £70,000, and William Miles handed his son a £100,000 cheque on his wedding day in 1795. Given monetary inflation in the past two centuries, all of these men were unbelievably wealthy, the equivalent of a millionaire at today's values. But despite Bristol's influence it was London that remained queen of the sugar trade, sending out as many as 320 vessels in 1804, compared to a total of 188 from all the other English ports and just over 80 from Scotland. Ten years later, despite both the French and United States war, there were nearly 800 British ships operating in the Caribbean.

Not all carried sugar. Jamaica produced some of the best coffee in the world and other islands produced cotton, particularly the beautiful Sea Island cotton, and dyewoods, ginger and mahogany, indigo and pimento. Molasses was used mainly for rum, although the United States developed more taste for this unique spirit than Britain. Yet the successful capture of French and Dutch colonies led to over-production of sugar with a consequent fall in prices and loss of profits.

Often the planter and the merchant were one and the same person but, even when they were not, tendrils of sugar cane inextricably intertwined both their lives and business. Societies such as the London Society of West India Merchants and the London Meeting of West India Planters and Merchants were major operators, but Bristol, Liverpool and Glasgow also possessed their own societies. The sugar planting Gladstones from Liverpool were ancestors of a prime minister, while Lord Penrhyn began his career as plain Richard Pennant, the Jamaica planter. The Lascelle family went one better – their sugar fortune helped one of their number become the Earl of Harewood. All over Britain, fortunes made from sugar cane hacked down by slaves enabled merchants to build fine houses and live lives of supreme comfort.

Further down the scale, sugar enriched people in less obvious ways. In the Caribbean there were men determined to rob the merchant of his lawful profit, with smugglers operating between British islands and the French and Spanish colonies. In Britain there were equally clandestine methods of earning a dishonest living. In an age before organised policing, docklands were notorious for theft and with such readily acceptable materials as sugar, coffee and rum, the West India trade was particularly susceptible to pilfering. The Thames-side thieves were organised into gangs with evocative names such as Night Plunderers, Mudlarks, Scuffle-Hunters and Light Horsemen, artful dockside dodgers who ripped off the merchants for uncounted thousands of pounds. It was not surprising that the West India Merchants continually promoted better law enforcement, but even the advent of the River Police in 1798 did not halt the plundering.

In 1801 the West India Dock opened in London, bringing all the Caribbean shipping into one area and thus making it easier to police. At that time nearly one third of British imports came from the sugar islands, and perhaps a sixth of her exports were destined for them. As an interesting irony, British shipping now carried New World silver to Europe while the British near-monopoly of the sugar trade, combined with her blockade of Europe, encouraged German and French scientists to explore sugar beet as an alternative. Britain received 95% of her sugar from the West Indies, with her only competitor the Cuban and French colonial sugar that neutral United States' ships carried.

However, it was not United States' shipping that created the downfall of the West India planters. The abrogation of the slave trade in 1807, followed by abolition of slavery within the British Empire in 1830, dislocated the economic roots of the sugar cane. Continual cultivation had denuded the soil of the islands, making them less able to compete with competition from dominions in the southern hemisphere, while British trade outwith the Empire increased. In time the expression 'rich as a West Indian' no longer had its old meaning, but with those riches fouled by the memory of slavery perhaps there is little to regret in its demise.

Chapter 13

Of Ships and Shipbuilders

> *'She starts – she moves – she seems to feel,*
> *The thrill of life along her keel!'*
> Longfellow: 'The Building of the Ship.'

There was a saying among the sailors of the Shetland Islands that the seventh wave always makes for land. It is easy to sit in safety and scoff at these old stories, but men like the Shetlander, the whaler of Nantucket or the Azores fishermen knew the sea in a way that people today can rarely fathom. Living in and on the water, not just their livelihood but their lives depended on their reading every mood and whim of the ocean. There were no mechanical aids to claw them out of danger, no coastguard or satnav system; they depended on their knowledge, intuition and skill.

There is the true story of Laurence Hughson of Skerries who was skippering a sixern back from the Atlantic deep sea fishing grounds, when the boat was smothered in sudden fog. When some of the crew began to worry, Hughson examined the sea, searching for the *Midder Di*, the mother wave, that underlying swell that headed for land. Following his sea sense, Hughson guided them back to Skerries; seamanship in the days of sail and oar was not only a highly developed skill, it also necessitated an art that technology can never fully replace.

The Shetland sixern was an interesting example of an Atlantic sea-boat, and a repertoire of the unique Shetland language of the sea. Open to the elements, it could be sailed with a single lugsail or rowed with each man having his own *kabe*, or wooden rowlock. Each of the six oars was held in place by a loop of rope, known as a *humbliband*, that was attached to the gunwale and which held the oar in place if the rower missed a stroke in rough weather. At sea the crew drank sour milk that was kept in *blaand* kegs, while there was a *skup* for baling and an *ouskery* to scoop up the herring. Perhaps Hughson's sixern carried a *looder*-horn, which was an ox-horn foghorn. Interestingly,

Dutch cod-fishermen in open dories on the Grand Banks used giant whelk shells to call to their mother ships when the fog rolled in. According to folklore, each Shetland fishing family could recognise the sound of its own horn and so knew that their menfolk were safe, however foggy the day or black the night. Sixerns could be around 70 feet long, 5 feet 6 inches in depth and 20 feet in beam, and were often imported from Scandinavia in kit form, as there were no trees on these northern islands.

There were many other vessels that evolved around the Atlantic coasts. Common in the late 18th century were the 'regular traders' that were built specifically for transatlantic trade. Either barques of around 250 tons or fully rigged three-masters between 250 and 500 tons, they carried coal or what was termed 'fine freight' on the westward journey, they could unload, barter and reload within a matter of weeks and make up to three round voyages a year. Vessels such as *Adriana* operated almost as regularly as ferries between Liverpool and Philadelphia between 1789 and 1801, while *Pigou* crossed bi-annually between Philadelphia and London from 1787 and 1804. Sailing between spring and autumn and refitting in the winter, it was with vessels such as these that United States seamen, shipowners and shipbuilders learned confidence and skill.

If the majority of Atlantic shipping in the 1780s was British, by the late 1790s the Stars and Stripes was more common than the Union flag. Partly this was due to excellent seamanship, but in July 1789 Congress contributed by slapping a duty of 50 cents a ton on every non-American built or owned ship, augmented by a 10% customs rise for goods imported in foreign ships. By contrast, United States vessels paid only 6 cents a ton, so even British merchants were persuaded to use American shipping. The French Revolution gave merchants a further reason to use neutral American shipping that had less chance of being attacked by privateers.

Even while North American-built vessels came to dominate Atlantic traffic in the early 19th century, their green wood construction contributed to a short lifespan and made them difficult to insure for more than a single voyage. Save for their timber, the most immediately obvious difference between European and North American vessels was the colour of their sails. In place of the baggy, duller flax canvas of the Europeans, United States' vessels used white cotton canvas. It was smarter, but European seamen swore that flax was easier to handle in frosty or wet weather. The United States Navy must have agreed, for they bought their flax canvas from Baxter Brothers of Dundee in Scotland. The comparative lack of men on United States' vessels would also be noticeable, as their vessels used smaller ropes and larger blocks, which perhaps did not look so smart, but certainly meant that the running gear snagged less and was easier to handle.

Among the distinctive smaller craft that evolved along the North American seaboard was the sharpie. Originally a New Haven oyster dredger of between 30 and 60 feet in length, the sharpie was flat-bottomed with a dominant centreboard. From around 1830 to 1860 these vessels flourished in the Chesapeake, and although the sloop-rigged skipjack eased them into retirement many were retained as pleasure craft. But of all the ingenuous North American shipping designs, perhaps the longest-lasting was the schooner. There are claims that when the first vessel of this type was launched in Gloucester, Massachusetts in 1713, one of the spectators called out 'There she scoons!' As 'to scoon' was a Scottish verb meaning to skip or dance across the surface of the water, this was an excellent description of the performance of these vessels, particularly when compared to the lumbering actions of the bluff-nosed merchant craft more common to the period.

If the Massachusetts schooner set the example, the Newfoundland firm of Kempe proved an adept pupil. In 1795 their 30-ton decked schooner *Sarah Kempe* slid into the Atlantic, forerunner of hundreds of the stout Newfoundland Banks schooners that braved the northern seas. Varying in size from 40 to 75 tons, many of those that did not fish the Banks pushed through the coastal ice on St Patrick's Day on their way to hunt for seals. British seamen termed these North American vessels 'plantation built' as they swarmed onto the Atlantic seaways.

A vessel from the dream of a sailing seaman's heaven, the original schooners were fore-and-aft rigged on both masts, but with square topsails on their shorter foremasts. Traditionalists would prefer the schooners to have just the two masts, but they have been built with more; the mighty *Thomas W Lawson* boasted seven masts. Despite being a monster of 5000 tons and 385 waterline feet, with masts a frightening 190 feet in height, the combination of skilled Massachusetts designers and steam technology ensured that *Thomas W Lawson* could sail with a crew of only 16. Small crews were one advantage of the schooner rig when compared to square-sailed ships. Unfortunately *Thomas W Lawson* was sunk off the Scilly Islands in 1907 with only a single survivor.

Schooners were one of the best North American exports. When the Nova Scotian shipbuilder George McKenzie built his own 45-ton schooner, he first sailed her to the West Indies then became a regular transatlantic trader. Crossing between Canada and Britain with cargoes of timber, McKenzie earned a reputation as a blue-nosed seaman, a hard-driving master mariner who never lost a man overboard. When his brother died at sea, McKenzie pickled the body in a coffin of rum until it could be buried in Nova Scotia. It was not until 1839, after 18 years as a seaman, that he settled in New Glasgow to open his own shipyard, and the vessels he produced were renowned for their quality.

As beautiful as the schooner, to many people the clipper is the epitome of wind-powered vessels. Although there is a tendency to refer only to a certain type of mid- to late- 19th century vessels as 'clippers', the term was used for many varieties of speedy sailing ship. One derivation of the name 'clipper' was that these vessels could 'clip' time off the passage of even the fastest packet ship. During the war of 1812 the Chesapeake-built blockade-runners and privateers were known as Baltimore clippers, and their long, lean hulls, raking stems and overhanging counters certainly foreshadowed the later more famous craft. Not until 1832, when Isaac McKim demanded a vessel that united the smooth lines of a schooner with the square-sailed qualities of a deepwater brig, was the instantly recognisable clipper ship formed. The result was *Ann McKim*. At 500 tons in weight, she was also long and low with the

...these vessels could 'clip' time off the passage of even the fastest packet ship.

raking stem of a schooner, but she paid for her speed with a limited cargo capacity and failed to make a profit. However, she had set a trend. John Griffith was one of the best early clipper builders and he disregarded the traditional tumblehome hulls and built long craft with limited wind-catching upperworks. The ships were superb and so was the timing. When the British cancelled the monopoly of the East India Company in 1833 they permitted competitors into India, and United States merchants whooped in to snatch up a massive share of the market.

They enjoyed certain advantages – their ships were both faster and more technologically advanced, their officers were better trained and often more sober and their crews worked harder. The hard discipline of the United States blood boats with the Down East master and bucko mates was legendary and it seemed that Britannia had miscalculated as American vessels pushed into every ocean of the world. The Royal Navy still held Neptune's trident, but Uncle Sam's mercantile marine was fastening Old Glory around the prongs.

Stimulating shipbuilding was the scent of gold. First in California in 1848, then in Australia in 1850, the discovery of gold led to a demand for ships that could carry passengers on ocean voyages with great speed, and return with relatively lightweight, valuable cargo. Simultaneously, in 1849 the British government repealed the Navigation Act, so allowing free competition for all colonial trade. The United States took full advantage, with their lean ships shouldering the slower British aside as they dominated the tea trade between China and London. Uncle Sam took to the sea in style, but however excellent the early clippers, the best was yet to come.

Occasionally there emerges into this world a man whose artistry is so far above his contemporaries that it can only be described as genius. Such a man was Donald Mackay of Boston, builder of some of the finest clipper ships the world has ever seen. Born in Nova Scotia, Mackay was not a native Bostonian, but as his ancestors had been among the loyalists who had left the newly-formed republic during the revolution, New England blood was as rich in his veins as was the Gaelic Scots in his name. Mackay was a true child of the North Atlantic, by blood, heritage and inclination. Bred in the port of Shelburne, Mackay grew up with the scents and sounds of Atlantic seafaring life and when he turned 16 he crossed the border to become an apprentice in a New York shipyard. Within a decade he was a master shipwright in John Currier's Newburyport shipyard in Massachusetts, and his expertise was so obvious that Currier offered him a partnership in 1841.

Mackay's first vessel, the 380-ton *Courier*, was launched in 1842 and became noted as one of the fastest coffee carriers on the New York to Rio de Janeiro route. As a partner of a man named Pickett, Mackay designed the fast packet *Joshua Bates* for Enoch Train's line that operated between Boston and Liverpool. After this success Mackay opened his own shipyard in East Boston.

In a five year spell Donald Mackay produced 17 ships, including five fast packets for Enoch Train's company. *Stag-Hound*, built in 1846, was considered the largest merchant vessel then built, but the prime clippers that made Mackay famous throughout the world eclipsed even her fame. In 1851 he built the California clipper *Flying Cloud* which sailed at a phenomenal 21 knots during her record 89-day passage between New York and San Francisco. Yet possibly more important than their speed was the stability of Mackay's vessels. Seamen in other ships, bucking and heaving off the Horn or wallowing in the tremendous swells of the Roaring Forties told awed tales of being passed by a Mackay vessel with all sail set and passengers dancing on a rock-solid deck. It was no wonder that rival shipbuilders envied the prestige of Donald Mackay, but none could match his skill.

Other record breakers emerged from Mackay's yard. There was the 285-feet long, 4500-ton *Great Republic* that sailed from Sandy Hook to Lands End in just 13 days. One of the longest ships of her time, *Great Republic* could sail under nearly full sail while other ships were putting reefs in their topsails. Then there was *Sovereign of the Seas*, launched in 1852 for the Swallow Tail Line – she was so fast on her New York to California route that James Baines of the Black Ball Line chartered her for the Australian wool trade. *Sovereign of the Seas'* immediate record of 65 days from London to Melbourne remained unbroken for 30 years. Baines promptly ordered four more of Mackay's vessels: *Lightning, Donald Mackay, James Baines* and *Champion of the Seas*.

For a while American clippers dominated the China tea trade, but although their vessels were fast, their softwood let in water and after a handful of hard-pressed voyages

Taeping *and* Ariel *in the great tea race of 1866.* Courtesy of the Billie Love Collection, Isle of Wight.

they became strained. There is no fault in this, for Mackay's ships were not designed with durability in mind. They fulfilled their intended function better than any other vessel of their time, and perhaps they stimulated the British response. For half a century the British had lagged behind their United States competitors, but now they began to fight back.

The British seaman retained the skills of the previous century, being adept with a halyard, sail needle or marlinespike, active aloft during a full gale and deft at the oars of a small boat, but they also had an 18th century attitude to time; speed was not a virtue. Their ships suited their talents; for decades the Tonnage Laws had disadvantaged the British shipping industry by taxing the length and breadth of vessels, but not depth. As a result British ships were built too short, too narrow and too deep, making them clumsy, slow, short, stumpy and oversparred. When these laws were repealed in 1854, British shipbuilding yards responded with an explosion of ships that swept any challenger from the trade routes, while inventive minds experimented with innovative design and technology. When British clippers slid from their designers' boards into the unsuspecting seas of the world, Britannia could remove the Stars and Stripes from her trident and unfurl the Union flag.

The majority of contemporary shipwrights followed the rule 'cod's head and mackerel tail', which meant following the general principle of floating timber. Logs are better towed with the thicker, butt end, forward so most cargo vessels were designed with rounded bows and a wide beam forward, tapering to a 'fine run' astern. Clippers were different – finer, sleeker and built of hardwood to be more durable, they not only outlasted most clippers built in North America but also delivered their tea in better condition. Even before 1854 there had been indications of a revival. Alexander Hall of Aberdeen had been building schooner-rigged vessels since 1839, and in 1852 their *Cairngorm* had sweeter lines than anything they had previously produced, and their clippers *Stornoway* and *Chrysolite*, although smaller than the United States' equivalent, were every bit as good. From 1855 the Greenock firm of Robert Steele & Company began a building programme that was to culminate in vessels like *Taeping* and *Ariel* that starred in the great tea race of 1866.

In 1853 Scotts of Greenock produced the first iron clipper, *Lord of the Isles,* nicknamed 'the diving bell' because she was so fine in bow and stern that she dived in at one side of the sea and out the other. When she caught fire nine years later outward bound for Hong Kong, her crew took to the lifeboats and reached Macao despite having to repulse two pirate attacks. If the lines of the diving bell were fine, then *Titania's* crew claimed she could sail astern up the Shanghai River. Clipper designers were among the first to understand that the speed of a sailing ship depended on her taper aft but, however fast and attractive these ships were, they were extremely difficult to control in following seas. Clippers were easily pooped – large waves which broke on the stern and rushed up the entire length of the ship, smashing, destroying and sweeping people overboard.

These were extraordinarily sensitive craft and many masters who were competent with slower vessels found themselves in difficulties when they commanded a clipper. They were unique, the fastest trading vessels of their day and even if *Cutty Sark*, arguably the most famous, was designed and built in Scotland and is preserved in London, it was the genius of the United States' designers and builders who originally evolved the breed. For the next couple of decades clippers presided over long-haul routes, but the opening of the Suez Canal, the development of multi-masted steel barques and continual improvements in steam technology ensured that their demise was already ordained.

The rise of British shipbuilding coincided with a decline in the United States marine. A financial depression in 1857 was followed by the outbreak of the Civil War, and as Americans butchered each other in a fratricidal frenzy, their share of sail-powered shipping dwindled. Nonetheless, Canada continued the North American contribution – in 1878 her 7000 ships made her the fourth largest ship-owning nation in the world. Like her southern neighbour, all the Canadian vessels were created from the great softwood forests, spruce, larch or juniper, and although strengthened by copper or iron they rarely lasted more than ten years. Yet they were amongst the best ships in the world, with both the White Star Line and the Black Ball Line ordering Canadian vessels.

Experiments with iron ships were not always successful with much of the early iron plate being rejected, but new technology was invented with rollers to flatten or shape the plate, massive shears for cutting and punches to create holes for the rivets. The use of iron and composite vessels expanded, but it was much later in the century that the Clyde produced the final, near-perfect example of the sailing shipbuilder's art, the steel four-masted barque of the 1890s. These ships could maintain a steady 12 or 15 knots while carrying 6000 tons of cargo, and were worked by a crew that would have been thought ridiculously small at the beginning of the century. Whereas the clippers are famous, these fine vessels have gone largely unrecorded, yet when the 352-foot long *Brilliant* was launched by Russell & Company in 1901 she was said to be the longest four-masted ship in the world.

Shipbuilding was a difficult, dangerous occupation with its share of disasters. In 1883 *Daphne* was launched while men were still working inside her. When she struck the water she rolled right over, trapping and killing over 100 men in Scotland's worst shipbuilding disaster. However, most launches were triumphant. In 1901 Stéphens built the first ship specifically to transport bananas from the Caribbean to Britain but *Port Morant* was hardly the most unusual vessel to have been built there. In a period of vast innovation, whatever was required would be built and whatever could be built was built on the Clyde. The great stern wheelers that thrashed up the Irrawaddy in Burma were constructed with the same careful skill as the ferries for the stormy Minch. A floating dock for one of the fast-growing ports of the Orient or a suction dredge for the Clyde; a fire float or a floating church during the 1843 disruption – ask and it would be built. Despite all these, perhaps the strangest vessel ever launched on Clydeside was the yacht *Livadia*, built by Elders of Fairfield in 1880. Designed by Russians for the use of their tsar, *Livadia* had the hull of a yacht placed on a steel raft, but the living space was that of a palace. Forty feet high and with three funnels and five masts, she boasted an illuminated fountain, a rose garden and a 10,000-bottle wine rack. Unfortunately when the tsar tried out his new toy he discovered he was prone to seasickness. Folklore claims that *Livadia* was used as a coal hulk before being broken up in 1926.

While the designer sat in his office and gained the plaudits, it was the riveter who was king of the shipyard. He was the best-paid worker and the man whose efforts put the whole thing together. At the end of his day's labour, with ears throbbing from the tremendous racket and sweat drying on his face and body, he could look up and admire the beauty he was helping create. Possibly pride compensated for the harsh conditions under which he laboured, for even in the late 19th century all work was performed outdoors with the vessel actually on the berth. Men could be working hundreds of feet above the ground, in frost or rain, with the nature of their contract augmenting their discomfort. They were employed only until the vessel they were currently building was complete, but fortunately there were so many vessels being floated into the Clyde that order books were rarely empty. Any spring tide could see as many as four separate launchings, but even so the pay was poor and the living conditions were terrible. Housed in tenements thrown up at great speed and with little regard to amenity or even a minimum of comfort, the workers had to take pride in the term 'Clyde built' that became a symbol of quality throughout the world. By deepening the river, the dredgers had reclaimed much land on the banks of the Clyde. Being flat and unoccupied, this land was perfect for shipyards although the narrowness of the river meant that launchings frequently had to be sharply angled.

From sail to power the Atlantic provided the finest shipbuilders in the world. In 1901 the Turbine Steamer Syndicate was founded with Denny's, Pearson Marine Turbine Company and the steamer owner Captain John Williamson, who was the pioneer of commercial turbine power. That same year TSS *King Edward*, built by Denny's, became the world's first turbine-powered merchant ship. During the next five years Denny's produced a further 16 turbine-powered vessels, among them the first turbine cross-channel ferry, and the first turbine ship in the Pacific. In 1911 McLaren Brothers of Dumbarton produced *Electric Arc*, a 50-foot launch with a propulsion method as revolutionary as steam had been. The 20th century had begun, and the changes of the 19th, however radical they appeared, were about to be more than eclipsed.

Chapter 14

Packet Rats

'Oh the times are hard and the wages low,
Amelia, where you bound to?
The western Ocean is my home,
Across the western Ocean!'
Brake-pump shanty, mid-19th century

Over the past few thousand years, ships have been used to carry just about everything, from elephants to gold and food to nuclear missiles. Nonetheless, one of the most important commodities is information and this, in the form of mail, was the original cargo of the packet boat. Throughout much of the 16th century England's attempt to conquer Ireland necessitated much military traffic between the two countries and both official documents and private correspondence were carried by sea. To ensure regularity of mail, it was carried on vessels that sailed between two fixed destinations and as State letters were known as 'the Packet', vessels that carried them became termed 'packet-boats'. In time this derivation became common for any vessel that carried mail on a regular basis, particularly if it operated on a fixed route.

In 1661 such a service began to operate between Harwich and Hellvoetsluys in the Netherlands, but it was not until 1689 that a packet service first sailed into the Atlantic, with the route between Falmouth in Cornwall and Corunna in north-west Spain. As one of the most south-westerly harbours of England, Falmouth occupied an excellent position for a packet port, with ships based there having an advantage over vessels from more easterly ports with respect to the Channel headwinds. As the Atlantic seaways increased in importance, Falmouth was selected as the base for 30 packet ships.

The Post Office packets were beautiful, three-masted vessels of between 150 and 200 tons, known as 'runners' for their speed, and could bite hard with the 18 or more cannons that scowled from their gunports. Unlike just about every government vessel of their time, the crew were all hand-picked volunteers and most were young, fit seamen. The packets must have contained comfortable cabins, for newly-appointed colonial governors and military officers of high rank and inflexible dignity preferred to travel by packet rather than by the larger and certainly better-armed Royal Navy ships. At a cost of 54 guineas between Falmouth and Jamaica, the packet passenger service was not the cheapest.

At any time there could be a collection of packet ships sitting in Falmouth, waiting to sail immediately the government mail was received. Only the larger were selected for the Atlantic routes, with the captains sporting uniform coats and distinctive hats similar to that worn by naval officers, for theirs was a position of responsibility and trust. It was communication that bound the ends of the Empire to the London hub, and the packets were the indispensable communicators, with standing orders to sail as soon as the weather permitted a double-reefed topsail. In that more leisurely age there were some seamen who would not poke their bowsprit out of harbour in anything like a blow and many who hove to at dark, so only fine seamen could follow the orders of a good packet captain. While their salary of up to £1000 a year reflected the standing of the captain, the perks were also evident – regular employment and the opportunity to load their own cargo onto the packet ship, making much profit while paying no freight charges. The position was often hereditary with sons following the keel furrows of their father. Even the ordinary hands, and there were around 60 of them on each ship, earned a wage that was in excess of the average seaman. They were also exempt from the press-gang. Fixed routes on a fast ship and an exemption from the Royal Navy made this a dream berth for many seamen and invoked intense envy from the less fortunate.

Yet despite these obvious advantages there were many packet captains who abused their position. It was not unknown for an indolent captain to plead sickness or urgent family business and remain in Falmouth while his command dug her prow into the long Atlantic rollers. Wartime appears to have exaggerated this tendency for there was one instance in 1793 when the French Revolution was still young enough to be an exciting novelty, that 12 Falmouth packets were at sea with only two captains between them.

Some packet captains turned the situation to their own advantage, using the comparatively heavy armament and the fine turn of speed of the packet to make a handy privateer. Others, less scrupulous, insured their cargoes at a high rate before surrendering to the first available privateer. History books, with their emphasis on seamen such as Nelson and John Paul Jones, forget to mention the more fallible and possibly more human characters who trod the decks of other ships. Not all seamen cared who won the current war, provided they came out with a whole skin and a healthy bank balance. When one particular packet ship appeared to be escaping a privateer after a long day's chase, he hove to and sent a boat to politely inform his pursuer that he had surrendered. There were even packet captains, less blatant if just as dishonest, who preferred smuggling to insurance scams. Or perhaps smuggling was not a matter of honesty: at a time when many officers of the Royal Navy favoured French brandy, why should the packet captains not supply it?

Being fast and efficient, packet boats were also perfect for carrying spies to mainland Europe, sitting with furled sails off Brittany or ghosting offshore while a ship's boat rowed, oars muffled, up the Loire. These would be tense hours, with the hands standing to their guns and lookouts scanning sea and coast for sight of the French. No doubt some captains capitalised on their smuggling contacts to pick up brandy as they landed agents, and perhaps there were spies who hitched a lift on a packet ship, only to relay information about the latest convoy to the Dunkirk privateers.

More conventional packets sailed to the Caribbean, Lisbon and Halifax and, despite the shortcomings of some captains, the majority were honest. Despite standing orders to toss the mail overboard if they were attacked, many captains preferred to slog it out with privateers. There was one case in 1798 when *Antelope*, Jamaica-bound from Falmouth, was attacked by a French privateer off Cuba. Already outnumbered three to one by the crew of the privateer, the packet captain must have speculated about the allegiance of his passengers, who included French royalists and a French ex-naval officer. He had no need – presumably realising that capture could mean death by guillotine, the French passengers fought alongside the crew of *Antelope* so that the privateer was captured and carried as a prize to Jamaica. Not all encounters were so fortunate since hostile vessels captured 19 Falmouth packets between 1793 and 1815.

By that time the speedy packet ships worked on routes that extended like fine threads in a global postal service that connected Britain to India and Halifax, Jamaica and Gibraltar. Ambassadors and governors, gouty generals and occasionally their imperious wives travelled with the mail, and if the equivalent is a Royal Mail postbus, then the passengers are privileged by the comparison. Not until paddle-steamers altered ocean traffic forever did the old sailing packets lose their position, but the name of 'packet ship' continued, being applied to any vessel that sailed on an established route between two fixed points.

Definitely the first and arguably the most famous of these later Atlantic sailing packets was the legendary Black Ball Line that operated between New York and Liverpool. To ensure that they could maintain a steady pace across the Atlantic, Black Ball liners had extremely strong spars and high quality rigging that could endure both the prolonged battering of the weather and the strain of holding a cloud of canvas for lengthy periods. At between 300 and 500 tons they were not the largest of vessels but, by leaving New York on the first and 16th of each month, they were amongst the most regular on the North Atlantic.

In a January day of blustery snow in 1818 Black Ball's first vessel, *James Monroe*, slid away from New York's East River, with the bellowing of onboard cattle and alarmed cackle of hens the only fanfare for the birth of a piece of nautical history. Perhaps some of the crowd who had gathered on the Manhattan waterfront would have felt pride when *James Monroe* became the first ship to cross the Atlantic six times in the same year; soon such a feat was commonplace among the packet liners. But there was another side to these vessels and this was the domain of the packet rats.

On the North Atlantic routes the term packet ship reached new heights of fame, while simultaneously plunging to new depths of notoriety. For if the Atlantic packet ships were more regular and reliable than just about any vessel afloat, and were commanded by officers whose skills were never less than superb, they were also renowned for the utter brutality with which they treated their crewmen, the packet rats.

Life at sea was never easy, and discipline by rope's end and seaboot too commonplace to merit a comment, but on board the packet liners the crews existed in a state of battened-down violence. To achieve their tight schedule in the frantic northern weather, the packet liners were probably the hardest-driven ships afloat, while to keep costs down a special type of man was recruited for the forecastle. These were the packet rats and if the name does not now bring a thrill of apprehension, then perhaps it should for the human rats were as predatory as those that lived in the animal kingdom. Yet this was also the time of the sea shanty, which helped the small crews work in unison. Mostly these were hard-work songs – sardonic, bitingly condemnatory – the rats' verbal retaliation against bullying mates and unreasonable conditions at sea. There was little other joy in the seagoing life of a packet rat.

Although the Black Ball Line was the first of the Atlantic packets, other shipowners soon elbowed in with their own lines and their names are as evocative as the cattle ranches of the old West. There was the Red Star Line, the Black X Line and the Swallow Tail Line which all competed on the North Atlantic, all sailed from New York and were all American-owned. North Atlantic packets were in a class of their own since no British shipping could match them for speed and reliability. And they knew it; the vessels had names so distinctive that it is almost possible to feel the pride as they flaunted the Stars and Stripes on the sea that washed Britannia's doorstep. There was *Independence, Ocean Queen* and the famous *Dreadnought* that men sang songs about:

> *'There's a saucy wild packet, a packet of fame,*
> *She belongs to New York, and the* Dreadnought*'s her name*
> *She's bound to the westward where the wide waters flow,*
> *Bound away to the westward in the* Dreadnought *we'll go!'*

East to west, west to east, *Dreadnought* carried the red cross of her house flag with jaunty arrogance as she slid clear of Sandy Hook and battered into the seas, striving for a fast fortnight's passage to the Mersey. What cared *Dreadnought* if the limeys boasted the largest navy in the world; she represented the most professional merchant marine. United States' ascendancy at sea increased in proportion to the size of the packet ships – from around 500 tons in 1815 they averaged 1200 by 1840. By then the Atlantic seemed to belong to Uncle Sam and damn the trident of the limey's Britannia. Although the American packet liners lacked durability with their softwood construction, they were light and fast. Less costly to build than British ships, they also had finer lines, with an average length to breadth ratio of 5.5 : 1 rather than 4 : 1, so they were sleek where the British looked tubby, a different class of ship manned by a different breed of seamen.

For a century and a half the sparse interior of New England had encouraged men to take to the sea, but in the opening decades of the 19th century the Erie Canal had opened up the fertile farmland of the Midwest. There had always been a trickle of farmers flitting to the frontier, but now people boarded barges and wagons to continue the westward journey that their European ancestors had begun. From being a sailing and trading nation, the United States was on the threshold of a period of internal colonisation as the western frontier dominated much of the next half century. As if in compensation, the American merchant marine continued to be officered by some of the most professional and best-educated nautical men in the world. And of all the merchant officers, the best were drawn to the packet service with its constant challenge from sea, commercial competition and, always, the packet rats.

Britannia, attempting to wrestle her trident clear of the accumulated seaweed of tonnage laws and complacency, had to agree. In 1837 a British Parliamentary enquiry concluded that the United States packet ship captains and officers were '... generally considered... more competent as seamen and navigators and more uniformly persons of education than the commanders and officers of British ships of a similar size and class.' There was no doubt that the packet captains were superb seamen. They were fast, dependable and sailed in all weather; they also sailed their own ships into harbour rather than choosing the safe option of being towed, but perhaps that was pure Yankee prudence as the tugs might expect payment. They also revealed that streak of competitiveness that distinguished the United States.

At one time sailing had been quite a leisurely business but in the 19th century things speeded up. Races between rival ships became common practice with Mississippi paddle steamers or Clyde ferries competing for custom, the great clippers racing from China to the Channel with tea and Bully Forbes (of *Marco Polo* and the Australian emigrant trade) proudly proclaiming that he captained the 'fastest ship in the world'. In 1837 one of the most famous packet races was held, with Captain De Peyster of the Black Ball Line's *Columbus* competing with Captain Russell of the Dramatic Line's *Sheridan*. Prestige was important, but the winning ship also expected to pick up a tidy $10,000 and a $50 bonus for each of the hands. The packet ships tore out of New York into the teeth of a North Atlantic February with the men facing sleet and lashing rain, murderous grey seas and constant hazing from their officers. But they could take it, they were packet rats, the toughest seamen afloat. Bloody-fingered, they hauled at stubborn canvas; foul-mouthed, they roared defiance at the sea; hungry for success, they forced speed from their ship while the Stars and Stripes flogged beneath the wicked sky. With her canvas threatening to rip free and her spars straining with the pressure, *Sheridan* battered her way across in just 18 days; Liverpool had never looked more welcoming as she slid into the Mersey. But she was two days behind *Columbus*.

Although these packet ships were faster than just about anything of their time, they were not primarily intended as racing craft. Ten to 12 knots was about average, 14 knots was good, while only the constant driving by the officers and the bloody-minded determination of the rats ensured that they crossed the ocean with any alacrity. There were legends told about the packet captains, dark tales of mixed awe, fear and admiration. There were Down East Yankee captains who nailed shut the forecastle door as soon as Sandy Hook was astern and kept the rats on deck or aloft for the remainder of the voyage. There were bucko mates who worked with a revolver at their belt and a knuckle-duster on their fist.

> *'There's London Pat with his tarpaulin hat,*
> *And Frisco Jim the Packet rat.'*

Only the best of captains could shake constant speed out of the packet ships and only the hardest of officers could control the packet rats. And both sides knew it, expected no quarter and offered none. Some packet ships such as *Southampton*, *Patrick Henry* and *Montezuma* crossed from New York in a bare 15 hard-driven days. Few could match the 14 days and six hours of *Independence* and none could compare with *Dreadnought* which crossed in a storming 13 days and eight hours during one voyage in 1859.

> *'Now the* Dreadnought*'s a-sailing the Atlantic so wide,*
> *Where the high rolling seas roll along her black side;'*

Dreadnought sailed under Captain Samuel Samuels, and her exploits could be placed alongside Donald Mackay's famous *James Baines* that crossed in 12 days and six hours. *James Baines* was a clipper, designed for speed and crewed by crack hands whilst *Dreadnought* was a packet ship crewed by rats - Samuels must have been quite a seaman. Like the vast majority of the packet masters, he was a New Englander but the rats were Scousers from Liverpool, Irish Paddies or the ubiquitous Danskers and Scowegians from Scandinavia. Only these men could endure the hardships of the packet ships.

> *'Beware them packet ships I pray,*
> *They'll steal your gear and clothes away'.*

The Down East skippers ensured that their ships were in top condition before they left port since that way they could sign on the dregs of the dockside rather than experienced deep water men. The rats came on board in shirts, trousers and seaboots; the lucky might carry some dunnage, but not for long. Mustered aft, they were harangued by the captain while the bosun and mate rummaged through the forecastle, removing offensive weapons, tossing bottles of liquor over the side and breaking the points off sea-knives. Those of the rats who had been to sea would expect this and would have taken precautions, but the unconcealed aggression of the officers would irritate those who had never sailed under the Stars and Stripes before.

The bucko mates believed it was impossible to control the rats without violence and knew that they were perfect for the job. They were men of iron and blood who ruled by the weight of their fists and the savage swing of a belaying pin; men who knew they could 'whip their weight in wild cats'. Once at sea, with the wind shrieking to the damned through ice-frosted rigging and the Atlantic pouring green and frothy over the bulwark, life onboard became a battle of attrition. As the century progressed, the seaman-like quality of the packet rats deteriorated and measures to control them slid from hard discipline to utter brutality. On average there were 40 rats aboard a

'...*Scousers from Liverpool*...' Photograph by the author.

packet ship, and if one's sympathy today lies with the rats, consider what life would have been like if they had control of the ship. Men who lived for drink and fought for pleasure, bitter-eyed and callous with a jaundiced view of the world, they viewed officers as a natural enemy and pity as a weakness.

Not that the bucko mates were any sort of gentlemen. One who achieved most notoriety was Robert Waterman of the Black Ball Line. In later life he was renowned as 'Bully' Waterman, one of the captains who took the forty-niners round the Horn to California at the expense of his crew. As the captain of *Sea Witch* he made record passages but as captain of *Challenge* he was tried for murder of one of his own crew. The packet ships were not suitable for soft-handed clerks.

The bucko mates had to be hard and any hesitation at sea could be fatal, for the man and for the ship. If a first voyager was ordered aloft on a night of biting wind, with the topmasts hidden amidst whirling flecks of snow and the wind plucking at tattered clothing and torn fingers, it would be natural for him to blanch. It was then that the bucko mate came into his own, blasting the man up the rigging with lung power or the whip of a rope's end. If the man already feared the mate he would be more likely to comply. Many of the first voyagers had no intention of becoming seamen, they wanted only a voyage across the Atlantic, a one-way ticket to the land of opportunity, the Californian goldfields and the promised gold-paved streets of New

York. Many lied about their sea experience in order to secure a berth and the mate had the thankless task of driving his ship with whatever material came to hand. Others were simply brutes, unable to understand anything other than brutality, but pitiless behaviour surely created as much trouble as it caused.

There was one Irish publican who had a knack of finding prime seamen for the packet ships. Surprised at how many experienced seamen appeared to frequent this man's pub, a ship's mate entered one day, claiming to be a first voyager searching for a berth. The publican placed a bull's horn on the table and invited the man to walk around it three times, before handing him to a mate whose vessel was short-handed. Without a qualm, the publican claimed that, to his certain knowledge, this man had been around the Horn three times!

Perhaps this particular story is apocryphal but the idea is correct. The bully mates were aware of the tricks ostensible seamen could fabricate in order to obtain passage across the Atlantic, so if they drove their men hard perhaps they were only venting some of their frustration at having to work with sub-standard material. But not only Down East Yankees had a reputation for roughness at sea, Nova Scotia bluenoses could be equally feared. One of these bully skippers is remembered as having built a massive house in the Annapolis Valley in Nova Scotia. According to sealore he drove his crews so hard that the stubborn died and the weak deserted, whereupon he retained their wages for himself. Given that the wage packet of a forecastle hand would scarcely raise a splash if thrown in a duck pond, there must have been another source for the captain's fortune.

Even for non-packet ships, life at sea was harsh. In the tropics there was the constant threat of disease and thirst while the stokers and engineers of steamships endured almost unimaginable heat. In the North Atlantic there was pounding by heavy seas and exposure to flesh-searing wind, with constant danger from storm or iceberg. Accidents and shipwreck were common and tuberculosis, the consumption that plagued overcrowded, damp accommodation, was widespread. Perhaps there would have been fewer accidents if the men had been better fed and treated. With the cheapest food possible, unheated quarters and officers who practised neglect and brutality as a matter of policy, it is not difficult to see why men slipped from aloft or lacked the strength to withstand the force of a deck-lashing sea. Even if the ship's master or the shipping company were better than average in their treatment of the hands, men could still be cheated by an unscrupulous steward or by crooked suppliers in port. There was seldom a doctor, so the best the injured could hope for was the ministrations of the ship's carpenter or, on the occasional long-hauler, the perhaps gentler hands of the captain's wife. Few, if any, packet ships had such a ministering angel.

Between around 1818 and 1850 it seemed that Old Glory flapping from the topmast of a packet ship had flicked the Union flag into the depths of the Atlantic. The United States built the best, fastest and cheapest ships and set the most professional officers and captains to command them. But possibly because of their continuing ascendancy, the packet ship owners failed to sense the change in the winds of trade. For once the North American preoccupation with progress faltered as ship owners assumed that the future was as safe as the present and discounted the steam ships *Sirius* and *Great Western* that thumped across the Atlantic in 1838. In the meantime, the packet rat clawed his way from ship to ship and endured the drinking shops and crimps of life ashore. In the poorest of doss houses he spent the night suspended across a rope in lieu of lying in bed. Others spent their meagre wages on the first available prostitute. Used to hell afloat, the packet rats could often be just as ill-used in the slums around the Atlantic docks, and if they were hard men by any standard, they were often well-matched by the women with whom they consorted.

> *'When I awoke next morning I had an aching head,*
> *And there I was, Jack all-alone, stark naked on the bed.*
> *My gold watch and my pocket book and lady friend were gone,*
> *Now all you bully sailormen take warning when ashore...*
> *For Yankee gals are tougher than the other side of Hell!'*

They are gone now, and nearly forgotten, these tough rats who infested the Yankee blood boats and treated the Atlantic with as much contempt as they treated themselves. They had their day and earned their dollars and would certainly scoff at any sympathy.

Chapter 15

The Coming of Steam

*I know nothing so perplexing and vexatious to a man of feelings
as a turbulent wife and steamboat building'*
John Finch

On the last day of March 1820, Donald McDougall's pipes played *Comet* through the newly-navigated Crinan Canal and into the glittering waters of the Sound of Jura. It was the culmination of a dream as the steamer's twin paddles flailed the ocean to a frenzy, spray rising to shimmer in the spring sun while a plume of smutty black smoke smudged the green hills of Knapdale. *Comet* was positive proof that a steam-powered vessel could operate on the open ocean, a portent of the future for shipbuilders and sailors over the entire world.

As far back as 1543 Blasco de Garay of Barcelona spoke of using steam for transportation, and if his foresight should have ensured the survival of his memory, his ideas were too far in advance of his time to be expanded. Not for more than two centuries did engineers seriously examine the application of steam power to shipping. While the Glaswegian James Watt improved the steam condenser, it was the French Marquis de Jouffrey who launched the first working steamboat in Lyons in 1783. Unfortunately the French failed to follow up their initial success and it was left to men from Great Britain and the United States to continue the experiments. James Watt linked with the Englishman Matthew Boulton, owner of the Soho Engineering Works near Birmingham, England, to form a firm that was to be a major player in the world of steam power.

On the other shore of the Atlantic, James Rumsay of Maryland spent 12 years of his life working on steam power before his first successful boat sliced into the waters of the Potomac. Steaming against the current, it achieved an eminently respectable 4 miles an hour by the unusual method of jetting water through the stern. Rumsay had been preceded by William Henry of Pennsylvania, who in 1763 attached a form of steam engine and primitive paddle wheels to a boat that he thrust out into the Conestoga Creek in Pennsylvania. When the boat sank it appeared to be the end of his adventure, but American steam engineers were a tight-knit bunch and Henry was acquainted with both John Fitch and Robert Fulton who shared his enthusiasm and were later to share his inspiration.

John Fitch is better remembered than Rumsay or Henry. A farm boy from Hartford County in Connecticut, Fitch had failed in many things from clockmaking to sailing before he turned to steam. His single coastal voyage had been marred by the hazing of the mate, while the failure of his marriage and his reputation for eccentricity were spoken of when he moved to Philadelphia. With the assistance of the watchmaker Henry Voight, Fitch attempted to build a steamboat and persisted through a series of failures until he celebrated a decade of United States independence in 1786 by launching a vessel of 60 feet. Although unwieldy in appearance with six paddles, the boat's success convinced Fitch to build another.

His aptly-named *Perseverance* carried passengers on the Delaware with an aplomb that was unfortunately not matched by any commercial fulfilment. Although *Perseverance* lost money Fitch was more than pleased: 'We reigned Lord High Admirals of the Delaware' he boasted, 'and no other boat in the River could hold its way with us.' The pleasure only lasted as long as his backer's patience. When they withdrew their funding Fitch withdrew his person to the Kentucky back country, where he committed suicide. Perhaps he was a failure in his own eyes but his achievement in building and running a steamboat from scratch surely represents a remarkable success.

Contrasting with the impoverished Fitch was John Stevens of Hoboken. The son of wealthy parents, Stevens spent his time in either a New York mansion or a summerhouse at Castle Point on the banks of the Hudson River. Using Fitch's steamboat as a model and buttressed by money, Stevens built his *Phoenix* entirely with United States' technology, including an American engine. By sailing her from the Hudson to the Delaware Stevens made the first, often-forgotten, steam-powered voyage into the Atlantic. *Phoenix* survived a typically stormy Atlantic inauguration to operate between Philadelphia and Trenton.

Meanwhile in Scotland, two men were working diligently to float their own steamboat. No stranger to novelty, Patrick Miller owned land in North America and Scotland, traded with continental Europe and was a shareholder in the Carron Iron Works, where the formidable carronade was produced. As if that was not enough, he turned his talents to marine propulsion. In September 1787 the Leith shipyard of Allan & Stewart produced Miller's first vessel, appropriately named *Experiment*. At 105 feet long, double-hulled and with five masts and no engine, her 30-strong crew used capstans, conical gears and sheer muscle power to drive her four paddle wheels. There was no problem in the sheltered waters of Leith harbour but when *Experiment* sloshed past the pierhead things proved more difficult. Despite all the exertions of the crew, *Experiment* only managed to paddle halfway across the Forth before a headwind stopped all progress. With *Experiment's* 11-hour voyage a failure, Miller recruited the mechanical skills of Leadhills-born William Symington and tried again.

On 14th October the following year, Britain's first steamboat slogged onto Dalswinton Loch. Symington's engine powered an ungainly looking vessel, with a pair of paddle wheels in between the twin hulls. At 25 feet long and seven in beam, this strange craft crawled through the water at a not unimpressive 5 miles an hour, and as she did not sink the attempt could be counted a success. Learning from each prototype, Miller moved onto the Forth and Clyde Canal. Retaining the double hull, his next craft was 60 feet long but, despite using a larger engine, her first voyage on 3rd December 1789 was a failure. Strong-willed and well-financed, Miller strengthened the paddle wheels and on Christmas Day his steamboat moved at a steady 6½ miles an hour along the canal.

While Miller moved onto other things, Thomas, Lord Dundas of Kerse provided financial support for Symington's continued experiments, and in 1802 he instructed the Grangemouth shipbuilder A. Hart & Company to build *Charlotte Dundas II*. With a length of 58 feet and a beam of 18 feet, she was powered by an updated version of Symington's engine and was the first truly successful British paddle steamer. Unlike the earlier attempts, *Charlotte Dundas II* was single-hulled, and the solitary paddle wheel in her stern made her a forerunner of the great stern wheelers that plied the Mississippi and Murray Rivers. However, *Charlotte Dundas II* never achieved such heights, she was used as a tug on the Forth and Clyde Canal, on one occasion towing two 70-ton barges for 20 miles against a headwind that would have defeated any sailing craft. Steam had arrived, in inland waters at least but not everybody was pleased. Objections that her wash would damage the banks of the canal sent *Charlotte Dundas II* into early retirement and, sadly, William Symington died in poverty. His work is hardly remembered and his name barely known outside Scotland.

In the United States, Robert Fulton was donning the steam-powered mantle of Fitch. A Pennsylvanian from Little Britain, the youthful Fitch had proved his inventiveness by launching a rocket, but more significant was his work in attaching paddle wheels to a fishing boat. It seems that similar ideas occurred to mechanically-minded people thousands of miles apart. After working as a portrait painter in England, Fulton partnered the Duke of Bridgewater on a couple of engineering projects before crossing to France. He was a neutral travelling from one belligerent nation to another, but it was perhaps natural that as a citizen of the United States he should voice his distaste at the Royal Navy's treatment of non-belligerent shipping. Even so, he offered his work on submarine mines and a torpedo to Britain after France had rejected him, so presumably the commercial aspects overrode any thoughts of morality. Britain, in turn, rejected him; presumably she was unhappy at any innovation that might jeopardise her traditional wooden-walled command of the seas. Returning to France, Fulton failed in an attempt to sink a British frigate with a 'diving boat' that he named *Nautilus*.

In that same momentous year of 1801 Fulton met Robert Livingston, the United States Minister who obtained the Louisiana Purchase from Napoleon Bonaparte.

Livingston now agreed to partner Fulton in operating a steamboat on the Hudson. In 1802 Fulton's initial attempt with a side-wheeler failed as the engine proved too heavy for the hull and the steamboat sank in the Seine. He tried again the following year but, although the steamboat remained afloat, it was too slow to be used for anything except display.

Fulton's request for a more powerful engine from Boulton and Watt was rejected by order of the British government, possibly because of his French connection, for when he returned to the United States his order was approved. By that time Fulton had examined Symington's engine on *Charlotte Dundas II* as she lay forlorn on the Forth and Clyde Canal. It was 1806 before Fulton began building the boat that made him famous and which really began the American steamboat age. Although the sceptical locals around New York's East River dubbed Fulton's creation 'Fulton's Folly', their sneers were silenced on 17th August 1807 when *Clermont* steamed into the Hudson River. The name came from the Hudson estate of Robert Livingston, and she was designed in the United States and built by the New York shipbuilder Charles Brown. At 133 feet long and 18 feet in breadth, she was much larger than any steamboat so far floated in Europe, and if her engine was built by Boulton and Watt all the rest was pure American. Fulton and Livingston were ready to exploit the government legislation that granted them a steamboat monopoly on the Hudson River.

After so many tribulations Fulton must have felt immense satisfaction as his boat steamed along the Hudson, her wash surging powerfully along the banks and her progress watched by the no-longer-jeering crowds. As *Clermont* sailed into the night the black smoke from her pinewood fuel became invisible but red-flecked sparks soared from her funnel to mark her passage. No doubt the clamour of her engine and churn of her paddle wheels woke the early-bedding farmers, panicked the cattle and infuriated mothers by keeping delighted young boys at the windows of their homes, but that was a small price to pay for progress. Namesake to namesake, *Clermont* rested at the Clermont estate after a full 24 hours of steaming. The triumph continued, all the way to Albany and back, then Fulton made minor alterations to his boat before starting the world's first steam ferry service. Thanks to Livingston's finance, Boulton and Watt's engines and Fulton's engineering skills, the United States had produced the world's first passenger-carrying paddle steamer.

While he was in Britain, Fulton had met the West Lothian-born Henry Bell, who had worked in a mill and a Bo'ness shipyard before spending two years as a mechanical engineer. While still a very young man Bell had experimented with muscle-powered wheel boats before turning to steam power. When both James Watt and the Admiralty rejected Bell's unsolicited views on ships' engines, he continued with the stubborn determination that seemed to characterise all the early steamboat engineers. Bell's vessels were to be pure Clydeside. John Wood & Sons of Port Glasgow built the vessel to Bell's design, with the Glasgow engineer John Robertson busy on the engine and John Napier & Son, also of Glasgow, manufacturing the boiler. For quite a while Bell had no name for the vessel he was creating but the sight of a comet flaring over Scotland gave inspiration and, early in 1812, *Comet* was launched on the Clyde. A little over 40 feet long, she was 11 feet 6 inches in beam, 15 feet over the paddle-boxes and drew about 4 feet of water. With only a 4 horse power engine she would never be fast and her appearance produced as mixed reactions from the good people along the Clyde as *Clermont* had along the Hudson. There were those who found her high smokestack ludicrous, particularly as it also acted as a mast for her single square sail, but surely Scottish Calvinism influenced the claim that brimstone and the devil's fire powered her somewhat erratic progress. However, if the first voyage of *Comet* ensured Henry Bell a place in history, to the hardy men and ghosting beauty of silent sail, it signalled the beginning of a long, permanent decline.

Despite early setbacks that necessitated lengthening *Comet*, reducing the paddle wheels from four to two and installing a more powerful engine, Bell's boat was a success. *Comet* commenced a regular service between Port Glasgow, Greenock and Helensburgh where Bell owned Bath's Hotel. On her maiden commercial run on Thursday, 6th August 1812 *Comet* sailed the 20 miles from Port Glasgow to Broomielaw in three and a half hours. She was not speedy – her normal time between Greenock and the Broomielaw was five hours although one cynical passenger is reported as saying she took nearer seven, three of which were spent on a shoal. Such was the pace of development in those thrusting, heady days that only a few months after her commercial launch, *Comet* faced competition from other steamboats. There was the 49-feet long *Elizabeth*, larger, faster and more powerful than *Comet*. Flat-bottomed to slide over the shoals of the Clyde, *Elizabeth* could travel from Glasgow to Greenock in only three hours but, for all her apparent superiority, she had a chequered life and faded from history soon after being transferred to the Mersey.

Comet struggled gamely to compete. After finding the short steep seas of the Forth unfriendly, Bell decided on a major gamble and in doing so made history. His Hebridean service to Oban marked the first ever regular ocean service for a steam vessel, but in December 1820 *Comet* was wrecked by the disturbance known as the *Dorus Mhor* between Jura and Scarba. It was a disaster that ended Bell's dream but only the beginning of an era. Steam power was about to enter the mainstream of shipping.

Steamships were venturing onto the oceans all round Britain. In 1815 the *Thames* sailed from Glasgow to Dublin and Lands End before beginning a service between London and Margate. In a squally day in 1816 *Elise* became the first steamship to cross the English Channel and three years later *Waterloo*, a schooner-rigged steamer, started a regular ferry service between Liverpool and Belfast.

In 1819 the United States sent *Savannah*, a sailing packet with a 90 horse power horizontal engine to challenge the Atlantic. Built in New York and complete with cleverly collapsible paddle wheels, *Savannah* crossed the Atlantic from Georgia to Liverpool in an historic 29 days. However, although she picked up boiler coal in Kinsale in Ireland she only used her engine for 80 hours of her crossing, so *Savannah* was less a steamship than a sailing vessel with an auxiliary engine, and on her return to the United States her engines were dismantled. Nevertheless, and quite understandably, her sailing date of 22nd May is National Maritime Day in the United States.

Two years later HMS *Rising Star* was the first steam warship to cross the Atlantic, but again she used her sails for the bulk of the voyage. The steam revolution continued apace with more than 40 steamship companies registered in London by 1825, and various claims made for the first Atlantic crossing by steam. The paddle steamer *Royal William* certainly crossed from Quebec to the Isle of Wight but she may have used wind power more than steam. However, there is no doubt about the crossings of *Sirius* and *Great Western*.

In 1838 the British & American Steam Navigation Company hoped to make the first all-steam Atlantic crossing, but when the company building their ship encountered financial problems, they had to charter another. *Sirius* was a Leith-built, wooden-hulled side-wheeler that normally operated in the Irish Sea. At 703 tons in weight, she left London on 28th March, picked up passengers in Cork and on 4th April headed into the Atlantic. Her 40 courageous passengers are the forgotten guinea pigs in this experiment, as with 450 tons of coal on board and travelling solely by steam power, *Sirius* slogged across the Atlantic to arrive in New York on 23rd April. She had consumed coal at such a desperate rate that only 15 tons remained, not enough for a full day's sailing, and had to burn both cabin furniture and a spare mast to keep steam up in her boiler. Yet *Sirius* was the first ship positively to cross the Atlantic from east to west with no propulsion other than steam.

Great Western was an entirely different case. Much larger than *Sirius* at 1320 tons and 236 feet in length, she had been designed specifically for the Atlantic crossing by Isambard Kingdom Brunel. With her four boilers and the two cylinder Maudslay side-lever engine installed, interior space in *Great Western* was restricted but there was no doubting her style. It was 8th April 1838 when she steamed out of Bristol, to thrust across the Atlantic at an impressively constant 8 knots, but with only seven passengers occupying the space reserved for 24. On 23rd April, the same day as *Sirius* but a little later, *Great Western* throbbed into New York harbour. She had been 15 days on the voyage and had 20 tons of coal left. *Great Western* was to become the first steamship to provide a regular service across the Atlantic.

The factor of refuelling was a constant preoccupation of the early steamship designers, for fuel storage space had obviously never been a problem for wind-powered ships. The trick was to provide a ship that could carry enough fuel to enable her to make long voyages while retaining sufficient cargo space to make her commercially viable. The problem was illustrated by the July crossing of another *Royal William,* which was so overladen with coal that the passengers could wash their hands in the Atlantic simply by stretching over the bulwark.

In 1840 the British government agreed to subsidise a steam packet service for carrying the Royal Mail across the Atlantic, and the contract was awarded to the British & North American Mail Packet Company. Three farsighted men had founded this company; David McIver, George Burns (who already ran a line between Glasgow and

Photograph of an engraving of the Great Western *passing Portishead on her maiden voyage to New York in 1838 (after a painting by Joseph Walter).* Reproduced by permission of the SS Great Britain Project, Bristol.

Liverpool), and a man from Nova Scotia whose name was to ring around the world – Samuel Cunard. The best- remembered of their four, near identical Atlantic steamers was RMS *Britannia*, a wooden-built paddle steamer of 207 feet and 1156 tons. On her first return trip she carried more than 60 passengers from Boston to Liverpool in 15 days, and was welcomed into the Mersey by massed crowds and a thunderous salute of cannon. On another occasion in 1844 when ice blocked *Britannia* in harbour, the stout people of Boston swarmed out in force and hacked a seven-mile long, 100-foot wide passage to the open sea. Government subsidies of up to 20% of their operating costs enabled the British steamship companies to compete favourably with the hard-driven United States' sailing packets, although the factor of travelling on a steamship may have encouraged some passengers. People have always felt the need to be fashionable.

Much of the success of the Cunard vessels was due to the Clydeside engineering skills. The same David Napier who had created the boiler for *Comet* moved into shipbuilding and ship design in a big way. Interestingly, on her maiden voyage to Dublin, his *Rob Roy* carried Charles McIntosh, the inventor of waterproof cloth. Perhaps the voyage encouraged his researches for *Rob Roy* steamed into a south-easterly gale. After the success of *Rob Roy*, Napier's experiments in the Firth of Clyde were to alter the basics of ship design for more than a century. He realised that steamships and sailing vessels reacted differently to the sea, with steamships operating more efficiently with a sharp bow compared to the more traditionally bluff, rounded bow of a sailing vessel. This simple innovation greatly improved the sailing performance of Napier's vessels.

'Bristol-built, Great Britain *was the first tranatlantic liner to be built of iron.'* Great Britain *in the Great Western Dock at Bristol.* Reproduced by permission of the SS Great Britain Project, Bristol.

As a young boy, Robert Napier, a cousin of David, was nearly pressed into the Navy and to prevent any repetition he was indentured to his blacksmith father. Robert proved a brilliant craftsman, with his *Eclipse* of 1826 even better than *Rob Roy* and by 1846 he was producing vessels capable of sailing at 20 knots. In the 1830s he engineered 280 horse power side lever engines that were in advance of anything else in the world and he soon became advisor to the British & North American Royal Mail Steam Packet Company. It was Robert Napier who produced *Britannia* and yet there were still reservations about steam power. Although a single steamship could make two voyages for a sailing ship's one, they were three times as expensive to build and their cargo capacity was restricted by carrying coal. Sailing ships remained more efficient as cargo carriers until further improvements reduced the size of marine engines.

Napier's Cunard ships had scarcely settled into their regular service when Brunel again introduced another of his specialities to the Atlantic. Bristol-built, *Great Britain* was the first transatlantic liner to be built of iron and the first to be propelled by screws rather than paddles. At over 3000 tons she was large, and her 1500 horse power engines put little *Comet,* built just 30 years previously, into perspective. As well as her 60 first-class passengers in elegant staterooms, *Great Britain* carried a host of steerage travellers on her first voyage to New York in 1845. However she was not a lucky ship and ran aground in Dundrum Bay and it took a man from Wick in Caithness, James Bremner, to rescue her.

Not until 1850 did the United States attempt to regain their once-secure dominion over the Atlantic. That year Edward Collins, backed by a colossal annual government subsidy of $385,000, constructed four steamships for the Atlantic routes. The Collins Line *Atlantic, Pacific, Baltic* and *Arctic* appeared technically more advanced than their British rivals and were certainly faster, but either the workmanship was faulty or the Atlantic was unkind, for both *Arctic* and *Pacific* were sunk. This disaster discouraged the United States' government into withdrawing its subsidy and a steam-powered Britannia had wrested the Atlantic trident back from Uncle Sam. But was it a permanent gain or only a loan?

Chapter 16

Hunters of the Icy Waters

*'There is no justice or injustice on board a ship, my lad.
There are only two things. Duty and Mutiny – mind that.
All that you are ordered to do is duty. All that you refuse to do is mutiny.'*
Advice of an experienced Greenlandman of Friendship to the
12 year old First Voyager, Robert Eastwick

Given the stark choice of eat or be eaten, early humanity took to hunting with all the enthusiasm necessary to survive and by the time they learned how to travel on the sea they were proficient in hunting skills. It is unlikely that whaling originated in any specific area; probably any whale that was driven onto any shore would be hacked into eatable gobbets, yet the Basque people may have been first to hunt the whales in their natural element. For two golden centuries whale hunting boomed along the Biscay coasts as the mediaeval Basque seamen endured the storms of the Bay to bring home the blubber. Their prey was the Right whale, so named because *Balaena glacialis* is one of the easiest to catch, slow moving and so docile that soon numbers in the Bay were declining and the whalers had to venture further out into the broad reaches of the Atlantic. For that they had to abandon their small open boats and adopt the more seaworthy craft that were being developed.

It was the 16th century before European mariners pursued the whales much further afield but with the discovery of the Banks of Newfoundland the whales along the eastern coast of North America were being hunted with the same expertise that had virtually exterminated them in European waters. Yet another whaling ground was presented to the avaricious Europeans when the Dutchman Willens Barents discovered Spitzbergen, but before they battered north the English hired a number of Basques to teach them the skills of the hunter. Once they had mastered the basics, the audacious English claimed a monopoly on this Dutch discovery and for a while the English Muscovy Company contested the whaling grounds with Dutch, Basques and Danes as well as their fellow Englishmen from Hull. It was a free for all in the bitter austerity of the north.

Spitzbergen became a boom island as the Dutch dominated by virtue of greater numbers. Their prefabricated town of Smeerenburg, or Blubbertown, was accurately if not evocatively named as the stink of huge vats mingled with that of sweating men who laboured to reduce monumental whales to marketable commodities. Smeerenburg would be a noisy, bustling place, filled with the raucous voices of thousands of northern men while the Spitzbergen crags contrasted starkly with the beauty of the aurora borealis. After a decade or so the ravages of hundreds of soft-iron harpoons diminished the hunting potential of the Spitzbergen seas and the whalers sailed their ships westward, towards Greenland. They supplied a growing demand for the whale oil that fuelled the lamps of ladies' boudoirs and the crusies of cottages while the baleen, or whalebone, that curtained the gaping mouth of the mammal, was heated into flexibility before being formed into stays and springs, needles and netting and whips. All the things deemed necessary for progressive civilisation.

By the mid-18th century British whalers seriously challenged the Dutch as Britannia hoped to add a harpoon to her trident. In 1733 the British government offered a bounty of 20 shillings per ton for every whaling ship of 200 tons or more. As few shipowners thought the reward justified the certain risk, the bounty was increased to first 30 shillings then, in 1749, to 40 shillings. Only then did British whalers sally forth in numbers; profit was a healthy reason for slaughtering the whales and the people who invested the money and reaped the bounty were seldom those who dared the bitter seas of the North. The British government was responding to the burgeoning Industrial Revolution, for whale oil smoothed the clattering machinery that controlled the lives of labourers and created profit for the few. Oil was also needed for the lamps that lit the best streets of expanding cities, making life more difficult for the hungry footpads and illuminating the path of the respectable, the godly and the factory owner.

The whalers scoured the iced waters around Greenland for the bowhead whale, the *Balaena mysticetus* that the whalers termed the Greenland Right whale, and whose demise ensured an average 100 barrels of oil. During the opening decades of the 18th century whalers rounded the ominously named Cape Farewell at the southern tip of Greenland and pushed northward into the Davis Strait. When they found waters that teemed with whales, British, Dutch and colonial craft eased into the creeks and indentations of Baffin Bay and Lancaster Sound, mustered off the rock formation of the Devil's Thumb and slaughtered the mighty mammals with a ferocity only sustainable by western technology and consumer demand. They were hard men, these Greenlandmen, but they saw nothing immoral in their actions, for morals are only applicable in their own epoch and this was the age of the hunter. It was April when the whaling ships, blubber boats to their detractors, staggered out of their British ports, from Hull and Whitby, London and Aberdeen, Dundee or Peterhead or Leith. Most carried a contingent of 'first voyagers' who commonly spent the first few days amusing the seasoned Arctic seamen by vomiting over the bulwarks and wishing they had remained at home. Between 1820 and 1880 Government regulations insisted that each British whaler carried at least five of these 'green men' in order to receive the bounty.

'It was April when the whaling ships staggered out of their British ports...' Whaler Eclipse *in the Arctic, 1880.* Reproduced by permission of Aberdeenshire Heritage.

The idea was to form a reserve of men from whom any future Arctic expeditions could be drawn, for men still dreamed of the Northwest Passage.

Life on a whaler was rough. Of all shipping, that of a Greenlandman had a reputation matched only by the packet rats. Foul language was expected, wild behaviour was normal, bullying and fighting just part of life, but still some men returned year after arduous year. There was at least one British whaling man who never missed a season for 60 years and died at sea aged 75 . But all seamen lived in conditions that could only be described as sub-standard. As late as 1906 the Merchant Shipping Act increased living space to each seaman to just 120 cubic feet, which was less than half that allowed to a convicted prisoner.

All the same the blubber boats left gaily, with the ribbons fluttering from their rigging, a memory of the previous night's party that left sore-headed men on board and thoughtful women on shore. Then it was north to Orkney or Shetland to augment their crew with the boatmen of the Isles. There would be boisterous scenes as the 'southern boys' surged ashore, and while the fiddlers scraped jaunty tunes in the overflowing whisky shops, special constables quietened the inevitable disturbances and many an island woman found a man to warm her bed for the night. After that it was sterner work with the whalers slogging westward, following the 58th parallel to avoid the fogs, icebergs and foulness of Cape Farewell. This was Atlantic sailing, with freezing spray coating the decks, glistening in the rigging and bidding a bitter welcome to the shocked first voyagers. But there was worse to come.

Once into the Davis Strait an experienced man was sent to the chilling loneliness of the crow's nest to seek whales and icebergs. Ice could be lethal, from the massive bergs whose radiance could be seen on the darkest night to the low 'washing pieces' that hid behind the white surge of surf. All the experienced Greenlandmen were acutely aware of the wind, for a northerly gale could thrust a berg deep into the vitals of even the most strongly-built ship. And they were strongly built, two layers of oak, a third at the bow and further reinforcements of internal oak beams for the strains and shocks that were an inevitable part of the whaler's existence. They might be ugly ships, bluff-nosed, broad and stout, but they were purpose-built for their task of probing in the worst conditions to be found even in the North Atlantic.

And even here there was the possibility of a kill. The man aloft would scan the sea for the spout of a whale, or for the dark smear of plankton that provided the whales with food. Men were on edge, hoping for a record catch, with the old stagers regaling the green men with tales of famous ships of the past as they treated the brutal cold with disdain. There might be other whalers to watch, or an encounter with the indigenous Inuit, or a polar bear lumbering over the ice. Already the small, fragile-looking whaleboats were suspended from davits over the grey water, but the hands knocked back their grog and looked for the whales. They were paid by results so the more kills, the higher their wages and the happier their wives when they returned home.

Some of these whalers became rightly famous, including the Whitby man William Scoresby. The son of a whaler, Scoresby first went to sea at the age of ten, and when his father signed him into a Lerwick school he slipped away and persuaded a boatman to row him to his father's ship. He may have longed for the security of the classroom when *Dundee* was trapped by ice, and the catch of only three whales must have been discouraging. Three years later Scoresby was officially apprenticed to his father. For the next seven years he was bound to obey his father's lawful commands, swore not to 'commit Fornication nor contract matrimony' nor to 'play at Cards, Dice, Tables or any other unlawful Games whereby his said Master may have any loss'. Furthermore he was to avoid 'taverns nor playhouses'. Considering that whalers were renowned as the 'wild southern boys', some of these restrictions seem interesting but Scoresby, like countless other young men, thrived rather than survived.

When he was 16 Scoresby was chief mate of *Resolution* when she reached a new furthest north of 81° 30' north, and perhaps the experience encouraged him to explore as much as hunt the whales. That same momentous year he met his future wife and his comment that there was '... no class of men that enjoys and appreciate so much the

Crew of S.S. HOPE—Eira Relief and Search Expedition, 1882.

'Wild Southern Boys'. The crew of the S.S. Hope *searching for the* Eire *that had been crushed in the ice in 1882.* Reproduced by permission of Aberdeenshire Heritage.

society of the softer sex, as sailors' tends to alleviate the rough image of whalers. But perhaps Scoresby was different; about the same time he decided to go to Edinburgh University, noticing several differences between Scottish and English cultures. 'Christmas seems here to be very little notice taken of ... the people here attend the churches very regular...'.

After a spell in the Royal Navy, where the brutality of some naval officers disgusted him, Scoresby returned to studying and whaling. On his 21st birthday he moved to Greenock to take command of *Resolution*, but his later career diverged from that of a hunter. As well as exploring the coast of Greenland, Scoresby published a scientific account of the Arctic, became ordained and studied terrestrial magnetism in Australia. He was a very deep thinking wild southern boy.

As the Davis Strait became hunted out the whalers were forced to seek fresh grounds in more dangerous seas. They learned the geography of the coasts, that the western side of the Strait was scoured by a cold current from the north and that south-western Baffin Bay was impassable until the middle of summer. Instead they followed the warmer north-flowing current up the eastern Strait to where the Devil's upright Thumb provided a constantly sardonic assurance of tribulations ahead. Hunting had often been a perilous occupation, especially for the prey, but successful whale hunts of the past had ensured that each ensuing generation had worse conditions to work in, fewer whales from which to make their living and worse weather to endure. Some of the weather in the icy north was terrible. In 1815 *Esk* was embayed by ice in a storm 'that was truly terrific' while the swells hid the mastheads of surrounding ships. There was always the ice, the bone-chilling cold, the possibility of frostbite and death, but despite such conditions the whalers sailed north. They were Greenlandmen and this was all the life they knew.

If they were skilful, or lucky, the lookout would point to the spout of a whale, bellow the longed-for 'Thar she blows!' and the entire ship would erupt into mad activity. Notwithstanding appearances this was organised chaos as the boat's crew clattered into the whaleboats that eased on greased davits into the water. On average a whaler carried six whaleboats and the boat-header in charge of the oarsmen had an extremely responsible position. With all six oars muffled he manoeuvred his boat behind the whale, with one of the foremost oarsmen ready to lift the heavy harpoon and strike. While the best harpoonists could slash the tendons of a surfaced whale's flukes so it could neither dive nor swim, most thrust the barbed iron weapon into the great bulk of the beast. Muscle power and soft iron against the animal's frantic desire to escape meant that not every victory went to the hunter. The boatmen had to retreat as soon as the harpoon was thrust in, for the flukes of the whale's flailing tail could pulp a man or smash a fragile boat. There were other equally ghastly forms of death. The harpoon line could tangle round a man, amputating an arm, a leg or a head; the whale could tow the boat in what American whalers knew as a 'Nantucket sleigh ride' until it became lost in the icy, foggy seas. If the rewards of whaling were high, so were the perils.

Even if the whalers were saved from all this, life was hard. Other whaleboats joined the first until a dozen harpoons transfixed the whale, a dozen lines stretched to half a dozen boats, but still the task was incomplete. A whale could remain submerged for half an hour or a lot longer but, once it surfaced, the boat-header would plunge a lance deep into its body. This killing was a messy business, with blood bursting from the blowhole of the whale to spread across the uncaring surface of the sea, but the boat-header was not convinced it was dead until he had thrust a lance through its eye.

The tow back to the parent ship could be both exhilarating and exhausting, and the men would chant some repetitive work song as they pulled, but there was still work remaining. While some men hacked whalebone from the head, others used great flensing knives to strip the blubber from the body. All the time a cloud of petrels covered the ship, squawking in a raucous background chorus to the sounds of butchery and the sea. Blood, grease and fat smeared every surface of the ship but the men were happy; the death of the whale meant they had earned money for their wives and families and publicans. After the crew had taken what civilisation demanded, the remnants of the whale were discarded. These stripped and ugly corpses, known as the kreng, could

Built on the lines of a Dundee whaler, Discovery *is a reminder of the whaling ships of the past.* Photograph by author.

remain along the edge of the ice, pathetic monuments to man's constant pursuit of profit.

Towards the end of the season the whalers changed tactics, hunting around the ragged coasts of eastern Canada. Lookouts on the headlands replaced the man in the crow's nest, but the same little whaleboats pushed out into the same appalling danger to hunt the whale in the same bloody style. This was tiring work and the whaling men were glad when the September ice forced the hunting ships back across the Atlantic. Some stayed for just one more whale and some stayed a little too long. As early as August in 1866 the Hull whaler *Diana* was gripped by ice in Pond Inlet in northern Baffin Island. When her consort, the steam whaler *Intrepid* crashed south to safety, *Diana*'s surgeon, Dr Charles Smith, wrote a despairing diary entry 'Our last chance of succour or of safety has now gone'. Given a choice of staying put or joining the pack ice that drifted south towards warmer waters, Captain Graville chose the latter. Life was harsh on *Diana* – food was rationed, the forecastle temperature sunk to 30° below freezing and by November, as *Diana* slowly slid south, it seemed the ice would crush them completely. 'This is a dreadful life' wrote Smith, listening to the thick oak creaking with the tremendous pressure outside. In December a storm opened the seams in *Diana*'s hull and surrounded her with ice, and any Christmas festivities were ruined by the death of Captain Graville.

When the New Year opened with *Diana* being circled by a black raven with a bracelet of ice around its neck, the superstitious – and whalers were amongst the most superstitious of all seamen – might have thought this an omen of bad fortune. Others, the better read, might have seen a message from the long-gone Norsemen. Ravens were Odin's birds, and these northern seas had seen Odin's seamen.

Perhaps the raven had brought a message, but more likely it was poor rations that caused scurvy to strike. Smith noted the tender gums, the outbreak of red spots, but he could do little to prevent the first death on 13th February. Before the month ended most of the crew were suffering, but March brought some hope as the Labrador Current eased them south. Even so, not until 17th March, St Patrick's Day, could *Diana* struggle free of the ice. All that remained was her voyage across the Atlantic.

In earlier years there had been other dangers for the whalers as the Royal Navy press-gangs targeted the Greenlandmen. The result can be imagined as the most powerful navy in the world tangled with tough seamen who were unwilling to fight for king and country. In 1798 His Majesty's sloop-of-war *Nautilus*, aided by the boats of the guard ship *Nonsuch*, attacked the Hull whaler *Blenheim*. Two men died in the ensuing battle of grapeshot, flensing irons and musketry as *Blenheim* beat off the press. It was not only the Royal Navy which learned that it was unwise to antagonise the Greenlandmen. In 1794 a French privateer captured *Raith* of Hull off the Shetland Islands, placed a prize crew of 16 Frenchmen on board and transferred the bulk of *Raith*'s crew to the privateer. Only the mate and a single seaman were left on board the whaler, but they waited until the prize crew celebrated too much, threw nine drunken Frenchmen into an open boat, nailed the others below and sailed *Raith* into Lerwick.

Not only whalers hunted in the north. The first European conception of North America was a continent protected by deep forests in which roamed a multitude of fur-bearing animals. The 17th century fishermen of the Gulf of St Lawrence traded for beaver furs, which were perfect as a covering for the felt hats that were currently fashionable in Europe. For decades Dutch and French disputed the trade, with their Iroquois and Huron allies clashing with tomahawk and arrow so that Europeans could flaunt a stylish hat. When the French explorers Groselliers and Radisson braved the Great Lakes wilderness, they realised that the Huron were merely middlemen for the Cree, but their attempt at private enterprise with this more northern tribe resulted in a hefty fine from French officialdom. However, if the French were unwilling to trade with the Cree, the English could try.

In June 1668 *Eaglet*, on loan from the Royal Navy, and the privately-funded 50-ton ketch *Nonsuch* hoisted sail on the Thames and steered for the furs of Canada, but when a storm forced *Eaglet* back only *Nonsuch* arrived at Hudson Bay. On 29th September she dropped anchor in James Bay. Groselliers, called Mr Gooseberry by the Englishmen, threw up a cabin and traded so profitably with the Indians that *Nonsuch* carried nearly £1400 worth of fur in her initial cargo, enough to convince the king to issue a royal charter. On 2nd May 1670 King Charles, without consulting the current occupiers, granted most of Ontario and Quebec, all of Saskatchewan and Manitoba, the southern section of Alberta and a sizeable slice of the Northwest Territories to 'The Governor and Company of Adventurers of England trading into Hudson's Bay'. It was the foundation of what was to become one of the most successful companies in the world.

While Europeans were ravaging the Davis Strait and the Hudson Bay Company was ruling an area many times larger than most countries, their southern neighbours were also indulging in successful whaling. While Martha's Vineyard and New London were major whale hunting ports, Nantucket was probably the busiest in the world. In the early 1760s that island possessed 40 of New England's 80 whalers, who hunted the seas and sold their catch in London before returning home. By the beginning of the next decade, as the colonial grievances were about to burst into a war that turned the world upside down, Nantucket, whose population was only about 6000, had around 125 whaling ships. Similar to the British whalers, they were around 90 tons in weight and sturdy but, whereas the British crews were paid a minimum wage plus a percentage, the New Englanders earned only if they made a catch. Unlike British ships, the New England whalers were more likely to sail south than north, probing into the Pacific for their prey. They hunted the sperm whale, whose intestines could contain the ambergris that was made into perfume, and if Herman Melville immortalised one fictitious captain, then there were many others whose exploits deserve to be better remembered. By supreme irony, it was a returning Nantucket whaler that carried the tea chests that were thrown into Boston harbour during the tea party.

Like other nautical areas of what became the United States, Nantucket was severely disrupted by the revolution. By 1783 the island could float a mere 16 ships, while over 1100 Nantucket whalers had been killed, captured or incapacitated by enemy action. Many had fought in the privateers, some with John Paul Jones in *Ranger* but the end result, however victorious for the new republic, was sad for the legendary island of whalers. There were conflicts too, between British and American whalers as they clashed on half-known islands at the edge of the world, but by 1814 the Federal Navy had cleared out most of the British whalers to make the Southern Seas a United States' lake.

When the harbour bar at Nantucket prevented the larger whalers from entering, New Bedford became the whaling capital of the western hemisphere. By the late 1850s there were 300 United States whalers based in New Bedford and the Southern Ocean knew the twang of New England, the red stripes of Old Glory and the thud of an iron harpoon. Over half the world's whaling ships hailed from New Bedford and, when not hunting, the whalers created scrimshaw work that reveals the incredible creativity of working men.

Back in the north, by 1860 steam power was quickly replacing sail, reducing the risk of ships being becalmed and enabling them to thrust aside the smaller pieces of ice. It was Sir John Ross, one of the Discovery men who sought the Northwest Passage, who first introduced steam to the Arctic and although his *Victory* was anything but victorious, the idea caught on. The success of screw steamers in the search for the missing explorer Franklin showed the potential of steam. When the Greenlandmen realised that *Pioneer*, with her 60 horse power engine, could smash through impressively thick ice, they experimented with steam whalers. The earliest of these vessels had only auxiliary steam power, but by the 1860s steam whalers were as commonplace as the new rocket-gun which replaced the hard muscle that thrust the harpoonist's lance. Technology continued; in 1865 the Norwegian Svend Foyn invented a swivel-mounted harpoon gun for the Arctic while New Englanders used a darting gun that fired a bomb straight inside the whale. With innovations like these it was hardly surprising that the whales were vanishing from the seas.

Whatever the changes, a whaler's job was to catch whales and his profit depended both on his success and the market price for whale oil. By the 1860s whale oil was competing against petroleum which eased it out of the market place within 40 years. Whalebone remained in demand, although major progress in the chemical industry led to the introduction of plastics that usurped even baleen's position. It is interesting to speculate whether moral indignation at the practice of whale hunting would have been so vociferous if plastic and petroleum had not been developed. Perhaps the morals of any age can be reflected by the chosen lifestyle of the majority of people, but there can be no argument with the raw, wild courage of the hunters of the icy waters.

Chapter 17

The Convoys

'With joyful pride we contemplate this latest deed of our navy.
It will not be the last.'
Kolnische Volkszeitung, the Catholic Centre Party
newspaper after the torpedoing of Lusitania.

For decades Europe had been splitting into armed camps as tension over colonies, trade and nationalism resulted in a build-up of political and military insecurity. In August 1914 the murder of an Austrian archduke exploded the Continent into war; the central powers of the German and Austro-Hungarian Empires on one side, the Allies of the British, French and Russian Empires on the other. From the uttermost edge of Russia to the placid shires of England, men clamoured to fight for their country, while great grey warships sat uneasy at their moorings or steamed into suddenly-hostile seas. After nearly a century free from major naval warfare, the Atlantic seamen of 1914 had only a partial understanding of what lay ahead. This First World War would be like no other, with few Nelsonian ship-to-ship contests and no galaxy of immediately recognisable heroes. Not that there was a shortage of courage, but a different sort of bravery was required to face a different type of warfare. Rather than the hours-long madness of a gunnery contest, seamen would have to endure the constant anxiety of being hunted by an unseen adversary. The major threat to the merchant mariner came from neither privateer nor battleship, but from beneath the waves.

As far back as 1620 a Dutchman, Cornelis Drebbel, rowed the first known submarine beneath the Thames and it was an American, David Bushnell, who created the first submarine warship. Technical improvements continued throughout the 19th century, so by 1914 the German U-boats, diesel-powered and equipped with periscopes and self-propelled torpedoes, were formidable engines of war. Obviously they had limitations, their thin hulls and lack of range restricted their use to shallow or coastal waters, but while the middle of the Atlantic was relatively safe, the approaches to the British Isles were severely threatened.

Through these approaches, either threading the intricacies of the Channel to London or the south coast ports, or rounding Ireland to the Severn, Mersey or Clyde, came the shipping of the world's largest trading network. If trade was the lifeblood of Empire, the approaches combined to form the jugular, and the Admiralty was aware that the Imperial German Navy could thrust with the assassin's stiletto of the submarine. Already the Navy had responded to the German threat by building a major new base at Scapa Flow in the Orkney Islands and a smaller base at Rosyth in the Firth of Forth. Now the fleets faced each other across the steep grey waves of the North Sea, national flags flapping belligerently at the stern of armoured dreadnoughts with a killing capacity greater than anything ever imagined before.

'Jellicoe was the only man on either side who could lose the war in an afternoon'.

With the Royal Navy superior in both numbers and gunpower there was little possibility that the German High Seas Fleet could defeat them in a gun-to-gun encounter. Even so, Admiral Jellicoe was not prepared to rashly seek battle. As Churchill said, 'Jellicoe was the only man on either side who could lose the war in an afternoon'. If the German Navy had won a major battle they would have swept British shipping off the seas, not with the stiletto of the submarine, but by the headsman's axe of the dreadnought. By remaining in Scapa and Rosyth, the Royal Navy virtually restricted the German surface fleet to its bases and immediately halted German trans-oceanic trade. By retaining a fleet-in-being, Jellicoe not only began the blockade that eventually strangled Germany, but also compelled the Germans to depend on the hidden submarine to whittle away Allied shipping. The sheer preponderance of British sea power encouraged the Germans to entice Neptune's trident to the dark underwater of the U-boat.

Not that the Germans did not try to use their surface vessels. German and British fleets clashed five times in the first two years of the war. In 1914 the British raided the German base at Heligoland and sunk three ships, but the German Admiral von Spee won the sunset battle of Coronel in the Pacific, only to be all but annihilated by Admiral Sturdee off the Falkland Islands. The British Admiral Beatty led his battle cruisers to victory at the battle of Dogger Bank and at the end of May 1916 the main battle fleets faced each other at Jutland. The original German plan was to lure Jellicoe into a trap of submarines and mines, but battles seldom go according to plan. The submarines withdrew as their fuel became exhausted, so Admiral Scheer used Hipper's battle cruiser squadron as a lure for only part of the British fleet. Instead Jellicoe, Evan-Thomas and Beatty led out the entire Grand Fleet.

From being the hunters, the Germans should have been the hunted, but treacherous winds affected the British signalling and when the rival battle cruisers sighted each other too soon they immediately opened fire. The giant grey ships battered each other, with the British silhouetted against the afternoon sun and the Germans proving excellent gunners. With three ships sunk, three remaining against five of Hipper's Germans, Beatty gave the 1916 version of Nelson's 'England expects …' 'There seems to be something wrong with our damned ships today. Turn two points to port'. That was, nearer to the enemy. However the crisis had already passed as Evan-Thomas led his force of powerful battleships into the fight. From then on Jutland degenerated into a running retreat punctuated by desperately darting destroyers and columns of smoke from damaged ships. Scheer fled safely back to port, after inflicting more casualties than he endured and, save for one abortive sortie later that year, never led his ships into battle again.

Also above the surface were AMCs, armed merchant cruisers, passenger liners or merchant vessels that had been converted into warships by the addition of guns and naval seamen. One of the most effective German AMCs was the 4788-ton ex-banana boat *Moewe*, that sank 27 ships in the Atlantic and for the whole of December 1916 prevented Allied troopships from leaving West African ports. *Greif* was less successful. Disguised as a neutral Norwegian, she left the Elbe in February 1916, but only managed two days steaming before the British AMC *Alcantara* eased over the horizon and challenged her. Two ex-merchant ships fighting for their country on the cold Atlantic Ocean. At a range of less than a mile the armed merchantmen exchanged torpedoes and gunfire until both were damaged and the *Greif* sunk by a second British AMC, *Andes*. Yet for all the skill of the German seamen, the occasional foray by surface vessels could only nibble at the huge volume of British trade and their nemesis was always sailing beneath the White Ensign. What the Royal Navy could see, it could sink, but surface seamen could not see beneath the waves, where lurked the long lean U-boats.

As early as 3rd September 1914, U.21 proved the killing capacity of the submarine by torpedoing the British cruiser HMS *Pathfinder*. When U.9 followed this success by sinking four more warships the Admiralty began the long, painful search for an effective countermeasure. However, it was the Russians who made the first naval breakthrough when on 13th October they recovered the naval signal book from the clutch of a German corpse on the grounded cruiser *Madgeburg*. As staunch Allies, they forwarded the book to London, where the Admiralty decoded it. The ability to understand German naval radio messages enabled the Royal Navy to trace their ship movements, which was to be one advantage in a naval war about to turn very bitter indeed. At the end of October the captain of U.24 sighted and torpedoed what he thought was a troopship. In fact he had sunk the French passenger steamer *Amiral Ganteaume*. It appeared that the Germans intended to use their underwater weapon with some ruthlessness.

But Britain could be equally ruthless. When she signed the Second Hague

Convention of 1907 that outlawed the laying of mines in international waters, the full implications of 20th century warfare were not realised. Mines were even more indiscriminate than torpedoes, designed to destroy without warning or conscience. Yet as soon as Germany littered the North Sea with these merciless killers, Britain retaliated with minefields of her own, then declared the entire North Sea a British military area. With each sunken ship a drop of her children's blood, Britannia proved capable of wielding her trident with pure maternal fury. Yet still the men at the Admiralty were perplexed how to counter the menace of the U-boats.

By international law, submarines had to issue a warning to every merchant vessel that they intended to sink and were obliged to allow the passengers and crew into lifeboats, or another place of safety. Early in 1915, U-boats torpedoed a brace of British merchant ships without warning, and the chancellor of Germany promptly announced that Germany had extended submarine warfare to any shipping carrying munitions or supplies to any Allied country. Shortly after the German defeat at Dogger Bank, the chancellor proclaimed that the waters around the British Isles were now an 'area of war'. While the United States protested, declaring this action 'an indefensible violation of neutral rights', Britain countered by claiming the right to intercept all shipping that might be carrying supplies into Germany. The loose blockade of the central powers was tightening.

But if shipping was important to Germany, it was vital to Britain and the stiletto thrusts of the U-boats were dangerously effective. Not all the submarines' victims were from the Allied powers. When U.28 torpedoed *Falaba* in March 1915, among the 104 dead was Leon Thrasher, the first American casualty of the war. Merchant ships, however, could sometimes strike back. When threatened by a surfaced U-boat, the Great Eastern steamer *Brussels* reverted to ancient Phoenician fighting methods and attempted to ram. The submarine dived to safety. Notwithstanding such isolated incidents, the toll of British and Allied shipping continued to mount. Statistics can only conceal the suffering of the people involved, civilian seamen and passengers suddenly torpedoed by an unseen submarine or sitting in an open boat watching their ship shot to pieces. Most sinkings are forgotten, sad ships sacrificed to a campaign that has been overshadowed by battles such as Mons, Ypres and the Somme, but in May 1915 the death of one vessel shocked the world.

Captain Walther Schwieger was a veteran submarine commander and his U.20 was hunting off Ireland for British prey. When the Cunarder *Lusitania* came into his sights he loosed a torpedo, sinking the giant liner in 18 minutes. Of the 1198 deaths, 128 were United States' citizens but, although American public opinion was outraged, President Wilson was not prepared to abandon his neutrality. Like so much else in that horrific war, *Lusitania* was a disaster that should never have happened. All merchant captains knew to steer clear of headlands which were notoriously popular with hunting submarines, but despite half a dozen Admiralty warnings of 'submarine activity off south coast of Ireland', Captain William Turner steered a straight course and kept close to land. Schwieger could hardly have made an easier kill. Although Germany issued an official apology, the gloating of their press was possibly a more accurate reflection of German public opinion.

But *Lusitania* was only one of nearly two score liners sunk in those four murderous years. Another was the White Star *Arabic*, torpedoed in the Irish Sea in August 1915. Shortly after, U.27 attacked the steamer *Nicosian*, carrying New Orleans mules, but failed to register a battered-looking vessel named *Baralong* that limped along under the Stars and Stripes. As U.27 prepared to fire, *Baralong* lowered her American ensign, raised the White Ensign and discarded the camouflage that had concealed two guns. When she opened fire, a dozen submariners leapt into the sea and swam to *Nicosian*. Believing that this was the submarine that had sunk *Arabic*, *Baralong*'s furious Royal Marines shot six of the fleeing men, hunted the remainder to the engine room of *Nicosian* and killed them.

After the sinking of *Arabic*, the Admiralty decided that British merchant ships should be armed, but *Baralong* was an example of the British fight back. Knowing that U-boats usually only torpedoed larger vessels, the Admiralty sent out a number of small merchant ships, each carrying concealed armament and a cargo of timber to increase their buoyancy if they were hit. These vessels were known as Q-ships. When a U-boat surfaced, the Q-ship crew lured it close with pretended panic, then raised the White Ensign and unleashed their firepower in a devastating counter ambush. In all, Q-ships sank seven U-boats and Captain Gordon Campbell won the Victoria Cross, but by 1917 few U-boats were willing to fight on the surface.

Other methods of anti-submarine warfare were attempted. Dazzle paint broke up the image of merchant vessels and 'protected approach areas' were meant to provide a secure cone of sea outside main British ports. Sloops and destroyers patrolled these cones, but when U-boats learned the secret codes that relayed the safe areas to merchant ships they sat waiting, sure of a target. In this murderous game of nautical poker, the submariners seemed to hold not only the aces but the trump cards as well, and with the fate of the world at stake the Allied gamblers could do little but bluff and pay their losses with the lives of merchant seamen. Britannia began to grow anaemic, her hold on Neptune's trident weakened. Even some of her children lost faith.

As the level of sinkings increased alarmingly many seamen, particularly from neutral nations, hesitated to sail for British ports. But when so many of her men were lost Britain was, as always, fortunate in her women. There was one instance when a neutral crew refused to sail, but the master's British wife stood before them. 'You may be interested to know' she told them 'that I am going to sea with my husband this voyage.' Either her courage or her scorn shamed that crew into sailing, and she did indeed accompany her man to sea, but losses continued to mount as the U-boats held the ascendancy.

In March 1916 Britannia lunged downward with her trident as the Royal Navy dropped the newly-developed depth charge into the sea lair of the U-boat. The depth charge was a drum of explosive detonated by a hydrostatically-controlled pistol whose spring was set at a pre-determined depth. Although the concept was sound, the depth charge was crudely delivered by being dropped over the stern of a warship. Nonetheless it destroyed its first U-boat on 22nd March off the south coast of Ireland. Six days later the Reichstag called for unrestrained submarine warfare. Their sinking of the French steamer *Sussex* brought immediate American protests and subsequent restrictions to their campaign. In future, the Germans promised, no merchant ships would be torpedoed until passengers and crew had been safely removed. Nevertheless the U-boats remained effective.

Despite Q-ships and camouflage, protected cones and depth charges, sinkings continued to mount, littering the bed of the Atlantic with the rusting carcasses of once-proud ships. In June 1916, U-boats sunk 109,000 tons of Allied shipping and effectively trapped the Grand Fleet within Scapa Flow. For all their massive guns, not even the super-dreadnoughts could leave Scapa without a large destroyer escort, and the more destroyers that were defending the fleet-in-being, the less were available for patrol work. When the U-boats sank one million tons of allied shipping that October, the Kaiser sent them a message of congratulation. The same month, in what appears like a propaganda exercise, U.53 sank five merchant vessels, two of them neutral, along the eastern seaboard of the United States. Currently crossing the Atlantic, the United States' ambassador to Germany commented that the 'odour of burning oil was quite noticeable for hours'.

Throughout these terrible years, the merchant ships continued to toil across the Atlantic, the blood of Britain, of Empire flowing along her maritime veins. Although the strain was greater, the blood thinner, there was no thought of surrender. British and Empire mariners continued to crew the ships that supplied the beleaguered islands, and if they grumbled about their working conditions, they surely had cause. The minute his ship was sunk, a seaman automatically became unemployed and his wages ceased. Although some of the better companies allowed a few weeks wages for shipless survivors, and the 'distressed seamen' clauses of the Merchant Shipping Act offered some help, most merchant seamen lost just about everything if their ship was lost. Not surprisingly, many British seamen jumped ship in the United States, looking for greater security and higher wages.

However bad things seemed, they could always get worse. German calculations indicated that by sinking 600,000 tons of shipping a month, they could force Britain to surrender after six months. At the end of 1916 U-boats were sinking around half that figure, but in January 1917 Germany declared a policy of unrestricted submarine warfare. Any vessel, Allied or neutral, entering a 'war zone' was liable to be sunk without warning. It was a calculated gamble – could Germany drain the blood from Britain before the United States was forced into the war? The 'Brooklyn Eagle' voiced the American point of view in a succinct statement: 'Freedom of the seas will now be enjoyed by icebergs and fish.'

As early as 3rd February President Wilson broke off diplomatic relations with Germany, but as yet there was no state of war. With the president apparently believing that U-boats would not deliberately sink a neutral vessel, the remainder of the month passed with the United States in uneasy peace. Sinkings of British and Allied ships continued to escalate. If the idea of unrestricted submarine warfare had been to starve Britain it nearly worked; if the Germans hoped to intimidate the British into surrender they were deluded. In January 1917 114 British and Allied vessels were sunk, together with 66 neutrals, so there was a justified sensation of vengeance when HMS *Farnborough* sank U.83 in February. Captain Campbell's Victoria Cross was perhaps symbolic, but the message was clear: Britain would not be defeated.

For months, however, that defeat appeared all too possible. By April, with one Allied ship in four failing to make port, Britain had only enough food to last six weeks and a reluctant government introduced rationing. Each ship that dipped onto the bed of the Atlantic meant food, supplies and munitions that would never reach the women in Britain or the men in the trenches; and mariners choking to death as the submarine slunk to safety in the deep Atlantic. Each ship was a further drain on Britannia's strength as, jubilant at the success of their submarines, the Imperial German Navy promised victory within a month. Only then did the Admiralty make what was possibly the most crucial decision of the entire war - they agreed to a convoy system.

Since 1914 the Royal Navy had declined to consider using their smaller vessels as escorts, attempting instead to keep their fleet-in-being in case the German High Seas fleet should emerge. But with nearly 500 merchant ships lost in the first quarter of 1917, starvation was more of a threat than defeat in a naval battle. Lloyd George, the prime minister, set down a convoy system. The idea was for a number of merchant ships, between 10 and 50, to be escorted to their destination by a force of warships. In theory each escort would consist of a cruiser, a dozen armed trawlers, two fast torpedo boats, six destroyers and two observation balloons for spotting submarines.

Between the conception and the confinement of the convoys the United States entered the war on the side of the Allies. In March the United States learned of the Zimmermann Telegram which promised the return of Arizona, New Mexico and Texas to Mexico should they invade America in the event of her entering the war. That same month U-boats sunk five more American merchant vessels and on Good Friday, 6th April, President Wilson declared war on Germany. The United States had unknowingly taken the first stride from isolationism to the foremost power in the world.

Now the U-boats had to starve Britain out of the war before the United States could properly use its vast resources. They made a good start, sinking 875,000 tons of Allied shipping in April, but on 10th May the first British convoy sailed from Gibraltar. The experiment was phenomenally successful, so the system was extended to the North Sea. At the end of May the first Atlantic convoy crossed from Hampton Roads in Virginia, with the loss of only one straggler. The relief must have been unbelievable; in June there was not a single sinking among the 60 merchant vessels which crossed from North America to Britain. Although the Germans could not yet have realised it, they had lost the Atlantic campaign and with it any chance of defeating Britain.

With United States Navy squadrons under the command of Admiral Sims joining the veteran Royal Naval units, merchant shipping began to feel confident about

PEACE

Thank GOD for peace on earth again,
Good will t'ward men once more.
Lift up your heart, 'twas not in vain
Our men went forth to war!
Conquered on earth, in sea and sky,
Cruel Prussian might shall cease.
And the whole world shall henceforth live
In amity and peace.

WHEN THE BOYS COME MARCHING HOME

The Armistice saw peace return...

completing the voyage they began. When the convoy system was introduced to shipping sailing westward as well as eastward, losses in the Atlantic shrunk to virtually nothing. Worldwide shipping collection points were established at Halifax and Panama, Rio de Janeiro and Port Said, Gibraltar and Dakar. Escorted convoys would eventually carry over one million United States soldiers to reinforce the war-weary Allies, escorted convoys would carry food and munitions and now, after years of defensive warfare, the Allied navies moved to the offensive.

Fresh minefields tested the skill and strained the nerves of the German submariners as they threaded free of the North Sea, destroyers and submarine chasers hunted the hunters and for the first time Allied shipbuilding began to match shipping losses. At the beginning of August Edwin Dunning, a Royal Naval pilot, flew from Scapa Flow to HMS *Furious,* making him the first man to land successfully an aircraft on an aircraft carrier. That same month there were mutinies on the German battleships *Prinzregent Luitpold* and *Friederich der Grosse*; the frustration of being starved by the Royal Naval blockade was effectively eroding German morale. In September Walter Schwieger, the U-boat captain who had torpedoed *Lusitania* and 48 other Allied ships, lost his U.88 to British mines.

If the U-boat campaign against merchant seamen could be considered vicious, then the blockade of the central powers also had its dark side. Up to a quarter of a million German civilians died of starvation that year and the Austro-Hungarian Empire redeployed seven army divisions to control food riots in Budapest and Vienna. In September Allied and neutral shipping losses slumped to 159 ships and by November that figure had fallen to 126. In April 1918 a daring attempt to stop the passage of U-boats by attacking Zeebrugge and Ostend achieved only partial success, but shipping losses dropped to 100.

By now United States shipbuilding was getting into gear, with 16 shipyards sliding fresh vessels into the sea. There were 50 bays at the brand new yard at Hog Island, 28 bays in a new yard in Newark and hundreds of ships were produced to replace the horrendous losses. In May 1918 14 U-boats were sunk, over 10% of the entire German submarine fleet, but the sea war continued with unrelenting bitterness. As late as October 1918 an Irish Sea ferry *Leinster* was torpedoed with the loss of 176 people, but the Royal Navy extracted revenge off Gibraltar by sinking the veteran U.34 that had sunk 120 merchant ships in three years.

The Armistice of 11th November saw peace return to oceans that would never be quite the same again. Of the 15 million tons of shipping that had been sunk, 9 million was British, but the Royal Navy had sunk 175 of the total of 195 German submarine losses. It had been a horrendous war and at the end people wondered if it had all been worthwhile; perhaps it had. A peace dictated by a triumphant German Empire would not have been pleasant for the world.

Chapter 18

The Contest of the Liners

Whereas the vast majority of people crossed the Atlantic in some degree of discomfort, either as hard-working hands on a merchant ship, bewildered emigrants packed in steerage or chained slaves in a despicable hell-ship, there were those who enjoyed the experience. In the days of the sailing ships even the most expensive of accommodation entailed certain discomforts – cramped cabins, seasickness and bad food were common – but when steamships became established on the Atlantic routes standards of comfort rocketed. First-class passengers on any on the great ocean liners travelled amidst luxury that most people could hardly even conceive.

It was Thomas Ismay, a far-travelled shipowner, who revolutionised standards on passenger steamers after purchasing the White Star Line in 1867. Although White Star had originally sailed to Australia, Ismay transferred the name and house flag with its famous white star to his Oceanic Steam Navigation Company that operated on the Atlantic crossing. Ismay ordered four steam passenger ships from Harland & Wolff of Belfast, stipulating high standards of comfort, with the result that White Star's *Oceanic* was remembered as one of the best of the early liners. Traditionally the best cabins were aft but Ismay placed them amidships away from the screw, which was noisy and created unpleasant vibrations. *Oceanic's* cabins were also spacious, with large scuttles for light and air, coal fires within marble fireplaces and fresh running water. Augmenting this personal comfort was a promenade deck that stretched across the ship, allowing the first-class passengers the opportunity to exercise without the necessity of brushing shoulders with those of lesser fortune, or those who actually had to work the ship. There was also a smoking room for the gentlemen. Well-bred Victorian ladies, of course, never smoked, but doubtless they were glad to be rid of their men for a while. William Pirrie, the White Star's chief designer, had spent much of his time and Ismay's money in inspecting some of the finest hotels in Europe to gain inspiration for *Oceanic's* interior. His talent, combined with Ismay's vision and the skilled workforce of Harland & Wolff, made *Oceanic* the forerunner of the great Atlantic liners.

White Star ships tend to be remembered more for comfort than speed, yet in the early years some challenged for the Blue Riband trophy that was awarded for the fastest Atlantic crossing. Sailing from Liverpool, the White Star ships continued to develop in comfort and increase in size until in 1911 the 45,324-ton *Olympic* was launched: the largest ship in the world. Despite these successes, the White Star name is forever associated with the 1912 loss of their even larger *Titanic*, surely the most famous shipping disaster in the world.

One of the chief rivals to the White Star and one of the most famous passenger lines of all time was the Cunard Line. Cunard had successfully tendered to replace the current transatlantic mail service that was operated by sailing brigs with one operated by steamships. Ordering four wooden paddle steamers from the Glasgow engineer Robert Napier, Cunard guaranteed an all-year-round, bi-monthly service between Liverpool and Boston. From the start Cunard's line was noted for its speed, with its most celebrated early ship, *Britannia*, achieving an average crossing of 15 days. In 1856 Cunard floated its first iron ship, *Persia*, and for the next century and a half the company constantly ranked among the front runners in the transatlantic passenger trade. The names read like a roll call of the world's finest liners; *Umbria,* 1884; *Campania* 1893; *Mauritania*, 1907; *Lusitania*, 1907; *Queen Mary*, 1936; *Queen Elizabeth,* 1938; *Queen Elizabeth II*, 1969. A century of conveyance on the Atlantic, with ship design progressing from comfort to luxury and each successive ship carrying passengers in a cocoon of privilege. Cunard ships competed aggressively for the Blue Riband, with *Acadia* donning the Riband as early as 1840, only to be beaten by the American Collins liner *Pacific* in 1851.

As the United States withdrew from first-rate passenger carrying following the demise of the Collins Line and the decline of the sailing packet trade, the Germans took their place. In 1856 the Hamburg-America Line was founded followed by North German Lloyd in 1857, although it was not until the latter decades of the century that they began to slacken the British grip on the Atlantic passenger trade. *Elbe's* 16-knot thrust in 1880 was impressive in itself, but it was the Kaiser's admiration of White Star's *Teutonic* in 1887 that really galvanised German passenger ship building. Kaiser Wilhelm was greatly interested in increasing German naval power and the prospect of a fleet of fast passenger liners that could be converted to armed merchant cruisers was immensely appealing. With German steel production steadily increasing it became obvious that the British would struggle to maintain their supremacy. The siren song of Lorelei was luring Neptune's passenger trident from the care of Britannia to the deceptive beauty of the Rhine.

But Cunard's liners were growing ever larger and ever more luxurious. In 1881 Cunard's *Servia* was launched; at 7400 tons she was larger than just about anything ever built, but she was distinctive for more than her size. Her speed of nearly 17 knots earned her the sobriquet 'Ocean Greyhound', her hull was of steel and she was the first liner to have electric lighting. In the theatre of North Atlantic liners, innovations were expected and each new ship had to compete in a highly competitive market. The Germans were well aware of this and Vulcan shipyards at Stetting challenged the British yards by producing *Kaiser Wilhelm der Grosse* for North German Lloyd. The Kaiser had to witness the birth of this 14,900-ton beauty, with her four tall funnels, impressive public apartments, stained-glass windows and paintings that enshrined all the nationalistic mythology of rejuvenated German history. Luxury entered a new dimension with *Kaiser Wilhelm* as German engineering expertise merged with German culture to create a Nordic god to rule over the Atlantic swells. She was also fast enough to whip the Blue Riband from the neck of Cunard's ocean greyhound on her Atlantic passage.

It was this vessel that encouraged White Star to produce a new *Oceanic* in 1899. Again built by Harland & Wolff, she outweighed *Kaiser Wilhelm* by a good 2000 tons, but Hamburg-Amerika was equally competitive – while White Star now searched for luxury, the German firm aimed for speed. Their *Deutschland* was smaller than *Oceanic* but fastened the Blue Riband securely around her quadruple funnels. *Oceanic*'s patrons consoled themselves with the luxury in which they lounged, for *Deutschland* paid for her speed with a raucous engine and a less comfortable voyage that unsettled many passengers and diminished her popularity. Nonetheless, *Deutschland* retained the Blue Riband until 1906.

Her German rival North German Lloyd gracefully withdrew from the speed stakes to concentrate, like White Star, on comfort. In the opening years of the 20th century *Kronprinz Wilhelm*, *Kaiser Wilhelm II* and *Kronprinzessin Cecile* made an immense impression with their twin screws, palatial accommodation and the four funnels that appeared to mark the apogee of the ocean liner. Advertised as ocean 'flyers' or 'express steamships' these vessels sailed from New York to Plymouth, Cherbourg and Bremen, taunting the British at the contest they had invented.

While German nautical reputation escalated, the United States, for so long strangely subdued on the Atlantic highway they had once dominated, at last re-entered the contest. An entrepreneur with the evocative name of Morgan created a company known as

Across the Pond

International Mercantile Marine, took over half a dozen British shipping firms and, astonishingly, bought the White Star Line. As the established British lines reeled in disbelief, Morgan announced his intention to control Cunard. White Star was bad enough, but Cunard was an institution - the chairman requested government help to block this blow to British prestige. The government responded with a low interest loan to build better ships and an amendment to Cunard's articles that barred foreigners from gaining control.

Two new Cunard ships were built and both made their mark on history. *Mauritania* was built on Tyneside, *Lusitania* on the Clyde; both had the most modern steam turbine engines and, like their German rivals, both flaunted four funnels. They entered the transatlantic service in 1907 with first *Lusitania* then *Mauritania* removing the Blue Riband from the Kaiser's grasp and wrapping it firmly around Britannia's trident. Although Kipling thought *Mauritania* was 'a monstrous nine-decked city', popular opinion tended to differ, with even Franklin Roosevelt immediately seduced by *Mauritania*'s style. 'She always fascinated me' he said 'with her graceful, yacht-like lines... .'

Perhaps it was the atmosphere of breeding that set the Cunard ships apart from their German rivals. There was nothing ostentatious about *Mauritania*, just the inherent style long associated with the British upper class. It was a thing that had evolved over centuries, an amalgamation of education, certainty, confidence and adaptation that was transmitted into the very fabric of the Cunard ships. Where the German vessels were overdone, perhaps overblown, their British rivals were dependably unpretentious, but with the right application of art placed exactly where it should be. They were a floating representation of all the finest qualities of upper-class Britain, an advertisement for the serene solid strength of Empire. Uniformed stewards swept silently through the elegant dining rooms, dispensing the best of fare on bone china plates and the best of drink from crystal decanters. Here the murmur of educated voices rose to the glowing chandeliers as gentlemen leaned back in their chairs and ladies preened themselves, flirted mildly and eyed their peers in the hope of finding fault or scandal. It was a comfortable environment for those who belonged; for those who merely aspired to belong it was a society to be envied.

Elegant ships also stirred further competition in an age where national pride was interwoven with company pride in a dangerous alliance of patriotism and progress. Flag waving was an international pastime, status was superseding the old Christian virtues and White Star pushed forward with *Olympic* and *Titanic*. Again they were built by Belfast's Harland & Wolff, two giants side by side under the Irish sky and when completed in 1911 *Olympic* was known as the 'world's largest ship'. She was also one of the most luxurious with squash courts, wide beds and an on-board swimming pool. The old time sailors that had crossed the Atlantic with Columbus or shared the hardships of *Mayflower* would have stared uncomprehendingly at this splendour. And when *Titanic* slipped quietly out of Belfast and down to Southampton there might have been some dismay at her title of 'the world's safest ship'. Tempting fate at sea was

156

never wise and already Neptune's vengeful trident was slicing at the Arctic ice. However safe she appeared to those who enjoyed first-class staterooms, there was no safety for the hundreds of steerage passengers who died in the North Atlantic. White Star had decreased the number of lifeboats in order to maintain the look of the ship. Style and appearance contributed to the deaths of very many people that day when nature's iceberg reminded the world that no ship should be deemed unsinkable. In a sense, nothing would ever be the same again for the passenger liners, for even luxury ships had been proved fallible.

Yet the contest on the Atlantic continued. The designers of Cunard and Hamburg-Amerika toiled over their drawing boards to dream up ever-larger vessels, and while Cunard produced *Aquitania*, Hamburg-Amerika came up with *Vaterland* and *Imperator*. These were the last of the pre-war giants, the dream ships of the old-world order; *Imperator* which sported a gaudy imperial eagle to make her longer than *Aquitania*, and *Vaterland* which represented the peak of the Kaiser's Germany. At 54,282 tons she was the largest ship in a world that was destined never to let her display her ample charms. When war placed an emphatic full stop on the epoch of European imperialism, the United States requisitioned *Vaterland*, changed her name to *Leviathan* and used her to ferry tens of thousands of American soldiers to the carnage of France.

Cunard lost 22 ships in the war but was compensated by the claimed *Imperator*, renamed *Berengaria*. The United States retained *Leviathan* while a third German giant, the uncompleted *Bismarck*, was transferred to the White Star Line as *Majestic*. As postwar austerity replaced the horror of 1914-18, passenger lines rebuilt their fleets with ships that lacked the splendour of the pre-war beauties. Smaller, more functional, probably more cognisant of reality, they reflected the sober change that four years of atrocity had wrought on the world.

Although the liners had carried hundreds of thousands of immigrants over the Atlantic, two-thirds of the passenger space had been reserved for those who travelled first-class. The postwar years changed this, as they changed so much in the passenger liner trade. After 1924 the United States slammed shut the door to free immigration, making the liners battle harder for paying trade. There were drinking cruises when Americans, starved of alcohol by government prohibition, boarded the majestic liners purely to stand at the bar. There was an end to the steerage class that had carried so many million people from hopeless misery in a European ghetto to hopeful squalor in dumb-bell apartments. There was the rebirth of French nautical pride as *France*, *Paris* and *De Grasse* crossed the Atlantic with electric lifts, electric hair dryers and an elegance that was purely Gallic. Later, in 1926, *Ile de France* was launched with an interior so uniquely styled that it has been termed 'floating Hollywood', a name that in itself reveals the cross-cultural exchange of the Atlantic. And there was a rising middle class.

These last were mainly from the United States, professional people with money to spend and a hankering to visit the old countries beyond the Atlantic. Not all were sober, sedate or sedentary for this was the age of the flapper and the bright young things that wanted to live life in the present. If the 1890s had been the 'naughty nineties' then this was the 'roaring twenties' and women with money were at last helping create a society that was desperate to escape from the past.

Those who could afford to travel first-class in liners could also escape from the present. With growing unemployment on shore, the passenger liners had no difficulty in recruiting the best staff, the most famous artistes and the most talented chefs to pamper their privileged clientèle. Only the rich and ultra-rich luxuriated in first class – they boasted a lifestyle that set them apart from ordinary mortals and more money than most would believe possible. Insulated by wealth, they could view the liner and the world through rose-tinted cocktail glasses; the ship was a floating amusement that carried them across the Atlantic. They knew they were the élite and nothing else really mattered, darling. In the evenings they danced and banqueted and flirted with others of their kind while by day they could enjoy the immaculate swimming pool, or lounge on the mahogany deckchairs while their great ship surged over the sea. They had no real reason to worry for everything was done for them; life was a glorious song enhanced by the hum of a liner's massive engines and the aroma of perfectly-cooked food.

As the rich partied and the flappers paraded, as the stewards padded and the seamen worked, unemployment queues lengthened and there were strikes and wars and rumours of war. But North German Lloyd launched the 32,300-ton *Columbus* to remind everyone how powerful Germany had once been, and followed that with *Bremen* and *Europa* to show that their fatherland had a future as well as a past. Few cared that it was United States' money that financed the latter two ships; the great republic was experiencing guilt about her part in the Treaty of Versailles. *Europa* entered the North Atlantic trade in 1929, the same year that her generous benefactor experienced the Wall Street crash. Grand enough to attract attention, her speed reclaimed the Blue Riband for Germany, but the 1930s saw other nations enter the competition for Atlantic passengers.

The Canadian Pacific Line had long taken passengers across to Quebec but in 1931 they launched *Empress of Britain* which boasted a palatial restaurant, two private dining-rooms, a mall, the Knickerbocker Bar and a glass-ceilinged swimming pool. *Empress of Britain* was arguably the first liner of real class to emerge since the war, and at 760 feet long she was one of the largest. There was no disputing her luxury, but her arrival coincided with the depression years and she failed to make the impact her style deserved. Other liners from other nations were also unsuccessful in capturing the plaudits of the earlier giants. Italy was next into the competition, producing *Rex* and *Conte di Savoia* in 1932. A newly-created Italian Line operated both, and although they were intended to enhance Italian prestige, both suffered inaugural mechanical problems. Despite this early handicap *Conte di Savoia* was the first Atlantic liner to boast a stabiliser, while *Rex* wound the Blue Riband round the sinister fasces of Mussolini. Dismayed at the success of their Italian neighbours, the French Line decided to build again, and *Normandie* was developed at Saint-Nazaire. Cunard began work on an as yet unnamed liner at John Brown's yard in Clydebank but only until the depression helped drain away her money. The skeleton of No 534 towered forlornly above a suffering town as unemployed men drew their dole and women cursed the rusting hull as a constant reminder of their poverty.

To some, *Normandie* was the best liner to ever cross the Atlantic. She was backed by government money, designed by a Russian named Yourkevitch and launched with a wave of emotion and a surge of Loire water that upended hundreds of spectators and provided splendid opportunities for the cameramen. Over 1000 feet in length and nearly 80,000 tons in weight, her absolute luxury was only enhanced by the reputation for speed that she gained when she flicked the Blue Riband from *Rex* to herself. If there was ever an award for extravagant opulence, *Normandie* would be on the short list – Art Deco and caged birds, apartments that would shame a five-star hotel and an efficient army of servants created an interior that surpassed luxury. Such a ship should have become a legend but, like *Empress of Britain*, she seldom sailed with a complete passenger list. Great liners might well proclaim the genius of their makers, but only government subsidies allowed them to display their national flag to the uncaring Atlantic. In the transatlantic crossing money-making remained secondary to national prestige.

It was years since Britain had produced a world-beating liner. *Mauritania* and *Aquitania* were beautiful but ageing and were no longer up to the standard demanded by the more discriminating passengers. With fewer customers and larger ships the Atlantic was a buyers' market. Cunard decided to raise a government loan, scrape the rust from project number 534 and retake their position as the best shipping company on the Atlantic. The government agreed to a £3 million loan, but with the condition that Cunard merge with White Star. This was not such an incredible proposal as it once would have appeared, for International Mercantile Marine had sold off White Star to the Royal Mail Group, who had since become bankrupt. The name Cunard-White Star sounded like a merger but in reality it was a Cunard takeover and soon the venerable White Star name was only a memory.

When work restarted in April 1934, Clydebank came back to life. With money in their pockets and pride in their work the shipbuilders shaped what was to become one of the most famous of all transatlantic liners and indisputably one of the finest ships ever to grace the seas. Originally it was intended to name 534 *Victoria,* but after a minor misunderstanding with King George V she became *Queen Mary.*

On 26th September 1934, with rain lashing at the assembled thousands, Queen Mary launched her namesake *Queen Mary* into the Clyde. At nearly 81,000 tons she was immense and if some critics claimed that her lines lacked the chic élan of *Normandie,* she was completely suited for the Atlantic and her interior could never be faulted. She was comfortable without being pretentious, welcoming without being overpowering, solidly and utterly secure. Overall, *Queen Mary* was a Clyde-built Cunarder: there can be no higher commendation.

In June 1936 *Queen Mary* faced her destiny on the Atlantic and crossed safely to New York. Crowds cheered her out of Britain, crowds cheered her into New York but *Normandie* still held the Blue Riband. Not for long – in August *Mary* became queen of

Queen Mary – a Clyde-built Cunarder. Courtesy of the Billie Love Collection, Isle of Wight.

the Atlantic, slicing to New York in three minutes less than four days and shrugging off a renewed French challenge to retain the Riband with a time fractionally less than three days 21 minutes. *Queen Mary* is perhaps the most affectionately-remembered of all the great liners. Later liners were faster, many were more glamorous or larger, but they all lacked the indefinable something that made the difference between merely a great liner and the majesty of a queen.

Rival companies did not kneel before *Mary*'s maritime throne, instead they planned a process of usurpation. With national prestige at stake, North German Lloyd hoped to build a mighty vessel that sailed a full day faster than the *Queen*. Simultaneously the Hamburg-Amerika Line intended putting three spanking new ships on the Hamburg – New York route, but the world of the Atlantic passenger trade was about to change. The evil cloak of fascism that had descended on Germany would only be purged by war, after which technological advances would have altered humanity's conception of travel. Transatlantic crossing would be timed in hours rather than days.

War created new roles for the liners. They became troopships, transporting the soldiers who fought the war or hospital ships that returned the broken men to the women for whom they had been fighting. But one more mighty ship was launched before the jet-stream of functional aircraft superseded the dreamships of glamour and romance. It was February 1940 when John Brown's yard launched the next queen of the Atlantic as *Queen Elizabeth*, larger than her royal sister, surged out of the Clyde and across to New York in a maiden voyage that was as utilitarian as the grey she was painted. From 1939 until 1945 the great liners, built for pleasure and profit, carried soldiers from half the world to fight soldiers of the other half. Many were sunk – *Empress of Britain; Athenia; Rex; Normandie* – dozens of beautiful ships, well-known or less well-known, were sacrificed for the cause of democracy.

The vessels that survived emerged into a different world. Although there was still a small place for transatlantic liners, aircraft carried many more passengers from continent to continent and large passenger ships were more frequently used for cruises. Things have come a long way since Samuel Cunard crossed from Halifax, but it is nice to know that a queen of the dynasty he founded still crosses the Atlantic.

Chapter 19

Crossing the Pond

There are many examples of humanity's longstanding interest in flight, from Leonardo da Vinci, who sketched a mechanical bird's wing, to John Damian, who attempted to fly from the ramparts of Stirling Castle. The culmination of Damian's flight into the castle midden revealed the reality of most early flying experience – it was best left to the birds. Not until the latter decades of the 18th century did humanity appear ready to take to the skies. In 1782 enlightened France was first to follow man's imagination with the practicality of the Montgolfier brothers' hot-air balloon, but not everybody accepted such progress. On one occasion the military was needed to escort one of the spectacular creations through a superstitious mob. It makes an intriguing picture, flickering torches illuminating the balloon as it passed through a corridor of people crossing themselves in fear. The French government tried to nullify the terror by explaining that the balloon 'cannot possibly cause any harm and … will some day prove serviceable to the wants of society'.

The first manned flight was also in France as Pilatre de Rozier and the Marquis d'Arlandes clambered into the wicker basket beneath their balloon on 21st November 1783. When the balloon was heated the world's first aeronauts lifted into the afternoon sky, above the hunting lodge of the king, above the Bois de Boulogne until, at an amazing 270 feet, the men raised their hats to acknowledge the cheers of the crowd below. After that gentlemanly gesture a breeze carried the balloon silently, swiftly, historically in the direction of Paris. At one stage the contraption hesitated but the aeronauts fuelled the fire beneath the balloon and it soared upwards to 500 feet. Once over Paris the aeronauts descended gracefully to the streets below. Humanity had risen to kiss the skies, but every balloon was still at the whim of nature's wind. It would be some time before powered flight was possible.

Throughout the 19th century there were many long distance balloon flights but in later years a succession of aerial pioneers burst through the flight barrier. Among the earliest and most neglected of these dedicated men was the Brazilian, Alberto Santos-Dumont, who flew the first airship in September 1898 by adding a petrol engine to a hydrogen balloon. As before, France was the world leader in manned flight, and France backed the Brazilian with all the fervour of an international hero.

If the aeronautic bug was biting deep in Europe, in the United States only a few people bothered to scratch. One was Samuel Pierpont Langley, director of Pittsburgh's Allegheny Observatory, who sent a steam-driven, 16-feet-long model aircraft on a half-mile trip down the Potomac River in 1896. Following this success, the United States government funded Langley to build a larger, engine-powered aircraft. Sailing across the Atlantic in pursuit of one of the newfangled internal combustible engines, Langley found himself scorned; nobody seemed to believe that his ideas on heavier-than-air flight would work. After an American engineer spent two frustrating years in an abortive attempt to build an effective engine, Langley's assistant Charles Manly plundered the most effective parts from the failure, took them to the Smithsonian Institute in Washington and worked on the project in person.

In October 1903, while Santos-Dumont was experimenting with his airships, Manly made the first recorded attempt at powered manned flight in a heavier-than-air machine. The aircraft moved forward, left the ground, toppled, and dropped both itself and its pilot straight into the river. When a second unsuccessful attempt drew derision from both press and public a possibly-embarrassed government withdrew its funding. Two months later Wilbur and Orville Wright succeeded where Manly had failed.

The Wright brothers were sons of a clergyman whose theological philosophy was balanced with practical scientific experimentation. In such an atmosphere it was natural for the young Wrights to play with model helicopters and kites and equally natural that they should open a bicycle shop, the fashionable industry of the period. Inspired by the gliding experiments of Otto Lilienthal, the brothers decided to combine their engineering skills with the theory of flight. The difficulty was neither the wings nor the engine, but effective steering and a method of balancing the machine while in flight. 'It seemed to us,' said Wilbur Wright 'that the main reason why the problem had remained so long unsolved was that no one had been able to obtain any adequate practice.' Moving to Kitty Hawk in North Carolina for its suitable winds, they experimented with gliders from 1900 until 1902 and not until they were satisfied with their flying machine's framework did they focus on a powered machine. The theory of twin propellers each rotating in opposite directions had been decided but the brothers found it difficult to work out the correct diameter, pitch and area for the blades. Not until December 1903 were these problems ironed out and the biplane made four separate flights. Self critical, the Wrights realised their creation needed work on its equilibrium, but when a system of transverse control preserved lateral balance the machine seemed adequate.

December 1903 – the biplane made four separate flights. Courtesy of the Billie Love Collection, Isle of Wight.

While the Wright brothers' innovations were being virtually ignored by even the American press, the success of Santos-Dumont in France in flying airships around the Eiffel Tower and out to sea caught the imagination of the British publisher Alfred Harmsworth. A self-made newspaper magnate, Harmsworth owned the *Observer*, the *Times* and the *Daily Mirror*, but it was his *Daily Mail* that offered a series of flying prizes. One was for the first man to fly the English Channel while another, in 1913, was for the first non-stop flight across the Atlantic.

The Wright brothers were fêted when they arrived in France in 1908. Not only did they give flying demonstrations to fascinated crowds, but they also competed for the Michelin Prize for the fastest flying machine and for the machine that remained longest in the air. However, disaster is no respecter of celebrity and in September Wilbur Wright crashed, killing his passenger, Lieutenant Selfridge. Over in Britain there were three airfields where fliers learned their trade – Hendon, Eastchurch and, most of all, Brooklands, deep in the Home Counties and in a world of its own. When not flying, the aeronauts either built flying machines or talked about them, and at night they slept within touching distance of their pride and joy. They were all young men in this noisy bachelors club, save for the maternal Mrs Billings who ran the indispensable and very English Bluebird Café. Among her clientèle were the Australian Harry Hawker, the ebullient Jack Alcock and the very young Frederick Raynham. While the English learned and discussed and drank tea flavoured with petrol, the slender Frenchman Louis Bleriot stepped into his monoplane at Calais, asked 'Ou est Dovre?', pointed his machine across the Channel and flew to England.

The Channel was only 22 miles across but the Atlantic was far wider and infinitely more dangerous.

While these trailblazing fliers were making tremendous progress with land-based aircraft, Glenn Hammond Curtiss of New York State was working on an aircraft that could take off and land on water. Like the Wright brothers, the Hamondsworth-based Curtiss owned a bicycle shop and he proved his mechanical skill by inventing a speedy motorcycle. From there he progressed to building the engine for the first United States army dirigible in 1905 and then united with a group named the Aerial Experimental Association to create a flying machine. Meetings were held at the Canadian home of one of the members, Alexander Graham Bell, and when a monoplane crashed into Lake Michigan during the 1911 Chicago aviation meet, Curtiss flew his hydro-aeroplane to assist the struggling flier.

In Britain, aviation meets and air races became frequent with pilots such as Raynham, Alcock and Hawker as popular as latter day sports stars. Every flight was an adventure and there were some spectacular crashes, but in those days of low altitude, low power and low speed the pilot usually emerged relatively unscathed. These were the heady, carefree days of audacious amateurism when men constructed their own machines, invented new manoeuvres and made up the rules as they flew; but such times did not last long. The outbreak of war in 1914 severely curtailed civilian aviation as the warring powers congregated on and above the battlefields of Europe.

For three years the United States stood aloof from the conflict but Curtiss did his bit for civilisation by building aircraft and flying boats for the Allies, and then for his own country when the United States became a belligerent in 1917. If necessity is the mother of invention, warfare is her wicked sister and machines initially designed for transportation were used for destruction. Four terrible years furthered progress and Curtiss worked on his NC – Navy Curtiss – flying boats. In July 1918, presuming that other things had occupied idle minds, the *Daily Mail* repeated its prize offer of £10,000 for the first aircraft to fly the Atlantic. There were certain conditions; enemy pilots were ineligible, the flight could commence anywhere in North America and finish anywhere in Europe but the maximum time allowance was 72 hours. The aircraft had to start and finish under its own power and although help during the flight was not permitted, a flying boat could touch down on the sea and take off again. The prize stirred the enthusiasm of the flying world, but not until peace brought the lifting of the Royal Aero Club's ban on the Atlantic race could British pilots participate.

As the shortest Atlantic route stretched 1880 lonely miles from Newfoundland to Ireland, pilots looked to that friendly, fog-bedevilled island as their jumping-off point. There were many hopefuls, many more dreamers and only a few genuine entries. One confident pair boarded a white-painted aircraft named *Shamrock*, pointed it in the general direction of North America and took off from Britain, westerly, against the prevailing winds. They did not quite make Ireland before the machine dived into the Irish Sea. When more serious contenders arrived in Newfoundland in 1919, they found the weather disappointingly inclement and facilities not always what they had hoped, but there was tremendous interest. The Australian, Harry Hawker, was there accompanied by a Scottish navigator named Mackenzie-Grieve and a single-engined Sopwith plane named *Atlantic*. Frederick Raynham and his navigator Morgan hoped to cross in a single-engined Martinsyde named *Raymor*.

There was also Jack Alcock and his navigator, Arthur Whitten-Brown, in a two-engined Vickers Vimy. As a captain in the Royal Naval Air Service during the First World War, Alcock had fought German aircraft with his Sopwith Camel and had bombed the Turks in a Handley Page bomber. Shot down and captured after a bombing raid on railway marshalling yards on the Bosporus, he had ended the war as a prisoner. Alcock subsequently became a test pilot with Vickers Aircraft. His navigator was one of those people who were more an example of Atlantic unity than of any national insularity. Glasgow-born of American parents, Whitten-Brown was as quiet natured as the Mancunian Alcock was ebullient. He, too, had served in the First World War, first as an infantry officer at Ypres and the Somme, then in the Royal Flying Corps. After being shot down and badly wounded, he had taught himself aerial navigation while a prisoner of war.

Never to be underestimated, the US Navy had entered three of Curtiss' flying boats and backed them by a splendid operation that could either be seen as brashly extravagant or as an example of typical American thoroughness, depending on the viewpoint of the observer. The US Navy had marked out the route of the flying boats with over 90 ships spaced out across the ocean. Some had aircraft radio receivers while others had equipment to read and report on the weather. It was like a knotted rope to support the flying boats, known as the Nancies, across the Atlantic. They were large machines, awkward-looking to modern eyes but among the finest available at the time and on 2nd May 1919 their route was reported as Trepassey in Newfoundland to the Azores and thence to Lisbon in Portugal.

On 16th May, after flying up from the United States, three Nancies took off from Trepassey and rumbled gamely eastward toward Europe. Vicious weather forced Nancy one into the sea and, despite the huge naval contingent, it was a little steamer named *Ionia* that rescued the fliers. After 15 hours of flying in equally bad weather the pilot of Nancy three collapsed. The flying boat ditched but the crew's skill and sheer courage took them to the Azores. Nancy four, commanded by Lieutenant Commander Albert Cushing Read, followed the route until fog obscured the knotted rope beneath. Read, another quiet navigator who answered to the nickname 'Putty', still managed to find Horta in the Azores, 1000 miles into the Atlantic. For days Read was stuck in these mid-Atlantic islands, unable to progress because of fog and gales so it was not until 27th May that the flying boat was able to continue towards Europe.

Again Read followed the guiding ships and nine hours later he guided his Nancy down into Lisbon harbour. Nobody could ever dispute that the Atlantic had been first flown by a United States Navy flying boat, but the 19 days on the crossing counted it out of any race prize. Nonetheless the world was delighted with the effort and when Read flew from Portugal to England he touched down in Plymouth, from where

Mayflower had sailed to colonise the New World. The circle had been completed, New World technology had returned Americans to their European roots, but Harmsworth's challenge still remained.

Harry Hawker, the Australian flier, was not far behind the flying boats in attempting to traverse the Atlantic, nor was Frederick Raynham. Both started their machines in Newfoundland on the same day, but while Raynham's aircraft crashed on takeoff, Hawker's Sopwith managed to stagger into the chill Atlantic air. Almost immediately they encountered the notorious Newfoundland fog, but it was engine trouble that forced them to give up their attempt after 14½ gruelling hours. Sighting a ship, they dived into the sea and were rescued by the Danish steamer *Mary*. Still nobody had managed to cross the Atlantic non-stop, but despite the difficulties there seemed to be a queue of willing volunteers.

On 14th June Jack Alcock and Arthur Whitten Brown readied themselves for the ordeal. Both wore flying suits and when questioned about his route, Brown said 'Our objective is Ireland, we shall aim for the centre of the target.' Like so many others in that pioneering period, their takeoff was a breathless, confused thing but the Vickers Vimy finally swayed into the turbulent Atlantic air just before two o'clock in the afternoon. It was not an incident-free trip. The radio was damaged on takeoff; they steered into the inevitable fog; one of the engine silencers burned itself out; they hit high cumulo-nimbus cloud but they continued, deafened by the engine and frozen by fog and wind. For hours wind buffered the Vickers Vimy so it made the most appalling aeronautical gymnastics, including a spin that nearly plunged it into the sea. As Alcock tried to climb above another huge cloud that loomed ahead, the aircraft became dangerously coated with ice. There is a story that Brown crawled onto the wing to hack ice from the air intake while the aircraft hurtled along at 100 miles an hour. If that is true, and neither Alcock nor Brown claimed it was, then the navigator was a man of superhuman courage. He was that anyway, for all these Atlantic pioneers willingly risked death to fly their machines.

Just before 8.30 on the morning of 15th June the Vickers Vimy arrived over Ireland. Alcock and Brown had flown the Atlantic for 16 hours and 12 minutes, non-stop and unaided, then they landed nose-first in a bog. Both fliers shared the £10,000 prize for the adventure and both were knighted.

On 2nd July that same year East Lothian in Scotland was the starting point for another historic flight as the airship R34, commanded by Major G. Scott, lifted off and ghosted westward. R34 took four days to cross the pond arriving in Mineola, New York two days after Independence Day. The return flight took just 75 hours, making R34 the first airship to cross and recross the Atlantic and the trouble-free nature of the flight seemed to offer serious competition to the heavier-than-air machines.

In the dark years after the First World War exploits like these raised morale but a couple of flights did not mean that the Atlantic airways had been conquered. Until the crossings were regular and commercially viable, surface ships still reigned supreme on the Ocean Sea.

The R34 took four days to cross the pond. Courtesy of the Billie Love Collection, Isle of Wight.

In July that same amazing year of 1919, a flight between Hendon in England and Le Bourget in France marked a dress rehearsal for daily commercial international flights which actually began at ten minutes past nine on the morning of 25th August 1919. Lieutenant E.H. Lawford piloted a DH4a from Hounslow to Le Bourget with one passenger and a valuable cargo of Devonshire cream, leather, grouse and newspapers. The world's first commercial international air passenger, George Stevenson-Reece, paid £21 for the two and a half hour flight. It was nearly inevitable that at some stage commercial flights should extend across the Atlantic, but although courageous individuals could risk their own necks, there remained tremendous problems for the available commercial aircraft. Apart from navigation and the foul weather there was the viability of carrying a necessarily small number of passengers.

For many years commercial flying over the Atlantic focused on the route between West Africa and north-eastern Brazil. This route was not only shorter, but also had the highest likelihood of both clear visibility and fine weather. Augmenting these advantages were the gentler winds that aided fuel conservation and the convenient refuelling stop at the island of Fernando de Noronha, just 300 miles east of Brazil. Perhaps a trifle aggrieved at the United States and British success over the North Atlantic, it was the French who attempted a regular service in the South.

Air travel developed fast in the 1920s and 1930s, with airlines forming and folding with a rapidity nearly as bewildering as the production of different varieties of machines. It was on 11th May 1930 that Jean Mermoz and his co-pilot Jean Dabry flew a Latecoere

28 flying boat from Dakar to Natal. Mermoz' flight took slightly more than 19½ hours, but as the machine was lost on the return flight the French government hedged its bets and ordered two types of four-engined flying boats, a Latecoere 300 and a Bleriot 5190. As mechanical failure was always a possibility, flying boats, with their ability to touch down on the sea, were often preferred to land-based machines. Nonetheless, a designer named Couzinet produced a land-based aircraft that he claimed could cross non-stop between Africa and South America. Again it was Mermoz who acted as pilot, but Couzinet had enough faith in his aircraft to join the four-man crew as the machine flew for over 14 hours to touch down successfully in Natal. It was 16th January 1933.

While France had made history in the South, Americans were making history in the North. In 1927 Charles Lindbergh had flown solo from New York to Paris in a flight of 33½ hours, much of it through fog. His *Spirit of St Louis* became a household name. Four years later, in 1931, an American woman named Amelia Earhart emulated his achievement in a 15-hour flight that gained her much fame and the Distinguished Flying Cross. Women would not be in the background in this new airborne era but in 1935 she disappeared while attempting to fly around the world.

By this time the Germans had recovered some of their fire and immediately entered the realm of competitive flying with airships. In 1932 the Deutsche Zeppelin Reederei began a regular service between Seville and Recife and, although the journey was nowhere near as fast as heavier-than-air services, it was usually more comfortable and continued operating fortnightly until 1937. In March 1935 the German air minister, an ex-fighter ace named Herman Goering, formed the Deutsche Zeppelin Reederei as the German State airline. One year later the LZ 129 *Hindenburg*, over 800 feet long and with a cruising speed of 77 mph, made its inaugural flight. Compared to the cramped conditions in even the largest of heavier-than-air craft, accommodation for the 50 passengers was splendid. There were lounges, writing rooms and even promenade decks to stretch the legs.

Hindenburg glided through ten trouble-free return flights that summer season, averaging around 65 hours to cross the Atlantic east to west and 52 hours west to east. While she rested for the winter, her accommodation was enlarged to embrace 72 passengers and a crew of 55. However *Hindenburg*, like *Titanic*, is more remembered for the manner of her end than for anything else. After arriving at Lakehurst, New Jersey on her first flight of 1937 she exploded, the hydrogen in her balloon caught fire and the majority of her passengers were killed. That single, terrible disaster destroyed public confidence in airships, leaving the future for heavier-than-air machines.

In the early 1930s the Germans had experimented with flying boats launched by catapult from a depot ship and in 1934 they began the first regular transatlantic mail service. The journey was intricate, involved and efficient. From Stuttgart, a Heinkel carried the mail to Seville where it was transferred to a Junkers that carried it to Bathurst in West Africa. A Dornier flying boat took over, refuelled at a depot ship in mid-Atlantic and continued to Natal with a second Junkers completing the route to Buenos Aires. Yet it was the Italians who stole everybody's thunder in December 1939 when they became the first to inaugurate a regular trans-oceanic passenger service. Despite the success of Linee Aeree Transcontinentali Italiene's flights between Rome and Rio de Janeiro, they lasted only two years until the Second World War forced the discontinuation of the service.

Despite the early achievements of Great Britain and the United States, it was Germany who persevered with the North Atlantic routes. In July 1929, a decade after the inaugural flights, the German liner *Bremen* launched a mail-carrying Heinkel He-12 seaplane 300 miles east of New York. The following year the German liner *Europa* made 24 catapult launchings, with both Heinkel 58s and Junkers 46as being thrown into the air. With the success of this method ascertained a depot ship, *Schwabenland*, was placed between the Azores and New York as one stage in a route that stretched between Berlin to New York via Lisbon.

Concurrent with their airship development, the Germans had made 14 Blohm and Voss Ha-139 flights over the Atlantic and were hoping to launch a routine service. In August 1938 a Focke-Wulf Condor flew from Berlin to New York in less than 25 hours, returning in 20 but, as with the Italians, German Atlantic progress was halted by the Second World War. Britain and the United States were also pushing forward the boundaries of air travel, again preferring flying boats to land-based aircraft that required a long, permanent and well-engineered landing strip. Imperial Airways and Pan American combined to start a service between New York and Bermuda in June 1937, which success encouraged further flights between Foynes in Ireland and Botwood in Newfoundland. That summer, while people spoke of the tragedy of *Hindenburg*, Sikorsky S23s flew between Southampton and New York without mishap. In early 1939 a regular flight began between New York and Lisbon, while June saw the first of thousands of Boeings begin an Atlantic service. Two months later the British Overseas Airways Corporation flew the first regular British airmail service across the Atlantic, shortly before the Second World War erupted.

On 13th September 1940, as the German radio gloated about the Luftwaffe's supposed destruction of Fleet Street, British aircraft were delivering Fleet Street newspapers into New York. Despite the efforts of French, Italian and German companies, it was the BOAC that operated the first regular transatlantic service, ferrying North American-trained pilots and various diplomats over and above the Atlantic. By the time war ended the Atlantic air crossing was virtually routine.

Then the real competition began. Companies from half the nations of Europe and all of North America vied with each other for the transatlantic routes. There was Air France and Sabena, Swissair and American Overseas Airlines, Svensk International and BOAC. Where once a handful of daring pilots had wagered their lives in a machine seemingly made of string and canvas, now the Atlantic air route was the most popular in the world. The success of the fliers virtually finished the Atlantic surface passenger trade. A service that had once been a necessity for millions of emigrants was now reduced to little more than a luxury cruise for the fortunate. The end of an era, but the Atlantic crossing has always been about progress.

Chapter 20

The Atlantic Lifeline

*'Unless a reasonable number of long-distance destroyers and
long-range aircraft come shortly a very serious situation
will develop on the Atlantic lifeline'*
Admiral Max Horton 19th November 1942, to the Admiralty.

On the same day that Britain declared war on Germany, Leutnant Lemp of U.30 torpedoed the passenger liner *Athenia* a few miles south of Rockall Bank. *Athenia* carried evacuees for the United States, and although 1300 survivors were hauled out of the water by nearby vessels, over 100 people died – 22 of these were United States' citizens. While Lemp possibly believed that *Athenia* was an armed merchant cruiser, the British Admiralty judged that the Germans had reverted to their First World War practice of unrestricted sinkings. By the 1936 Submarine Protocol, it was illegal to sink any merchant ship 'without having first placed passengers, crew and ship's papers in a place of safety'. Lemp's mistake resulted in an immediate hardening of attitudes on both sides. Even if some subsequent U-boat commanders acted humanely, the image of the hidden assassin was already imprinted in Allied minds.

Resolved not to repeat their mistakes of the last war, the Admiralty immediately organised convoys and ordered what they hoped would be adequate numbers of escort vessels. They would all be needed, for the redoubtable ex-submariner Carl Donitz commanded the U-boats. By the outbreak of war he possessed 57 vessels but reckoned he would need 300 to defeat the power of the Royal Navy.

In the early months the so-called phoney war was punctuated by acts of incredible bravery. In November 1939 Lt-Commander Maloney of the Royal Navy was sailing a captured merchant vessel into a British port when a U-boat surfaced dead ahead. Raising the white ensign, Maloney increased speed to ram, but gunfire from the submarine set his ship alight. The smoke attracted a couple of armed trawlers, who chased away the submarine before rescuing both British and German seamen from the merchant ship.

Individual actions, however brave, could do little to stem the inevitable. Donitz organised his U-boat commanders into wolf packs, ordered them to keep in radio communication with each other and spread them to form a wide net across the Atlantic. Commanded by highly-trained officers, the U-boats rode on the surface so that the British asdic could not trace them and struck by night. To the German people they were heroes, to the Royal Navy they were dangerous enemies, and to the merchant seamen they were ruthless killers.

This Atlantic war was unrelentingly brutal with men drowned in the freezing water, roasted by the gasoline of torpedoed tankers or choked by diesel oil from stricken ships. It was a war of incredible bravery, epitomised by the fight of *Rawalpindi,* an armed merchant cruiser with eight six-inch guns, against the battlecruiser *Scharnhorst* and her sister ship *Gneisenau.* 'Enemy battlecruisers sighted' Captain Kennedy reported as he moved to attack. It was a one-sided battle, but Kennedy's last stand delayed the battlecruisers so they had to withdraw before larger units of the Royal Navy steamed up. Even unarmed merchantmen could fight back, as one U-boat discovered when her torpedo missed SS *Clan MacBean* in October 1939. Ignoring the fire from the submarine's bow gun Captain Coultas attempted to ram, forcing the U-boat to submerge with its gun crew still on deck.

Every front in the war was important, but the Atlantic was the lifeline. Without supplies from North America, without the fighting material and fighting men from Canada and the United States, Britain may well have been defeated. And if Germany had obtained the shipbuilding and industrial strength of Britain and the oilfields defended by British armies in the Middle East, she might well have attacked across the Atlantic. Perhaps speculation is profitless, but could Russia without allies have withstood the might of Germany? And could an isolated and ill-prepared United States, without Britain as a base and stepping stone, have defeated a combination of rampant Germany and Imperial Japan? Control of the Atlantic ensured that neither of these scenarios occurred, and it was the skill of the Allied navies that ensured that the lifeline held intact. The Atlantic convoys kept Britain, the never perfect but always persevering representative of democracy, alive and fighting.

By declaring a neutrality zone, Roosevelt's Panama Act of 2nd October 1939 agreed with American public opinion. However, by banning all belligerent ships from an area extending from the Canadian border to Cape Horn, and extending up to 1000 miles out to sea, Roosevelt had effectively aided the Allies. German submarines could no longer operate in the western Atlantic without challenging American neutrality.

In the meantime the claws of Hitler's surface fleet slashed at the sinews of Allied trade. After running riot in the South Atlantic, *Graf Spee* was trapped by a small force of British and New Zealand cruisers and scuttled herself in Montevideo harbour. The attempts of the pocket battleship *Gneisenau* and cruiser *Koln* to endanger Allied merchant shipping was thwarted by the Royal Navy, but the heavy cruiser *Admiral Scheer* had a more immediate impact. On 5th November 1940 she attacked a 37-ship convoy bound for Britain. Captain Fegen, commanding the armed merchant cruiser *Jervis Bay,* ordered the convoy to scatter while he steamed to engage. With her six-inch guns hopelessly outranged by *Admiral Scheer's* eleven-inch, *Jervis Bay* still held back the raider for 30 minutes, allowing most of the convoy to escape. Captain Fegen and many of his crew were killed.

The sea war was not going according to the plan of either side. By this date Admiral Donitz still had less than 60 effective U-boats, and British reliance on asdic had proved over-optimistic – many improvements were necessary before submarines could be effectively traced underwater. German acoustic and magnetic mines had sunk scores of Allied vessels by the middle of February 1940, particularly in the North Sea, and Donitz used the mines to provide cover for his U-boats. Where mines could be blamed, U-boats were allowed to disregard the 1936 code and sink without warning. 'Do not rescue any men, do not take them along, and do not take care of any boats from the ship' Donitz ordered.

German fear and hatred of the Royal Navy which had defeated them in the previous war appeared to extend to the Luftwaffe, for the savagery of their air raids on Clydebank and Plymouth showed more than mere professionalism. When the Luftwaffe raided Clydebank they destroyed or damaged all but six of the houses. When they attacked Plymouth, defended only by the destroyers *Jackal* and *Mauritius*, they augmented their official bomb load by hurtling down pieces of metal, tools and spikes to rip the tyres of ambulances and fire engines. Refused permission to visit their families in the town, some of *Jackal's* crew imprisoned the first lieutenant, obtained permission from Lord Mountbatten and went ashore. Mountbatten reputedly had the ringleaders arrested at a later date and in a different port.

Although their invasion of Norway ended in practically every major German ship sustaining damage, it also gave Germany many new Atlantic bases and increased the length of coastline hostile to the Allies. The obvious threat to Iceland and the Faeroe Islands induced the Allies into occupying both. In the meantime the convoy war continued. After their intelligence obtained Royal Navy codes, the U-boats knew the position and routes of the convoys nearly as well as the British did. When France fell many destroyers were diverted from convoy duties to counter the expected German invasion, with the result that the U-boats enjoyed their 'happy time' and merchant shipping losses mounted. The shortage of escort vessels meant that even submarines were pressed into service, but more common were the hastily-constructed corvettes that were based on the Middlesbrough-built whale catcher *Southern Pride*. The original flower class corvettes were slower than surfaced U-boats and rolled badly in an Atlantic winter, but they filled an unpleasant gap in the convoy defences. Later designs were faster, more suited for the Atlantic and more powerfully armed.

British naval losses at Dunkirk had been heavy, but on 30th August 1940 President Roosevelt announced a lend-lease deal that sent 50 elderly but reconditioned and much appreciated destroyers from the United States to the Royal Navy in return for a long lease on bases. It was September before the Royal Navy claimed their new vessels in Halifax, Nova Scotia, and the matelots discovered that their American counterparts had left various articles of genuine goodwill on board, from pumpkins to pencil sharpeners. Donitz also received reinforcements in the shape of 27 Italian submarines, but soon realised that many Italians possessed different ideas about Atlantic warfare. One Italian commander, Salvatore Todaro, actually towed a packed lifeboat 600 miles to safety. Perhaps Donitz did not approve, but Todaro's conduct reveals an essential decency that not even fascism could submerge. Other submarine commanders appeared less charitable. On 17th September 1940 Kapitanleutnant Bleichrodt in U.48 torpedoed *City of Benares* which was carrying child evacuees to the sanctuary of North America. A Miss Cornish looked after seven survivors for a week in an open lifeboat; 77 other children died. That same month convoy HX 79 lost ten ships in five murderous hours.

The Allies responded by altering convoy routes northward and allocating more escorts and some aircraft but they were opposed by U-boat commanders such as Otto Kretschmer, an ace who sunk 44 merchant ships. While submariners were recommended to fire a spread of four or six torpedoes from a range of 3000 yards, Kretschmer often crept within the escort screen to sink a ship with a single torpedo. On 3rd November 1940 he torpedoed the British armed merchant cruisers *Laurentic* and *Patroclus*, while during a single three-day battle in March 1941 he sank five ships and damaged a sixth. Then Kretschmer, known as Otto the Silent, encountered a hunter every bit as skilled as himself; Commander Donald MacIntyre of HMS *Walker* depth-charged his U.99 to the surface. The successes of MacIntyre's 5th escort group helped to end this particular 'happy time' for the U-boats.

Kretschmer was one of a trio of U-boat aces recently neutralised by the Royal Navy. Also in a POW camp was Gunther Prien, whose U.47 had torpedoed *Royal Oak* after penetrating the defences of Scapa Flow in October 1939. In his short, violent career, Prien sunk 28 merchant vessels before meeting HMS *Wolverine*. The third ace, Joachin Schepke, had died when HMS *Vanoc* rammed his U.100. But men like Kretschmer can never be discounted. As a POW in Bowmanville, Ontario, he managed to contact Germany to arrange a submarine pick-up for escaped prisoners of war. Unfortunately for the Germans, the Canadian military had recaptured the runaways before the U-boat arrived off the St Lawrence.

Three dangerous submariners down, scores still at large and even with the lend-lease destroyers the Royal Navy was short of escorts, with around half the escort fleet damaged or under repair. At the beginning of 1941 thousands of men were transferred from the services to the shipyards, and the Admiralty equipped some merchant ships with catapult-launched aircraft but, even so, convoy losses in the approaches to the south and north of Ireland were unacceptably high. Churchill ordered the temporary abandonment of the southern approach route and moved the headquarters of western approaches to the Mersey. When Admiral Noble took over he immediately set up repair bases in northern England, Northern Ireland, Scotland and Newfoundland. Meanwhile the neutral United States continued to repair many Allied ships.

While the Germans used Focke-Wulf aircraft to spot the convoys, the Allies countered with British and Canadian long-range aircraft. Many of these aircraft were

American-built Lockheed Hudsons and Catalinas, and they scoured for U-boats from bases in Iceland, Britain and Canada. The happy time was well and truly over for the German submarines. In April an American destroyer USS *Niblack* had depth-charged a suspected U-boat and later that month the United States pushed their neutrality zone even further east. Nonetheless neither the President nor Hitler wanted America in the war. In Britain, one ship was built for every three sunk.

On 18th May 1941 Germany unleashed *Bismarck*. Completed earlier that year, the 45,000-ton battleship was the most modern and amongst the most powerful in the world and when combined with the heavy cruiser *Prinz Eugen* she posed a massive threat to every Atlantic convoy. As the German ships entered the Denmark Strait they were shadowed by a brace of British cruisers, while heavy units of the British Home Fleet sailed out of Scapa and other vessels moved to cover the convoys. On 24th May HMS *Hood*, an elderly but beloved battleship, backed by the untried *Prince of Wales*, met the Germans, with the result that *Hood* was sunk, *Bismarck* damaged and *Prince of Wales* withdrew to join the stalking cruisers. An air attack from *Victorious* further damaged *Bismarck* as the Royal Navy closed in. On the 25th *Bismarck* and *Prinz Eugen* parted company but after the death of *Hood* the Royal Navy were after blood. Sailing south-eastward for France to repair her damage, *Bismarck* vanished into the Atlantic. There were worried men in the Admiralty until aircraft located the giant German ship, then the Royal Navy presented the bill. This was about more than convoy protection, this was about the pride of the Royal Navy and angry men who had seen their friends killed. On the evening of the 26th torpedoes damaged *Bismarck*'s steering and reduced her speed; she was harassed by destroyers until finally the battleships *King George V* and *Rodney* closed, battered her with their big guns until, again torpedoed, *Bismarck* sank.

Her destruction was one major success for the Allies but a second and even more significant came that same month when the Royal Navy captured U.110 off the Hebrides. Although the same Lemp who had torpedoed *Athenia* commanded U.110, his death was irrelevant compared to the intact Enigma machine that was aboard. Now the Allies could read the U-boat codes.

British successes had forced Donitz to concentrate his U-boats in mid-Atlantic, beyond the range of watchful long-range Catalinas. In the summer Germany attacked Russia, in August Churchill met Roosevelt and 269 squadron Coastal Command captured a complete U-boat. By decoding the German messages, Admiralty knew which convoys were under U-boat threat, and the Royal Navy intercepted and destroyed U-boat supply ships in mid-Atlantic. And all the time day by day, ship after precious ship crossed the Atlantic laden with Canadian wheat and Canadian manpower, West Indian sugar and United States food and military supplies. If the United States was not yet at war, she provided the wherewithal to keep what remained of the democratic world fighting. In the meantime the hugely-expanded Royal Canadian Navy played a significant part in controlling western seas. Farm boys from Saskatchewan and Alberta, Ontario and Manitoba, learned their sea lore the hard way, riding herd around vital Allied convoys

On 5th September U-652 attacked the destroyer USS *Greer* 125 miles off Iceland. Later that month the United States Navy began escorting convoys between Newfoundland and Iceland. On the 7th December Japanese aircraft attacked Pearl Harbour and Singapore and four days later Hitler declared war on the United States. It was now open season on any shipping, anywhere in the world and trade along the Atlantic seaboard of the United States was extremely vulnerable to submarine attack.

Donitz knew this as well as anybody else and in January 1942 he launched his improved, long range U-boats against American shipping. At that time there were no convoys along the United States' east coast, and the U-boats enjoyed another happy time. Ship after ship, tanker after tanker was torpedoed as they sailed singly and unescorted along the coast. Behind them, the towns of Florida flared with brilliant lights, a tourist contrast to the dark scenes out at sea as nearly 500 merchant ships, over 200 of them tankers, died, taking thousands of seamen with them. By rejecting hard-learned British advice, Admiral King condemned scores of ships to be torpedoed. Only after six months of slaughter did the United States introduce a convoy system, and then they looked for escorts.

After sending so much to Britain, the United States had little left to escort her own ships and now it was Britain's turn to supply much-needed warships to America. Two dozen anti-submarine trawlers, more Coastal Command aircraft than she could spare and ten hard-working corvettes crossed the Atlantic to keep the lifeline intact. Admiral Adolphus Andrews, the United States Navy commander of the eastern sea frontier, began the inevitable fight back. When U-boats attacked her shipping, Brazil declared war and the United States' occupation of Brazilian bases proved invaluable for convoy protection. An interlocking convoy system radically reduced shipping losses, so after August 1942 the western Atlantic and Caribbean were virtually secure for the Allies.

In mid-Atlantic the situation deteriorated as a new generation of larger, more modern U-boats used 'milch cow' submarines to refuel and re-arm, enabling them to remain longer at sea. Of the 400 U-boats in the German Navy, perhaps 81 operated in the Atlantic at any one time and despite the losses to the Allied navies, Donitz' intensive training ensured that the quality of submarine officers remained high. Sinkings rose in the second half of 1942 until the strands of the lifeline seemed about to part. As the year turned, 30 convoys might operate simultaneously in the Atlantic, with about 670 merchant vessels escorted by nearly 150 warships. Most valuable were the tankers that carried fuel, or the troopships that carried the young manhood from a score of Allied nations to the battle zones of Europe and North Africa.

The wolf packs hunted across a broad front, and immediately a U-boat sighted a convoy it reported to headquarters at Lorient, who whistled up the other members of the pack and directed them to the attack. Sailing on the surface, the wolves congregated around the group leader who selected their targets, and once the torpedoes were loosed the submarines submerged and fled before the escorts could retaliate. It was very professional, very calculated and highly effective. But the capture of the Enigma machine meant that the Allied navies could also read the orders from Lorient and could attack the packs as they mustered.

All the time the war of technology continued – the Allies hunted surfaced U-boats with radar, traced submerged U-boats with asdic and bombarded them with depth charges. While the early depth charge throwers were crude, later improvements included the 'hedgehog' that could propel the lethal canisters in a net around the submarine. Clever U-boat commanders could respond by discharging oil or air bubbles to deceive the hunter.

At the end of 1942 Donitz guessed that the Allies were preparing to invade Africa, but his instincts let him down as he ordered his U-boats to cover Dakar rather than the north-west of the continent. Simultaneously Admiral Horton, commanding the eastern section of the Atlantic, organised support groups to hunt and destroy the U-boats. Initially four such groups were created and, under commanders such as Captain Walker, proved extremely effective. Squadrons of Halifax and Liberator aircraft began to patrol the central sector of the Atlantic, which the Allies knew as 'the Gap', the Germans as the 'black pit' but which both knew to be the decisive area of the war. German surface ships were still dangerous, but a raid by the heavy cruiser *Hipper* and *Lutzow* on a Russia-bound convoy found the Royal Navy eager for battle – *Hipper* was fortunate to escape with relatively minor damage. Even so, 1943 opened on a low as seven tankers were sunk in a convoy of nine, and it appeared that the U-boats were in greater strength than ever.

Only with colossal shipbuilding efforts could enough merchant ships be built to replace the losses. In 1942 the United States began a 'Ships for Victory' programme, aiming to launch three ships a day, a target which they achieved that October. *Joseph N. Teal* was the deciding vessel, having been constructed in an amazing ten days at the yard of Henry J Kaiser. 'A miracle of God,' Kaiser proclaimed, 'and the genius of free American workmen.' *Joseph N Teal* was one of thousands of Liberty ships, mass-produced and prefabricated. Ironically, the Sunderland Company of Newcastle-upon-Tyne had laid down the original design as far back as 1879, but they were simple, robust and carried a large cargo. With so many men fighting, up to a third of Kaiser's workforce were women, and women were also involved in the construction of *Robert E. Peary* at Richmond, California in four and a half days. Frequently underestimated but never defeated, British women also built ships and one, Second Engineer Victoria Drummond, commanded her engine room on an Atlantic convoy.

The Atlantic battle climaxed in the first half of 1943, during a season of savage storms that reduced air cover for the Gap. To combat Donitz' submarines the Allies had twelve escort groups; one United States, four Canadian and seven British, plus two British support groups and one United States Navy group. The year began with a strong wolf pack attack on convoy SC 118, where 13 ships were lost but three U-boats sunk. Convoy ON 166 was next, escorted by Captain Heineman's United States' escort group A3. First blood went to the US Navy as the Coastguard cutter *Spencer* destroyed U-225, but as they entered the Gap seven more U-boats attacked. Five merchant vessels were sunk, plus another U-boat.

As the months passed the tempo increased. There were about 100 U-boats hunting the convoys, and ship after ship was sunk, with the attendant loss of men. By March the lifeline was fraying fast as Britain had just two months of munitions remaining, but if 97 merchant ships had been sunk in only 20 days, the Allies had accounted for 15 U-boats. The technological struggle was just as intense, with the Luftwaffe working on the Heinkel 177 and Messerchmidt 264, long range 'Amerika' bombers intended to bomb New York. Despite the losses in the Gap, British proposals that Admiral King use some of the Liberators at present patrolling peaceful areas of the Pacific were turned down. Only the intervention of Roosevelt saw a squadron of the US Army Air Force located in Newfoundland, and with their help the Gap was nearly closed.

Allied tactics in the Gap were to cover each convoy with both a support group and long-range aircraft. In addition there were some small aircraft carriers, 'baby flat-tops' to the United States seamen, but the basic war continued between escorts and submarines. A convoy conference was held in March, deciding that while the United States' support groups would remain under the command of King, Horton would assume control of Canadian as well as British groups. All the time, land-based aircraft patrolled the Bay of Biscay attacking U-boats as they poured westward to the Gap. While escort groups defended the convoys, support groups followed up by hunting the often-damaged submarines, allowing them as little peace as the U-boats allowed the underpaid, underarmed and often under-appreciated merchant seamen.

In April a 17-strong wolf pack targeted convoy HX 231 and although four U-boats were accounted for there was also shipping loss. A massive pack of 39 submarines attacked convoy ONS 5, and in an Atlantic nightmare of flaring ships, drowning men and raging gales, 12 merchantmen were sunk, but the escorts took revenge on six U-boats. As April drew into May it became clear that the U-boat attack was being blunted. There were fewer, larger convoys protected by more escorts, but still over 100 U-boats lurked in the Gap.

During May, out of 894 merchant ships convoyed through the Gap, only 32 were lost and after the 17th there were no losses in the northern section. The support groups, British, Canadian and American, had overturned the U-boat successes. Escort ships had sunk 11 submarines, aircraft had destroyed 10 more and had assisted in sinking another three. It was no wonder that Donitz reported that 'U-boat losses in May therefore reached unbearable heights'. Even more significantly, he withdrew his U-boats, later to declare 'We had lost the Battle of the Atlantic.'

Although there was much heavy fighting ahead, never again would the U-boats pose such a serious threat. If submarines increased in size so did convoys, and the Bay of Biscay saw bitter encounters between packs of heavily-armed submarines and Coastal Command aircraft. Support groups roamed the Bay, and HMS *Starling* sank two U-boats in a hectic seven hours. In July a total of 19 U-boats were destroyed in the Bay. The U.S. Navy swept through the seas off Brazil, sinking every U-boat they found, while air patrols continued their heady success rate.

In Autumn Donitz tried again in the Atlantic, but despite some sinkings and a new acoustic torpedo he realised he was losing submarines faster than they could be replaced. In December the desperate German Navy resorted to their surface vessels again, sending out a battle group centred on *Scharnhorst* to attack convoy JW 55b for Murmansk. Again the Royal Navy was ready, with the cruisers *Belfast, Sheffield* and *Norfolk* repulsing *Scharnhorst*'s first and second assault. When Admiral Sir Bruce Fraser attacked in *Duke of York*, for the first time in her career *Scharnhorst* faced a ship as powerful as herself, and was sunk in possibly the last ever purely capital ship to capital ship action in European waters. The year that had started so well for the German Navy had ended in disaster.

Donitz continued to attack, but despite the use of magnetic torpedoes and snorkels, there were more U-boats being sunk than ever before. When Donitz mustered 70 submarines to attack the D-day armada, Coastal Command aircraft and escort ships from just about every Allied navy harried them right across the Bay of Biscay. Allied naval supremacy ensured that the invasion of France proceeded with little molestation, and the wolf packs had been tamed. In the single month of April 1945 57 U-boats were sunk, and by the time Germany admitted defeat 781 had been accounted for. Over 150 surrendered but 221 were scuttled or blown up by their own crews. The cost had been high; thousands of ships were sunk and many thousands of men died to keep the seas free. There are some poignant memorials to these men, from the Cross of Lorraine that recalls the Free Frenchmen who were based in the Clyde, to the massive monument in Battery Park, Manhattan for the Americans who sailed from New York but never returned to the light of Liberty's torch.

The professionalism and skill of the Allied navies, but most of all the sheer courage of the merchant seamen who had refused to be cowed, had defeated the wolves. Why had the merchant seamen persisted, despite an appalling casualty rate? Not for money - the average British merchant mariner earned shockingly low wages and any improvements during the war were surely less than they deserved. It is impossible to define any single reason, for each individual had his own, but there must have been something that empowered these men. They were not uniquely aggressive, yet there was surely a degree of sheer bloody-mindedness that made them refuse to give in. They had sailed because they had to, because it was their job and surely, in many cases, just because Hitler had to be defeated. Their courage strengthened each strand of the Atlantic lifeline and enabled the world to be cleansed of a great evil.

Chapter 21

The Challenge of Pleasure

'A wet sheet and a flowing sea,
A wind that follows fast,
And fills the white and rustling sail,
And bends the gallant mast.'
Allan Cunningham.

After being a place of mystery and a frontier for adventurers, a route for the desperate and a killing ground for predators, the Atlantic was not the most obvious stretch of water in which to seek pleasure. However, humanity can frequently surprise even itself and in 1966 two original individuals decided they would row from the New World to the Old. Both had been members of the British Parachute Regiment, but while John Ridgeway was an experienced sailor, Chay Blyth had barely rowed a boat in his life.

They set off from Cape Cod, that most evocative of American headlands, and for 92 days they hauled their open dory *English Rose III* across the Atlantic. Perhaps he had been a novice at the start, but by the time he reached the Aran Islands off Ireland, Blyth had earned his title of Number Two in the boat and was destined for a career of adventurous voyaging. Others followed in the wake of Ridgeway and Blyth, so the Atlantic has been crossed by a weird assortment of adventurers, some rowing alone and one audacious man even swimming across for charity. He was from the United States, where eccentricity for a good cause seems to be encouraged as a way of life. Much more common are the yachts that batter their way through gales and murderous seas, for yacht racing is a long-established pastime.

In 1851 the Royal Yacht Squadron offered a cup as prize for a yacht race around the Isle of Wight. Sixteen yachts entered the race; 15 were British, the other was a schooner of 170 tons built by George Steers of New York and named *America*. On 22nd August John Stevens skippered *America* to victory and from that date the United States dominated what is arguably the most famous yacht race in the world. In honour of

The United States dominated what is arguably the most famous yacht race in the world.

Stevens' victory, the name of the race was altered from the 'Hundred Guineas Cup' to the 'America's Cup'.

Yachts were originally developed as state vessels that displayed the dignity and pomp of monarchs or high officials, but in 1661 the first recorded yacht race was held. The competitors were Charles II in *Katherine*, and the Duke of York in *Anne*, but although their race on the Thames attracted some interest, yachting as a sport had a stuttering start. It was not until 1720 that the oldest surviving yacht club, the Royal Cork Yacht Club, was founded as the Water Club of Cork and another 55 years before the Royal Thames Yacht Club started. The United States had to wait until 1844 for their famous New York Yacht Club. The success of the latter made the long delay well worthwhile, but prior to that date many maritime citizens had sailed for pleasure without the formality of membership of any society. The Chesapeake in particular might have been created for cruising.

In the beginning, most British yachts were the playthings of the ultra-rich who raced for bets that ranged from £100 upwards. Crewed by professionals and modelled on the design of revenue cutters, yachts could often be monstrous in size although few were as large as the 493-ton barque *Brilliant* of G.H. Ackers. Well into the 19th century the traditional yacht design continued, but the stunning victory of *America* in 1851 shattered British complacency. With her finer hull design, her cotton sails and, perhaps most of all, her sheer audacity in winning a sport that many British considered to be their own, *America* was the precursor of a new line of yachts. In 1857 the America's Cup was formally presented to the New York Yacht Club and subsequently became possibly the most sought-after trophy in the history of yachting.

Many yachting Britons were desperate to bring the cup back across the Atlantic and from 1870 a series of challenge races were held. The names of the challengers include some of the most famous in British, Australian and Canadian yachting history, vessels such as Sir Thomas Lipton's *Shamrock*, the Canadian *Countess of Dufferin* and the Australian *Southern Cross*, but just about all had to defer to the Stars and Stripes. *Mischief* and *Mayflower*, *Defender* and *Constellation*; the United States' yachts have almost invariably proved superior. Until 1937 the America's Cup was contested between the largest of racing yachts, but new rules in the aftermath of the Second World War saw them restricted to the International 12 metre class, with the trophy going to the best overall in seven races. The American stranglehold was loosened only once, when the Royal Perth Yacht Club wrested the trophy to Australia in 1983. Four years later, in 1987, the bicentenary of the founding of Australia, half the yachting world seemed to congregate at Fremantle, Western Australia, where the cup was recaptured by the United States, but however much it dominated international prestige, the America's Cup was only one of an increasing number of racing events.

In 1875 the British designer E.H. Bentall built *Jullanar* with 'the longest waterline, the smallest frictional surface, and the shortest keel' of any contemporary yacht. She was also one of the most successful ever launched, winning many races and with her design influencing yachts such as *Britannia* and *Satania*. In the United States the Rhode Islander Nathaniel Herreschoff designed a 30-foot catamaran named *Amaryllis* that left all racing opposition floundering in her Narragansett wake. Until then the local yachtsmen had used broad-beamed sandbaggers, but Herreschoff's triumph led to a temporary interest in twin-hulled vessels. Longer lasting was the Herreschoff-designed *Gloriana* with a revolutionary hull form and a cutaway forefoot that managed to astonish those sailors that followed her to the finishing line. After such success it was not surprising that Herreschoff should be chosen to design yachts for the America's Cup.

By the beginning of the 20th century even the minor yacht races were becoming extremely organised. Races had a handicap system so that smaller yachts had an increased chance of competing, but as measurement was judged entirely on length, many vessels were designed shallow and broad. Known as 'skimming dishes' these yachts were useless for anything other than racing and were virtually outlawed by the international yachting conference of 1906. After 1925 the large J-class yachts dominated the major races. These could stretch to nearly 90 feet, were again crewed by yachting professionals and were so exorbitantly expensive that only the wealthiest of the élite could afford them. The Second World War ended such extravagance.

As the popularity of the sport spread to an increasing, and increasingly prosperous, middle-class, most races were between smaller vessels. With yacht clubs introducing one-design classes that relinquished the singularity of separate yachts in order to test the skills of the sailor in fair competition, designers worked less for individuals than for mass-producing boatyards. Lighter materials than the traditional hardwoods further revolutionised yacht building as fibreglass hulls became the norm, and scientific research improved sail design and rigging. With all these alterations it would almost appear that the challenge has been removed from sailing, but appearances can often be deceptive.

As so often before, once humanity had managed the basics of sailing in home waters, they looked to the Atlantic for the next challenge. As early as December 1866 the New

...fibreglass hulls became the norm

York Yacht Club was the motive force for the first transatlantic race. Three schooners, *Fleetwing*, *Vesta* and *Henrietta* sailed from Sandy Hook to Cowes hoping for the $30,000 prize. It was an innovative gesture and although *Henrietta* won without major mishap it was to be many years before such a race was organised on a more regular basis. However, a race was held between the schooners *Dauntless* and *Cambria* from Queenstown in southern Ireland to New York in 1870. Perhaps because such long-distance racing remained very much a rich man's pursuit, it failed to capture public interest. It was 35 years before the German Kaiser proposed another race across the Atlantic, but that same year saw a resurgence of interest in long- distance racing. A schooner with the somewhat prosaic name of *Atlantic* won the eight-yacht Atlantic race of 1905, but there was nothing prosaic about her fast time of twelve days and five hours. Around the same time the Bermuda and Fastnet races were introduced. The Bermuda Race was held between New York and Bermuda, the Fastnet between Cowes and the Fastnet Rock, and both could produce conditions to challenge the most seaworthy of racing yachts.

Whatever the pleasures of sport, the sea remains a dangerous place. Any death is a tragedy, and the danger of offshore racing was proved without a doubt during the Fastnet race of 1979. Although 303 yachts started that race only 85 finished, and it was due to the bravery and skill of the rescue services that the death toll was prevented from being any higher. The statistics speak for themselves, but cannot conjure up the frantic conditions of sailing a racing yacht through an Atlantic storm. The only consolation of this tragedy was the almost immediate review of yacht design by the Department of Ship Science at the University of Southampton.

Perhaps the Fastnet is the most prestigious ocean race, held alternately with the Bermuda race, but it is only part of a series of encounters in which the Admiral's Cup is the prize. From 1960, perhaps inevitably, the single-handed transatlantic race has become a more regular event with a four-year span between races for the competitors to recover their strength and, no doubt, rebuild their bank balance. The inaugural race saw some of the world's legendary yachtsmen competing including the 59-year-old

Francis Chichester, an adventurer who had already been the first man to fly solo to Australia and who had won yacht races while in his fifties. In 1960 Chichester, always supported by his wife, had recently defeated lung cancer and now hoped to defeat the Atlantic in his new 39-foot sloop *Gipsy Moth III*. Like so many earlier English mariners, Chichester was from Devon and his 40-day voyage won the race. Two years later Chichester again pitted himself against the Atlantic when he crossed in a record 33 days, a time he further reduced to 30 days in the 1964 race when he came second to the Frenchman Eric Tabarly.

After pushing back the frontiers of yachting by sailing single-handed from Plymouth to Sydney, Chichester completed the circumnavigation in his 53-foot ketch *Gipsy Moth IV*. The Queen was waiting for his arrival at Greenwich, and knighted him with the same sword that Elizabeth of England had used to knight Francis Drake after his circumnavigation. Still not satisfied, Chichester entered the 1972 transatlantic race, but declining health forced his retiral.

The same Eric Tabarly who had been victorious in the 1964 race adopted Chichester's mantle. An officer in the French Navy, Tabarly is, quite simply, one of the best single-handed racing yachtsmen in the world. He both planned and sailed five world-renowned yachts, all carrying the *Pen Duick* name. It was in *Pen Duick II* that he won the 1964 transatlantic race and three years later he entered, and won, the Royal Ocean Club's Morgan Cup, the Channel race, the Fastnet race, the Plymouth to La Rochelle race and the Benodet Race. His second place in the Sydney-Hobart race that same year must have been a bit of a disappointment. The following year he came second in the transatlantic race, following that by winning the 1969 transpacific race in *Pen Duick V.* It is somehow reassuring to know that this century can still produce such personalities.

It is perhaps even more reassuring to know that women are increasingly attracted by yacht racing, thus dispelling the myth that it takes a brawny muscleman to sail a racing yacht. There have always been women at sea, of course, from Betsy Miller who captained a Saltcoats collier in the 1800s to Mary Anne Talbot who was a powder monkey at the Glorious First of June, a midshipman in HMS *Vesuvius* and a second mate on a United States' merchantman. Nonetheless, only in this century were women able to take their rightful place in the yachting world and, as the yachtswoman Clare Francis has often proved, that place was frequently amongst the leaders.

Educated to degree level in London, Francis withdrew from an excellent career to sail. Her first major voyage was in the 32-foot *Gulliver G*, sailing single-handed across the Atlantic for a bet, after which she was half the only all-female crew in the Round Britain Race. Next came the single-handed race to the Azores and in 1976 the single-handed transatlantic race. For all that modern technology has done for sailing, this is still a major undertaking, a minimum 2800-mile ordeal from Plymouth at the western tip of England to Newport in Rhode Island. On a good day the North Atlantic can be unpredictable, on a bad day it is horrendous and even with electronic equipment and radio links a sailor can be incredibly alone if help is needed. To put that in perspective, it was expecting a single person in a small sailing boat to undertake the same journey that Columbus had only attempted with royal backing.

At a little over five feet tall, Clare Francis would not only be the first British woman to enter the race, she would also be the smallest competitor. In a borrowed boat that was named *Robertson's Golly* after the sponsor, Francis crossed the start line on 5th June 1976. She knew that one newspaper had classified the race as 'the toughest race in the world' but to her it was 'simply a great adventure'. Both Francis and *Robertson's Golly* proved adequate for the task, although the Atlantic revealed much of its nasty side. Storm force winds provided views of white tipped waves that extended to the horizon, and as gale followed gale Francis grew weary. There were fogs that tested her nerve, whales that chased the yacht, bad radio reception and one morning there was the horrific thrill of waking to find that *Robertson's Golly* had passed right between two icebergs. Things that seem like trivial irritations on land become extremely important when single-handedly crossing the Atlantic and there was the sheer physical fatigue of constantly-interrupted sleep. The chilling cold of the Newfoundland Banks fog was depressing and news from family and friends was cheering, but the prospect of *Robertson's Golly* being tossed around by the Great Rip of the Nantucket Shoals was terrifying. However, the climax perhaps made it all worth while - when Francis arrived in Newport she was not only the fastest woman racer but also the first British monohull competitor to arrive. Not all were so lucky, or so skilled.

Of the 125 yachts which had begun the race only 78 managed to finish, and five of these were outwith the correct time. Forty yachts had pulled out for one reason or another, five yachtsmen were rescued and two, a Canadian and a Briton, disappeared. The winner was the ubiquitous Frenchman Eric Tabarly in his *Pen Duick VI*, a 73-foot long giant that was originally intended for a crew of a dozen. The French competitors appeared more intent on winning than on merely taking part, although at 236-feet long *Club Mediterranee* was surely too long to be a serious contender. Other French yachts were light, fast and professional. The British were more laid back, preferring to party than to worry and to sail than to race. One yachtsman, Jock MacLeod, had designed his *Ron Glas* to be controlled wholly from the cockpit, where he sat drinking whisky. Columbus would have been amazed and his crew probably envious.

Yachting is only one example of this new concept of nautical pleasure. For centuries the sea was a grim place to work, an area of hardship, hard knocks and hard work, as the various sayings certainly prove: 'the sea and the gallows refuse no man'; 'worse things happen at sea'. Together with the army, the sea was the last resort of the scoundrel, a place of punishment for offenders, and an unpleasant alternative to prison. Recently some people have inverted that to think of the sea as a place of romance; there has been interest in the clippers, in the days of the sailing navies and in the poems of John Masefield. Perhaps there was always an element of pleasure for a few – the rich on the pleasure yachts, the gold-braided officers on the quarterdeck of a flagship and those men to whom it was a calling rather than a necessity.

Tall ships in Leith, 1997. Photograph by the author.

Almost as soon as technology chased away the old ways, humanity revived the sailing ship and reinvented an interest in wind and oar-powered vessels. There is the Tall Ships Race, when scores of wind-powered vessels sail from port to port, cruising the Atlantic, the Baltic and the North Sea in a display of multi-masted majesty that is as heartstoppingly beautiful as any man-made spectacle can be. There are sail training ships from most maritime nations backed by an amazing variety of yachts, and in every port they visit people gather to greet them in their thousands and tens of thousands. The ancient heritage is revived in the best possible way, without the hunger and heartache that accompanied the working vessels which crossed the Atlantic for so many centuries. Other sailing traditions also continue – there was even a mutiny aboard a Polish tall ship in the 1999 race.

Even when the tall ships are elsewhere and the harbours return to their more mundane function of importing and exporting food and all the consumer goods that society believes it requires, there are still nautical exhibitions, maritime museums and restored ships. One excellent example is at the tiny port of Portsoy, near Banff in north-east Scotland, which has an annual traditional boat festival where fine examples of small working boats can be seen. Festivals such as this reveal the interest not only in nostalgia, but also in acquiring some hands-on experience in sailing these fascinating craft. The Atlantic Challenge is possibly one of the most international of traditional seafaring competitions. Here teams from seafaring nations around the Atlantic, including the United States, Britain, France, Canada and Denmark, race gigs modelled on a 1796 French pattern. On these vessels two of the masts have dipping lug sails, the third has a standing lug spanker, and there are also ten 18-foot long oars; sailing or rowing them is a real test of seamanship, not to mention character. The very fact that people are willing to attempt sailing something as complex and unwieldy as this reveals that modern life has not yet sapped the world of its vitality.

The United States also has its share of reconditioned sailing ships, a reminder of a heritage second to none. Where better to sail than in the Acadia National Park in Maine where the gaff-rigged schooner *Grace Bailey*, nearly 120 years old and as beautifully kept as if she had just slid off the slipway, is only one of a small fleet of sailing vessels. *Grace Bailey* was one of the traditional working schooners of these waters, carrying timber from the southern states, rum from the West Indies and granite from Maine to New York. Like most of the vessels of the Maine Windjammer Association, *Grace Bailey* sails from Penobscot Bay, where schooners grace Camden, Rockport or Rockland, facing towards their domain on the long Atlantic waves. The ghosts of old-time sailors would feel perfectly at home in Penobscot Bay as *Natalie Todd* or *Bay Lady* slide out on the morning mist, with the gurgle of water beneath the bow and the healthy groaning of timber the only sounds to disturb the circling sea birds. Passengers on these schooners may assist in hauling on ropes and raising the great white sails. Some, the lucky, can sail south to the Florida Keys and visit the Dry Tortuga National Park. Here, near to the island that Columbus first landed, in sight of the Florida Channel through which the Spanish *flota* sailed majestically, the modern tall-ship sailor can experience the real birth of the New World.

The children of the New World were conceived on the waves, nurtured by the fat-bottomed merchantmen and disciplined by privateer, pirate and man-of-war. Taught by the adventurous, filled by the hungry, part of the New World at last outgrew its parents, to break away in a teenage tantrum and mature into the nation that helped save democracy. It is a complex history, punctuated by tragedy and excitement, prizes of incredible wealth and stories of inspiring courage, but the backbone was always the bare-footed sailor who hauled on the rough ropes and the Atlantic itself with its eternally-seductive horizon.

Glossary

asdic (Allied Submarine Detection Investigation Committee) underwater sound-ranging equipment to detect submerged submarines which is now known as sonar.

barracoon stockade within which slaves were penned while awaiting transportation to the Americas.

barque a three-masted vessel, square-rigged on the fore and main, fore and aft rigged on the mizzen.

brig a two-masted, square-rigged vessel.

Chipangu old name for Japan.

cockpit either the well of a yacht from where the vessel is steered, or the area of a sailing ship used by midshipmen, and as an impromptu hospital in action.

curragh leather boat of the Celts, still used today in parts of Ireland.

Discovery Men name given by the whalers to the explorers who searched for the North West Passage.

dumbbell tenements form of tenement housing in 19th century United States cities, so-called because of their shape.

dunnage luggage at sea.

filibuster pirate or other ocean raider; originally a French term.

forecastle or fo'c's'le originally the fore castle of a mediaeval ship, later the accommodation space for the crew in the forward section of the ship.

frigate warship – in sailing days vessels used for scouting and general duties but of inferior gun power to line of battleships. In the Second World War frigates were revitalised as anti-submarine warships larger than corvettes but smaller than destroyers.

galley a vessel propelled primarily by oars.

grain boier a specialised Dutch vessel for carrying grain.

Hanseatic League trading association of various German cities. Its network extended to many ports of north Europe.

herring buss Dutch vessel used for catching herring.

line of battle line of fighting sailing vessels. This formation enabled each ship to bring her broadside of heavy cannon to bear.

Lizard, The or Lizard Point the southernmost promontory of England.

lugsail four-sided sail, usually on small vessels.

mizzen aftmost mast on a sailing vessel.

nao an ocean-going ship of the fifteenth century.

pink a small, square-rigged vessel with a narrow stern.

pinnace either a small, two-masted sailing vessel, or an eight-oared, later sixteen-oared, ship's boat.

scrimshaw carvings performed by whalers, especially American, on whales' teeth or walrus' tusks.

sloop a type of small anti-submarine escort vessel in the Second World War.

spanker an extra sail on the mizzenmast to use a following wind.

thralls slaves of the Norsemen.

tumblehome inward slope of a ship above the point of maximum width, used in days of sailing navies so that the heavy cannon in the lower decks had more space.

weatherly able to cope with bad weather, less likely to be droiven to leeward by the wind.

Bibliography

Alcock, Sir J. and Whitten-Brown, Sir Arthur, 1969. *Our Transatlantic Flight.* William Kimber, London.

Andrews, Charles M., 1921. *The Fathers of New England* in The Chronicles of America Series. Yale University Press, New Haven.

Andrews, Charles M., 1934. *The Colonial Period of American History: The Settlements.* Yale University Press, New Haven.

Andrews, K.R., 1978. 'The English in the Caribbean 1560–1620' in Canny, N.P., Andrews, K.R. and Hair, P.E.H. (Eds.) *The Westward Enterprise: English Activities in Ireland, the Atlantic and America, 1480–1650.* Liverpool University Press, Liverpool.

Andrews, K.R., 1964. *Elizabethan Privateering: English Privateers during the Spanish War 1585–1603.* Cambridge University Press.

Babington, Anthony, 1971. *The English Bastille.* Macdonald & Company, London.

Baines, Dudley, 1991. *Emigration from Europe 1815–1914.* Macmillan, Houndsmills, Basingstoke.

Bartlett, C.J., 1963. *Great Britain and Sea Power.* Clarendon Press, Oxford

Body, Geoffrey, 1985. *British Paddle Steamers.* David & Charles, Newton Abbot.

Bonsor, N.R.P., 1975. *North Atlantic Seaway: an illustrated history of the passenger services linking the old world and the new.* **1–4** , Arco Publishing, New York.

Brooks, Clive, 1989. *Atlantic Queens.* Haynes, Sparkford and Newbury Park, California.

Canny, Nicholas (Ed.,) 1994. *Europeans on the Move: Studies on European Migration 1500–1800.* Clarendon Press, Oxford.

Carpenter, Rhys, 1973. *Beyond the Pillars of Hercules.* Tandem, London.

Castlereagh, Duncan, 1971. *The Great Age of Exploration.* Readers Digest Association Limited, London.

Chalmers, Rear-Admiral W.S., 1954. *Max Horton and the Western Approaches.* Hodder & Stoughton, London.

Collins, John Stewart, 1976. *Christopher Columbus.* Macdonald & James, London.

Columbus, Christopher, 1947. *The Journal of his first voyage to America.* Jarrold, London.

Cooper, Patrick, 1934. *Hudson's Bay Company: A Brief History.* Hudson's Bay House, London.

Costello, John and Hughes, Terry, 1977. *The Battle of the Atlantic.* Collins, London.

Crone, G.R., 1969. *The Discovery of America.* Hamish Hamilton, London.

Davies, R.E.G., 1964. *A History of the World's Airlines.* Oxford University Press, New York and Toronto.

Davis, Ralph, 1962. *The Rise of the English Shipping Industry in the 17th and 18th Century* (Davis & Charles, Newton Abbot.

De Gramont, Sanche, 1975. *The Strong Brown God: The Story of the Niger River.* BCA, London.

De la Varende, Jean, 1955. *Cherish the Sea: A History of Sail,* Sidgwick & Jackson, London.

Devine, T.M., 1975. *The Tobacco Lords: A Study of the Tobacco Merchants of Glasgow and their Trading Activities c 1740–90.* John Donald, Edinburgh.

Dillon, Myles and Chadwick, Nora, 1973. *The Celtic Realms.* Sphere, London.

Dulles, Foster Rhea, 1955. *America's Rise to World Power 1898–1954.* Harper & Row, New York, Evanton, London.

Dunn, Richard S., 1978. 'Experiments holy and unholy 1630–1' in Canny, N.P., Andrews, K.R. and Hair, P.E.H. (Eds.) *The Westward Enterprise: English Activities in Ireland, the Atlantic and America, 1480–1650.* Liverpool University Press, Liverpool.

Edey, Maitland A., 1974. *The Sea Traders.* Time Life Books.

Edey, Maitland A., 1975. *Lost World of the Aegean.* Time Life Books.

Erickson, Charlotte, 1976. *Emigration from Europe 1815–1914.* A. & C. Black, London.

Fayle, Ernest C., 1948. 'Shipowning & Marine Insurance' in C. Northcote Parkinson (Ed) *The Trade Winds: A study of British overseas trade during the French wars 1793–1815.* George Allen & Unwin Ltd., London.

Fayle, Ernest C., 1927. *The War and the Shipping Industry.* Humphrey Milford, London.

Fayle, Ernest C., 1948. 'The Employment of British Shipping' in C. Northcote Parkinson (Ed.) *The Trade Winds: a study of British overseas trade during the French wars, 1793–1815.* George Allen & Unwin Ltd, London.

Fisher, Sydney G., 1921. *The Quaker Colonies* in The Chronicles of America Series. Yale University Press, New Haven.

Forester, C.S., 1957. *The Age of Fighting Sail.* Michael Joseph, London.

Foss, Michael, 1974. *Undreamed Shores: England's Wasted Empire in America.* BCA London.

Francis, Clare, 1977. *Come Hell or High Water.* Pelham Books, London.

Francis, Daniel, 1984. *Arctic Chase.* Tops'l Books, Breakwater Books, St John's, Newfoundland.

Gilbert, Martin, 1994. *First World War.* Weidenfeld and Nicolson, London.

Gill, Crispin, 1970. *Mayflower Remembered: A History of the Plymouth Pilgrims.* David & Charles, Newton Abbot.

Grove, Eric (Ed.), 1994. *Great Battles of the Royal Navy.* Arms & Armour Press, London.

Handy, Amy, 1996. *The Golden Age of Sail.* Todri Productions, New York.

Harden, Donald, 1962. *The Phoenicians.* Thames & Hudson, London.

Harper, Colonel J.R., 1966. *78th Fighting Frasers: A Short History of the Old 78th Regiment.* Dev-Sco Publications Ltd, Chomedey, Laval, Quebec.

Heaton, Professor H., 1948. 'The American Trade' in Parkinson C. Northcote (Ed.) *The Trade Winds: A study of British overseas trade during the French wars 1793–1815.* George Allen & Unwin Ltd.

Horsfall, Lucy Frances, 1948. 'The West India Trade' in Parkinson, C. Northcote (Ed.) *The Trade Winds: A study of British overseas trade during the French wars, 1793–1815.* George Allen & Unwin Ltd.

Hope, Ronald, 1990. *A New History of British Shipping.* John Murray, London.

Israel, Jonathan, 1982. *The Dutch Republic and the Hispanic World*. Clarendon Press, Oxford.

Jackson, Gordon, *1978. The British Whaling Trade*. Adam & Charles Black, London.

Jane, Cecil (Translator), 1968. *The Journal of Christopher Columbus*. Anthony Blond, London.

Jones, Gwyn, 1964. *The Norse Atlantic Saga*. Oxford University Press, London, NY, Toronto.

Kemp, Peter, (Ed.) 1979. *The Oxford Companion to Ships and the Se*a. Granada Publishing, London, Toronto, Sydney, NY.

Kiernan, V.G., 1991. *Tobacco: a History*. Hutchinson Radius, London.

Lorimer, Joyce, 1978. 'The English Contraband Tobacco Trade in Trinidad and Guiana 1590–1617', in Canny, N.P., Andrews, K.R. and Hair, P.E.H. (Eds.) *The Westward Enterprise: English Activities in Ireland, the Atlantic and America, 1480–1650.* Liverpool University Press, Liverpool.

Lubbock, Basil, 1948. 'Seamen' in Parkinson, C. Northcote (Ed.) *The Trade Winds: A study of British overseas trade during the French wars 1793–1815*. George Allen & Unwin Ltd., London.

Lubbock, Basil, 1914. *The China Clippers*. Brown, Son & Ferguson, Glasgow.

Lubbock, Basil, 1924. *The Colonial Clippers*. Brown, Son & Ferguson, Glasgow.

Lubbock, Basil, 1955. *The Arctic Whalers*. Brown, Son & Ferguson, Glasgow.

Lubbock, Basil, 1948. 'Ships of the Period and Development in Rig' in G. Northcote Parkinson (Ed.) *The Trade Winds: A study of British overseas trade during the French wars, 1793–1815*. George Allen & Unwin Ltd, London.

Liddel Hart, B.H., 1970. *History of the First World War*. Cassell & Co, London.

McEvedy, Colin, 1967. *The Penguin Atlas of Ancient History*. Penguin Books, Harmondsworth.

McGrath, Patrick, 1978. 'Bristol & America 1480–1631' in Andrews, K.R., Canny, N.P. and Hair, P.E.H. (Eds.) *The Westward Enterprise: English activities in Ireland, the Atlantic and America 1480–1650*. Liverpool University Press, Liverpool.

MacGregor, Alasdair Alpin, 1971. *Islands by the Score*. Michael Joseph, London.

MacInnes, Professor C.M., 1948. 'The Slave Trade' in Parkinson, C. Northcote (Ed.) *The Trade Winds: a study of British overseas trade during the French wars 1793–1815*. George Allen &Unwin Ltd, London.

MacLennan, Dorothy Duncan, 1946. *Bluenose: A Portrait of Nova Scotia*. Collins, Toronto.

McAuley, Robert, 1997. *The Liners: A voyage of Discovery*. Boxtree, Macmillan, London.

Miller, Nathan, 1995. *War at Sea: A Naval History of World War II*. Scribnet, New York.

Morgan, Kenneth, 1993. *Bristol and the Atlantic Trade in the Eighteenth Century*. Cambridge University Press, Cambridge.

Morris, James, 1979. *Heaven's Command: An Imperial Progress*. Penguin, Harmondsworth.

Nugent, Walter, 1992. *Crossings: The Great Transatlantic Migrations, 1870–1914.* Indiana University Press, Bloomington, Indianapolis.

Paine, Ralph D, 1919. *The Old Merchant Marine* in Johnson, Allen (Ed.) The Chronicles of America Series. Yale University Press, Newhaven, Toronto, London.

Parkinson, C. Northcote, 1977. *Britannia Rules: The Classic Age of Naval History 1793–1815*. BCA, London.

Parkinson, C. Northcote, 1948. 'The Seaports: London' in Parkinson, C. Northcote (Ed.) *The Trade Winds; A study of British overseas trade during the French wars*. George Allen & Unwin Ltd, London.

Parry, L.H., 1978. 'The English in the New World' in Canny, N.P., Andrews, K.R. and Hair, P.E.H., (Eds.) *The Westward Enterprise: English Activities in Ireland, the Atlantic and America, 1480–1650*. Liverpool University Press, Liverpool.

Parry, J.H., 1966. *The Spanish Seaborne Empire*. Hutchinson, London.

Pocock, Michael, 1986. *Inshore – Offshore*. Conway Maritime Press, London.

Prebble, John, 1969. *The Highland Clearances*. Penguin, Hardmonsworth.

Quinn, David Beers, 1985. *Set Fair for Roanoke; voyages and colonies 1584–1606*. University of North Carolina Press, Chapel Hill and London.

Richman, Irvine Berdine, 1919. *The Spanish Conquerors* in Johnson, Allen (Ed.) The Chronicles of America Series. Yale University Press, Newhaven and Toronto.

Riddell, John, 1988. *The Clyde: An illustrated history of the river and its shipping*. Fairlie Press, Fairlie.

Rowe, Percy, 1977. *The Great Atlantic Air Race*. Angus & Robertson, London, Sydney.

Runciman, Walter, 1924. *Before the Mast and After*. T. Fisher Unwin, London.

Sanchez-Albernoz, Nicolas, 1994. 'The First Transatlantic Transfer: Spanish migration to the New World 1493–1810' in Canny, Nicholas (Ed.) *Europeans on the Move: Studies on European migration 1500–1800*. Clarendon Press, Oxford.

Salter, J.A., 1921. *Allied Shipping Control: An experiment in International Administration*. Humphrey Milford, London.

Severin, Tim, 1978. *The Brendan Voyage*. Arrow, London.

Severin, Tim, 1985. *The Jason Voyage: The Quest for the Golden Fleece*. Arrow, London.

Shammas, Carole, 1978. 'English Commercial Development and American Colonisation 1560–1620' in Canny, N.P., Andrews, K.R. and Hair, P.E.H. (Eds.) *The Westward* Enterprise: English Activities in Ireland, the Atlantic and America, 1480–1650. Liverpool University Press, Liverpool.

Smith, Richard K, 1973. *First Across: The U.S. Navy's Transatlantic Flight of 1919*. Naval Institute Press, Annapolis.

Smyth, Alfred P., 1984. *Warriors and Holy Men: Scotland AD 80–1000*. Edinburgh University Press, Edinburgh.

Stamp, Tom and Cordelia, 1975. *William Scoresby, Arctic Scientist*. Caedmon of Whitby Press, Whitby.

Thompson, Holland, 1921. *The Age of Invention* in The Chronicles of America Series. Yale University Press, New Haven.

Thomson, George Malcolm, 1975. *The North West Passage*. Martin Secker and Warburg Limited, London.

Tindall, George Brown and Shi, David Emory, 1997. *America: A Narrative History*. W.W. Norton & Co., New York, London.

Ward, W.E.F., 1969. *The Royal Navy and the Slavers: The Suppression of the Atlantic Slave Trade*. George Allen & Unwin, London.

Wardle, A.C. , 1948. 'The Post Office Packets', in C. Northcote Parkinson (Ed.) *The Trade Winds : A study of British overseas trade during the French wars 1793–1815*. George Allen & Unwin Ltd, London.

Warren, Mark D. (Ed.), 1970. *Ocean Liners of the Past – Lusitania*. Patrick Stephens, Yeovil.

Warren, Mark D. (Ed.), 1970. *Ocean Liners of the Past – Mauritania*. Patrick Stephens, Yeovil.

Winston, Alexander, 1969. *Privates & Privateers*. Arrow, London.